WORD LORE

THE
HISTORY
OF
200
INTRIGUING
WORDS

GRAMERCY BOOKS
NEW YORK

This 2006 edition is published by Gramercy Books, an imprint of Random House Value Publishing, by arrangement with Random House Reference, divisions of Random House, Inc., New York.

Gramercy is a registered trademark and the colophon is a trademark of Random House, Inc.

Random House
New York • Toronto • London • Sydney • Auckland
www.randomhouse.com

Page design by Nancy Sabato
Illustration by Mark Matcho
Typeset by North Market Street Graphics
Printed and bound in the United States of America

Library of Congress Cataloging-in-Publication Data

Word lore : the history of 200 intriguing words.
        p. cm.
    Previously published as: The Mavens' word of the day collection: word and phrase origins from Akimbo to Zydeco. New York : Random House Reference, 2002.
    ISBN 0-517-22661-8
    1. English language—Etymology.

PE1574.W67 2006
422—dc22

2005052708

10 9 8 7 6 5 4 3 2 1

Table of Contents

-able vs. -ible

Susan B. Haglock wrote: How do you know when to use **-ible** or **-able** as a suffix? The word *collectible* looks right to me, but *collectable* does not, and yet I have seen both. *The Oxford English Dictionary* says it depends on whether the root word is a Latin word that ends in *-ire,* but I don't usually know that either.

Of all the vagaries in English spelling, this one seems to cause the most frustration and confusion, particularly when the word you want isn't in your dictionary.

Theoretically, you should feel free to construct an adjective out of a verb or root plus a common suffix even when your dictionary fails to show the full form. These two suffixes are highly productive and both mean 'capable of, susceptible of', or 'fit for VERBing', or 'able to be VERBed'. Both suffixes are ultimately derived from Latin. If word histories were neat, we could say that **-able** comes from forms with *ābilis* and **-ible** from forms with *ībilis;* that both suffixes passed into English through Old French; and that one comes from Latin verbs with infinitives in *-āre* and the other from Latin verbs with infinitives in *-ere* or *-ire*. But there are many exceptions, and in any case, knowing all this is of little practical help in predicting spellings.

As with so much in language, there is no guaranteed solution. But when you're ready to tear your hair and fling your dictionary to the other side of the room, here are a couple of hints to help increase the odds of getting it right.

(1): **-able** is often used after a full verb (although sometimes a final *-e* is dropped before the suffix is added): *ap-*

proachable, addable, teachable, photographable, acquirable. In contrast, **-ible** is often used after roots: *credible, visible, permissible.*

(2): Frequently, the **-able** spelling is correct when there are related derived forms with suffixes starting in *-a.* The **-ible** spelling is similarly part of a group where other suffixes start with *-i.* For example, **-able** words may be related to words with *-ance* or *-ation.* Thus *acceptable* has *acceptance; accusable* has *accusation;* and *applicable* has *application.* The **-ible** words often have *-ive* or *-ion* related forms. Thus *combustion, permissive,* and *audio* hint at *combustible, permissible,* and *audible.*

Would that these tricks were *infallible.* (For example, borrowings from different languages lead to *fallible* but *fallacy,* a misleading pairing.) With some words, both suffixes have come into use (as with *collectible/collectable*). You may find other counterexamples for these two hints, but perhaps they can be a start.

$\sim$*EP*

agenbite of inwit (uh-GEN-bite uv IN-wit)

CHESTER ZENONE WROTE: Can you shed any light on the meaning of the phrase **agenbit of inwyt?** I've been able to find *inwyt* (or *inwit*), meaning 'inward knowledge', but have searched several dictionaries in vain for the term *agenbit.*

I'm wondering where you encountered this phrase. It's not in the average person's vocabulary!

Agenbite of inwit is an archaic phrase that originated as the title of a French treatise on morality. It was translated into English in 1340 by Dan Michel, a monk at Canterbury. The title (originally spelled *Ayenbite of Inwyt*) means 'the remorse of conscience', literally, 'the again-biting of inner wit'. The English word *agenbite* is a translation of both elements of the Latin verb *remordere* 'to bite again', the source of English *remorse*. The English word *inwit* usually means 'an inner sense of right or wrong', but its more general meaning is 'reason, intellect, understanding, or wisdom'.

The phrase **agenbite of inwit** has been revived by modern writers. James Joyce used it at least eight times in *Ulysses* to portray Leopold Bloom's character as being afflicted by the repeated bite or wound of introspection, self-analysis, and self-awareness: "They wash and tub and scrub. Agenbite of inwit. Conscience. . . . Venus had twisted her lips in prayer. Agenbite of inwit: remorse of conscience. It is an age of exhausted whoredom groping for its god. . . . Agenbite of inwit. Inwit's agenbite. Misery! Misery!"

In the 1960s Marshall McLuhan discussed the psychic numbness caused by the idolatry of technology: "With the telegraph Western man began a process of putting his nerves outside his body . . . Since the telegraph we have extended the brains and nerves of man around the globe. The electronic age endures a total uneasiness, as of a man wearing his skull inside and his brain outside. A special property of all social extensions of the body is that they return to plague the inventors in a kind of agenbite of outwit."

More recently, the film critic Richard Corliss described Humbert in the movie *Lolita:* "The agenbite of inwit gnaws at him, robs him of the malefic majesty that makes screen villains entertaining."

~CGB

akimbo (uh-KIM-boh)

REBECCA REAY-YOUNG WROTE: Can you please tell me the origin of the word **akimbo**? I can't find this information anywhere.

Akimbo, which means 'with hand on hip and elbow bent outward', first appeared around 1400 in an anonymous continuation of *The Canterbury Tales* called *The Tale of Beryn:* "The hoost . . . set his hond in kenebowe." In the 17th century, the word was spelled *on kenbow, a kenbow, a kenbol, a kenbold,* or *on kimbow.* The forms *akembo* and **akimbo** are found in the 18th century, with **akimbo** gradually becoming standard.

The word's origins are murky. One suggestion is that it comes from the Icelandic word *keng-boginn,* 'crooked', but there is no evidence that *keng-boginn* ever meant anything other than 'crooked'—or that **akimbo** ever meant simply 'crooked'. Also, if this theory of the word's origin is correct, there ought to be an earlier English form such as *keng-bow,* but there isn't.

Other suggestions trace **akimbo** to Middle English *cambok,* 'a curved stick or staff' (from Medieval Latin *cambūca*) or to *a cam bow,* 'in a crooked bow'. However, there is no extant form of **akimbo** spelled with *cam;* and the earliest form of the word, *kenebowe,* is a long way from *cam.* It seems logical that the *bo* part of the word is related to *bow,* but no one has been able to document the connection with certainty.

The *Middle English Dictionary* proposes (with a question mark) that **akimbo** might be related to Old French *chane* or *kane,* 'pot or jug,' combined with Middle English *boue,* 'bow'. In that case, the word **akimbo** originally meant 'bent like the handle of a jug'. Intriguing—but, again, there's no evidence. So we're left with "etymology unknown."

~GSM

albeit (awl-BEE-it)

ERIK HALLBERG WROTE: One of my favorite quotes is from Albert Einstein, who said, "Reality is merely an illusion, albeit a very persistent one." **Albeit** seems to work as a fancy form of *but,* which is a perfectly good word most everyone uses correctly. Is **albeit** therefore simply a verbal flourish, a synonym of *but,* or is there more to the story? *All be it* would appear to be the building blocks of **albeit,** in the sense of "all that it is." To my mind, this would work if the idea was broken down into ". . . but when you consider the whole of it . . ." Am I trying too hard to make literal sense of an odd word?

Albeit may be an odd, archaic-sounding verbal flourish, but as a conjunction it has been flourishing since Chaucer's time. As you imply, it literally means 'all (completely, entirely) though it be'. The actual meaning of **albeit** is closer to 'even if or even though; although (it be)', and just like *although/ though,* it is sometimes used to begin a clause: "He can ask for a loan, albeit I do not think he will get it." Here **albeit** implies an opposition or contrast, and yes, it is very similar to *but.*

However, the Albert Einstein quote shows the more common use of **albeit** in a concessive phrase, one that expresses a conceding, yielding, or admitting. In this use **albeit** can mean 'conceding or admitting that; in spite of the fact that', and the word *notwithstanding* can sometimes be substituted.

In the word **albeit,** the verb *be* is the third person singular present subjunctive. (The corresponding indicative form would be *is.*) In subjunctive constructions, the order of subject and verb is sometimes reversed: "Be it ever so humble..." (Patrick Henry's exclamation, "If this be treason, make the most of it," is an example of a subjunctive construction in which subject and verb are in the usual order.)

Historically, the adverb *all* has been used with the conjunctions *if* and *though,* and often the order was reversed, producing "all if, all though." The phrase "all though" was originally an emphatic form of *though,* which later became *although.* Sometimes the conjunction *if* or *though* was dropped if the verb was placed before the subject, leaving *all* as an apparent conjunction, in the sense of 'even if or even though; although'. So the phrase *al be it* meant 'although it be', which later became the one-word form **albeit.**

~CGB

all told

PAT ANDERSON WROTE: While visiting Microsoft in November 1999, Vice President Al Gore mentioned that "All told, it was a wonderful visit." Please elaborate on the meaning and origin of **all told.**

This idiomatic expression first appeared in print about 1850. It's used as a sentence modifier with or without a separating comma: "There are five actors all told/All told, there are five actors." In this particular use, *told* is the past tense and past participle of the verb *tell,* though not in the familiar sense of 'to narrate; relate'. As far back as Old English, *tell* has had another sense: 'to count one by one'. An example from Defoe's *Robinson Crusoe* (1719–20): "He could not tell twenty in English, but he numbered them, by laying so many stones in a row, and pointing to me to tell them over." In this sense, *tell* can be used with various adverbs: "He told down/up/off/over the stones."

Aside from counting off rosary beads ("The nun tells her beads") or counting votes or voters in an election ("The Speaker told the House"), this meaning of *tell* is archaic, recorded up through the late 1800s. It survives mostly in the fixed expression **all told,** which basically means 'all (being) counted'. But there is another fixed expression that uses this sense of 'to count'. When we *tell time,* we really 'count or keep track of the hours'. Another survival of this sense is seen in the word *teller,* 'a bank clerk who counts money'.

Tell (like *enumerate*) has the basic sense 'to mention numerically; count'. But it can also mean 'to mention one after another, as in a list'. So the expression **all told** means 'all (being) counted; all mentioned one after another'. Its more general meaning is 'in summation; in all; altogether', the sense used by Al Gore. First he mentioned great things about Microsoft. Then he summarized his list of Microsoft's merits by saying "All told, it was a wonderful visit."

Now you know that "The farmer told his cattle" means that he counted them, not that he dished them the dirt about the chickens. Also you realize that "The new recruits were told off" can mean not only that they were reprimanded, but also that they were counted off (set apart) from the rest of the company.

~CGB

-alm

ROY SABLOSKY WROTE: Why is the *l* silent in *palm, calm, balm* (probably there are more)? And does it seem to you that there's a trend toward pronouncing it, even though that makes the speaker seem a bit thick?

Certain pronunciations come and go over the centuries, and the sound (l) before a consonant is one particularly slippery customer. The well-known words that share the **-alm** pattern, like *alms, balm, calm, palm, psalm,* and *qualm,* are now, according to both American and British dictionaries, commonly pronounced with the "broad a" of *father* and without the (l) sound.

D. W. Cummings's *American English Spelling* (1988) states that in these words, "the *l* began to appear in English spellings in the 15th century, and it is not clear whether it reflected an actual pronunciation or was simply another instance of the Early Modern period's enthusiasm for Latinate respellings." Another theory is that the added *l* influenced the change from an older "short a" pronunciation to a "broad a" (Arthur Bronstein, *The Pronunciation of American English,* 1960).

If we grant that this *l* was at one time pronounced, dropping it represents a natural simplification resulting from its vowel-like nature. Before (m), for example, if the tip of the tongue doesn't quite get to touch the upper gum ridge, an (oo)-like vowel is heard instead. Eventually, even that much may be dropped. The 19th-century historical philologist A. J. Ellis wrote disparagingly of this in his two-volume *Early English Pronunciation* (1869): ". . . when a consonant followed, it was more convenient to leave out the (l), and the lazy or nimble tongue, as usual, took the most convenient or shortest road, and (l) disappeared."

Conversely, an (l) sound in modern American English pronunciations of *calm, balm,* etc., if not acquired in childhood, represents a spelling pronunciation—that is, one in which the speaker is guided more by the printed form than by what is traditionally heard. Today, pronunciations like (kahlm) and (bahlm) are criticized by purists.

Pity the poor student of English as a Second Language. The (l) sound is also missing in the usual articulations of *talk, should, half,* and *yolk.* Yet there it is in similar words like *elf, halt, milk,* and *elm.* For *golf,* the pronunciation *without* the (l) is criticized! Then there's the proper name *Ralph,* which is (ralf) in the United States and (rafe) in Britain. What's a person to do?

~*EP*

anniversary

SHAR FELDHEIM WROTE: What is the obsession with **anniversary?** I hear people say "one-month anniversary," "one-week anniversary," and other such nonsense. The worst was the "One Hundred Centennial Anniversary" on CNET. [But] . . . weeks, months, and centennials are not "anniversary" dates.

The Latin combining form *anni-* does indeed mean 'relating to a year'; the Norman French word *anniversarie* came from the Medieval Latin *diēs anniversāria,* or 'day recurring yearly'. During this process, the adjectival *anniversāria* got turned into a noun, **anniversary,** so that if you really want to be a stickler about all this, you should always remember to say "anniversary day" rather than "anniversary."

Why note that? Because language changes—it's always in flux. And English speakers, through the centuries, have been very acquisitive; if we haven't got a word for a concept, and some other language has, we'll borrow it and change it to suit our needs, thank you very much. Now we have a situation in which there's a concept we want to express, that of celebrating the passing of a period of time that is shorter than a year, and we haven't got a word for it. We can either make one up, usually on the analogy of another word in the same range of meaning (think *prequel*), or we can expand the use of a word that seems to fit the bill (think *gay*). Enter *three-month anniversary,* a borrowing from ourselves.

It's a telling commentary on our modern lives that we feel the need to celebrate the fact that a relationship has lasted a month, or that we've managed to stay away from cigarettes for three weeks. The use of **anniversary** to mark these occasions is still mostly a spoken phenomenon, and many speakers will curl their fingers in a "quote" sign when they use the word in this way. However, I've found evidence on Internet chat groups of people using this construction without any self-consciousness whatsoever:

> "let's see . . . yesterday was the one month anniversary of our first kissmass"
>
> "a very happy 3 month anniversary to the one man who completely changed my life"
>
> "still want to smoke however . . . tomorrow will be 3 weeks . . . I do subconsciously think about anniversary dates . . ."

Evidence such as this shows that people are becoming less aware of the connection with *annual,* in much the same way that we no longer consciously think of, say, *Oxford* as 'the place where oxen ford the river', and will happily use the suffix *-ford* in place names where no ford ever existed.

By all means, avoid the use of **anniversary** for periods of less than one year if it bothers you. However, I wouldn't count on being able to plug the dike forever. As for "One Hundred Centennial Anniversary"—well, we can all have a good laugh about that one.

~*WRN*

Antilles (an-TIL-ez)

BILL FREY WROTE: Every reference tells the geographic location of the **Antilles;** none I can find gives the origin and meaning of the term. Possibly it is simply *anti* and *illes* or, 'the islands across over there'. Can you help?

These islands, subdivided into Greater and Lesser Antilles, are sometimes—but not always—known as the West Indies—in other words, the Caribbean Islands. The Greater Antilles consist of the bigger islands: Cuba, Hispaniola, Jamaica, and Puerto Rico. The Lesser Antilles consist of all those other smaller islands: Guadeloupe, Martinique, Dominica, St. Lucia, Montserrat, Antigua, etc. They are often further subdivided into the French Antilles and the Netherlands Antilles. The noun **Antilles** is always plural.

The *Encyclopædia Britannica* says: "The term Antilles dates traditionally from before Europeans discovered the New World, when 'Antilia' referred to semimythical lands located somewhere west of Europe across the Atlantic. On medieval charts it was sometimes indicated as a continent or large island and sometimes as an archipelago. After discovery of the West Indies by Columbus, the Spanish term 'Antillas' was commonly assigned to the new lands, and 'Sea of the Antilles' in various European languages is used as an alternate designation for the Caribbean Sea."

Donald Johnson's 1994 book, *Phantom Islands of the Atlantic: The Legends of Seven Lands That Never Were,* devotes an entire chapter to *Antillia,* as he spells it. Johnson says that the first map—called a portolan chart—ever to show the word *Antilia* was made in 1424. Portolan charts, created before Columbus's discovery of America, were navigational charts that contained the accumulated knowledge of sailors and navigators. (*Portolan* basically means 'getting to a safe port, haven'.) These charts were made in the 13th, 14th, and 15th centuries, and some are quite accurate. On the 1424 chart, which was made by a Venetian cartographer, you can actually see the word *Antilia* next to a big, rectangular island.

"Throughout the fifteenth and early sixteenth centuries," Johnson writes, "Antillia's position on maps is consistent." That position is always around 700 miles west of the Azores. The inference is that because different sailors from different countries noted Antilia on charts, it must have existed. Some speculate that Antilia referred to Cuba.

Columbus apparently knew of Antilia. "Cartographers as well as historians," Johnson continues, "felt that the Antillia on old maps represented a foreknowledge of the New World. After the discoveries of Columbus, they accordingly transferred Antillia to a new position in the West Indies." But what of the origin of the word *Antilia?* In a 1954 study on the 1424 portolan chart, scholar Armando Cortesão wrote:

> *Antilia* is composed of two Portuguese words: "ante" or "anti" and "ilha," an archaic form of the Portuguese "ilha," i.e. 'island'. It is, therefore, a purely Portuguese word and it was meant to designate an island—discovered perhaps at the beginning of the fifteenth century by some unknown navigators, probably Portuguese.

Scholars are still battling over this one.

~RG

aspire, aspirate, and aspiration

MIRANDA STECYK WROTE: The word that I'm curious about is **aspire.** I was recently reading a book that referred to a character's **aspirations,** and it struck me how similar this was to the word **aspirate.** I checked with a friend in the medical field, who explained that to **aspi-**

rate was essentially to inhale fluid into the lungs. So, in this sense one could die of **aspiration.** Are **aspire** and **aspirate** related in any way?

Intimately. **Aspire, aspirate,** and **aspiration** all have embodied in their origins the idea of *breath* and/or *breathing.* They— and similar words such as *inspire, respire,* and *conspire*—can be traced back to the same Latin root *spīrāre* 'to breathe, respire, to be breathed upon or into'. If we trace the origins of *spīrāre,* we arrive at the Sanskrit word *picchorā,* 'flute', a breathy instrument indeed.

Aspire and **aspiration** are siblings, while **aspirate** might be called their cousin. The word **aspire** means 'to have a desire for something higher'. **Aspirations** are those desires. **Aspire** comes more recently from the Latin word *aspīrāre.* The *Oxford Latin Dictionary* gives many meanings for *aspīrāre* including 'to emit air or breath'; 'to instill, infuse (an emotion or quality) into a person or thing'; 'to exhale perfume, be fragrant'; and 'to have a longing for'—there you have today's most common meaning. Another of the definitions of *aspīrāre* is '(of a flute) to play an accompaniment'. **Aspire** first came into print in English around 1425. *The Oxford English Dictionary* gives the original meaning in English—now obsolete— as 'to breathe into or forth'. It cites an example from Sir Thomas More's *The apologye made by hym* (1533): "To spreade his beames upon vs, and aspire hys breth into vs."

Now, to the cousin, **aspirate.** Its first meaning in *Random House Webster's Unabridged Dictionary* is 'to articulate so as to produce an audible puff of breath, as with the first "t" of "total"'. According to *RHWUD,* it can also mean 'to inhale (fluid or a foreign body) into the bronchi and lungs' or 'to remove (a fluid) from a body cavity by use of an aspirator'. Here's an example of the latter meaning culled from the 1880 *Nation:* "He proposes to aspirate the vapours of the chambers." I don't think you can die of **aspiration** as you would, say, of a heart attack. You certainly can die in the act of **aspirating** something—as poor Mama Cass did—though. And isn't drowning the ultimate **aspiration?**

~*RG*

As you wish

BRADLEY WROTE: I understand that the phrase **as you wish** comes from a Latin phrase that means 'I Love You'. Inconceivable!

As you wish (for those of you out there who haven't either read the William Goldman classic *The Princess Bride* or seen the Rob Reiner film version) is what Westley says to his true love, Buttercup, all the while she's treating him like dirt for most of chapter one, until that is, she realizes she is madly in love with him. Every time he said **"As you wish"** to some demand or other of Buttercup's, Westley reveals when they confess their love to each other, "you were hearing wrong. 'I love you' was what it was, but you never heard, and you never heard."

So, the question is, is there a phrase in Latin that sounds like **As you wish** but really means 'I love you'? A little research uncovered the phrase *cupio omnia quae vis,* literally meaning 'I desire all things which you wish'. While comparable to the innocuous "I am entirely at your service" in English, it is interesting to note that the verb *cupio* ('desire') used in this phrase has a sense that is synonymous with "love." *Cupio* has found its way into English in the form of *Cupid,* the Roman god of love, the verb *cupidity* (eager or excessive desire, greed), and *concupiscence* (sexual desire, lust). Good stuff, but not exactly what you'd call a smoking gun. This leaves the word *vis,* from the verb *volo, velle* ('to want, to wish for [something]'). Is there a similar elasticity of meaning, and a more direct connection to English?

Skip forward about two millennia to modern-day Italian, and we find the phrase *volere bene,* in which the Italian verb *volere* ('to wish, to want, to desire') becomes "to love." The phrase *ti voglio bene,* literally 'I want/wish/desire you well', translates as "I love you." According to Battisti and Alessio's etymological dictionary of Italian, *volere* was substituted for the Latin verb *amare* ('to love') in this phrase in the Italian dialect. How might this have happened? A quick peek back at the Latin verb *velle* reveals it has another, love-related sense, which is 'to desire to have, to want (a particular thing or person)'. It is perhaps this very overlap in meaning with the verb *amare* that allowed for the switch to *volere bene* in the Italian.

OK, you say, but we still haven't found anything that relates any of this to English. A survey of reference books on English quotations, proverbs, and sayings yields absolutely zilch for **As you wish** or any variation thereof. I find a bit of encouragement from Shakespeare, however, whose love-conquered King Ferdinand in *Love's Labour's Lost* (1594) quotes in parting to his Princess: "Thy own wish wish I thee in every place!" Could this be a secret code for 'I love you'? What can we dig up in *wish*'s past? Some lustful skeleton in its etymological closet? As it turns out, there is one in there among the dusty old bones. The Middle English *wisshen* and Old English *wyscan* whence *wish* descended are akin to the Latin *venus,* which has various meanings related to sexual love, but is most well-known as the name of the Roman goddess of love (and Cupid's mother). We now find ourselves to have come full circle, with but a tenuous link to English, and no real answer at hand.

It was an interesting journey nonetheless, and all on the subject of love, which is in my mind a worthwhile pursuit. After all, "true love is the best thing in the world, except for . . ." well, I'll let you fill in the blanks.

~HL

☞ awe, awesome, and awful

THE RED TORNADO WROTE: Do **awful** and **awesome** come from the same root? The two words are opposites, one a negative and one a positive, yet it seems like they should have similar meanings, like *wonderful* and *wondrous.*

Awful and **awesome** share the same root word, **awe.** At one time they meant essentially the same thing, 'full of awe, profoundly reverential'. **Awe** first appears in its Old English form in a 9th-century manuscript. At that time, it meant 'immediate and active fear, terror, dread'. This terror and fear were typically inspired by God. The meaning passed gradually into 'dread mingled with veneration, reverential, or respectful fear'. The word has had a whole other career as a verb, basically instilling the emotions that the noun described and, really, following the changes in meanings, too. Shakespeare uses **awe** twenty times, and sometimes his sense of the word seems surprisingly modern. In *The Merry Wives of Windsor,* for example, Falstaff, speaking of Ford, says: "I will awe him with my / cudgel: it shall hang like a meteor o'er the / cuckold's horns."

Awful is a much older word than **awesome** and came into use at more or less the same time as **awe.** It first appeared in written English in 885 and simply meant 'awe-inspiring'— something, or someone, who inspired fear or dread. By the 17th century, though, **awful** also had the meaning of 'sublimely majestic'—clearly the opposite of what it means today. (**Awesome** didn't appear on the scene until the late 16th century.)

Today, the first meaning of **awful**—in most American dictionaries, at least—is 'extremely bad, unpleasant'. We can thank America for that. The *Dictionary of American English on Historical Principles* declares **awful** an Americanism and traces its first appearance in print to 1809. John Pickering, in his 1816 *Vocabulary, or, Collection of Words and Phrases Which Have Been Supposed to Be Peculiar to the United States,* wrote: "In New England, many people would call a disagreeable medicine awful, or an ugly woman an awful-looking woman."

The contemporary definition for **awesome** is, simply, 'inspiring awe'. However, I would bet that most Americans use the word in its slang sense, 'very impressive'. The changing usage of **awesome** and **awful** has inspired ire and dismay for some time now. A panel convened by the *Harper Dictionary of Contemporary Usage* in the 1980s discussed the liberties taken with **awesome.** The subject was the tendency for people to use **awesome** not to convey 'reverence, dread, and wonder', but simple admiration. The example given the panel was from the sports pages: "[Yankee pitcher Goose] Gossage's fastball has been good this season, but it hasn't been awesome." Poet John Ciardi said this was "a weakened sense extension. Such extensions are a farce." But the last word went to James J. Kilpatrick, a political commentator, who said about applying the word to Gossage's fastball: "The meaning is exact: inspiring reverence, dread, and wonder. Ask any batter who ever faced him."

~RG

ax and ask

SAM SHERWOOD WROTE: There is a guy in my office who has a heavy Southern accent, and he says **ax** instead of **ask.** When questioned he claims it's a regional pronunciation (Mississippi area), but it sounds to me more like a regional mispronunciation. There is also a man in my office from the Bahamas, and he too says **ax.** Can you explain?

Thank you for asking (aksing) this question.

While the pronunciation (aks) for **ask** is not considered standard, it is a very common regional pronunciation with a long history. The Old English verb *āscian* underwent a normal linguistic process called *metathesis* sometime in the 14th century. Metathesis is what occurs when two sounds or syllables switch places in a word. This happens all the time in spoken language—think NUCLEAR pronounced as (NOO-kyuh-ler) and *asterisk* pronounced as (AS-tuh-riks).

Metathesis is usually a slip of the tongue, but, as in the cases of (NOO-kyuh-ler) and (AS-tuh-riks), it can become a variant of the original word. This alternative version in Old English was *āxian* or *ācsian,* as in the "Wife of Bath's Prologue" in Chaucer's *Canterbury Tales* (1386): "I axe, why the fyfte man Was nought housband to the Samaritan?" *Āscian* and *āxian* co-existed and evolved separately in various regions of England. The *āscian* version gives us the modern standard English **ask,** but the *āxian* variant **ax** can still be found in England's Midland and Southern dialects.

In American English, the (aks) pronunciation was originally dominant in New England. The popularity of this pronunciation faded in the North early in the 19th century as it became more common in the South. Today the pronunciation is perceived in the United States as either Southern or African-American. Both of these perceptions understate the popularity of the form.

The (aks) pronunciation is still found frequently in the South and is a characteristic of some speech communities as far north as New Jersey, Pennsylvania, Illinois, and Iowa. It is one of the shared characteristics between African-American English and Southern dialects of American English. The wide distribution of speakers from these two groups accounts for the presence of the (aks) pronunciation in Northern urban communities.

So in fact, your colleague is correct in calling (aks) a regional pronunciation, one with a distribution that covers nearly half of the territory in the United States and England.

~*HGB*

bachelor's degree

ARLENE ROTH WROTE: During a recent conversation about using politically correct language, someone commented that he had been instructed to use the term "4-year degree" rather than **bachelor's degree.** Does the word *bachelor* in the terms *bachelor of science* or *bachelor of arts* really refer to an unmarried male? If not, what is the history of the term?

All the uses of the word *bachelor* ultimately can be traced to the same source, although quite how each distinct meaning developed isn't completely known. So, the 'unmarried male' meaning is related to the word in the term **bachelor's degree,** but it is not the primary meaning. Bear with me for a bit of history, and we'll get to what *bachelor* means in this sense.

Several of the Latin-based languages have forms of this word that are similar; we get ours from the Old French *bacheler.* The etymologists' best guess is that this comes from Latin *baccalāria,* a division of land, and the masculine and feminine adjectives *baccalārius* and *baccalāria,* used to refer to the people who worked on that land. It may ultimately refer to grazing land, on the theory that *bacca* comes from *vacca,* 'a cow'.

So, a *baccalārius* was most likely a tenant farmer in the earliest sense. In Medieval Latin, this term meant 'a junior member of a guild'; in the spelling *bacheler,* it was also used from the late 14th century in English to mean the same thing. The earliest use of *bacheler* is in the late 13th century, to mean a knight who is very young or who is still a squire in service to another knight. The idea of a bachelor being an apprentice comes from this usage. Now the connection becomes clearer: about the same time that *bacheler* began to be used to refer to an apprentice tradesman, *bachiler* was also applied to an apprentice student—one who had passed the lowest level of training but was not yet a master of the subject. (No one seems to have mastered the spelling of *bachelor,* which didn't settle down until the 18th century.)

The sense of 'unmarried man' also appeared in the late 14th century, so what you have here are contemporaneous and related meaning developments seeming to come from the same source, rather than one meaning progressing and changing through the centuries. Young knights, students, and apprentices were all men, and rarely married, so the connection isn't hard to see.

Still, I wouldn't get too upset about using **bachelor's degree.** It really just means 'apprentice-level degree'; the fact that, long ago, only unmarried men got that degree is about as relevant today as the god Thor is to *Thursday*.

~WRN

bag and baggage

ANDREW KARBOVSKY WROTE: In *Romeo and Juliet* I came across a passage: "Out, you green-sickness carrion! Out, you baggage!" (angry Capulet to his daughter). I have come to the conclusion that there are some woman-describing words that simultaneously mean 'a promiscuous woman' and 'a pert or flirtatious girl' (*hussy, wanton, minx*) or even 'a girl or young woman' (*wench, quean*). These meanings are more or less connected and can be regarded as different points of view concerning the same object. But what about *baggage?* How does its meaning of 'luggage' correspond to other meanings of 'a prostitute' or 'a pert young woman'?

Originally **baggage** was just luggage, or specifically, portable equipment for an army. About 1550 it was first recorded as an adjective to describe worthless or contemptible things. Thirty years later it was used of worthless or contemptible people: "This baggage fellow Burrus" (North's translation of *Plutarch's Lives*).

At about the same time, the noun **baggage** was first used in the sense 'a worthless or disreputable woman; a prostitute'. The specific reference to women (rather than to men or objects) became established by the 17th century, but by the 20th century it was already considered dated and offensive. This sense of **baggage** often appears in military contexts, because disreputable women (and also soldiers' wives) often rode in the baggage trains that accompanied armed forces, along with the army's equipment and supplies. William Robertson's *Phraseologia Generalis* (1693) records the term: "A baggage, or Souldier's Punk, Scortum Castrense" (A baggage, or soldier's whore, a whore of a military camp). Occasionally **baggage** referred to children as well as women. It seems that females, young and old, were worthless encumbrances, or were lugged along like heavy luggage.

Sometimes **baggage** described a pert or saucy young woman, and like *wench* and the other words you mention, it was used in an endearing though condescending way: "I believe the baggage loves me" (William Congreve, *Old Batchelor,* 1687).

The term **bag** in the sense 'an unattractive or unpleasant (old) woman' dates from about 1922, but well before this date it had the meaning 'a promiscuous woman or prostitute'. In these derogatory senses referring to women, **bag** may be an abbreviation of **baggage**.

~CGB

barbarian

BETH PIZIO WROTE: I don't know if I'm the first person to mention it, but I would have sworn that **barbarian** was borrowed into Greek from Latin, since the word *barba* meant 'beard' in Latin. Therefore, the Greeks called bearded foreigners "barbarians." Did my Latin teacher just not know what she was talking about? Inquiring minds want to know!

I received several e-mails of this type in response to my posting on COWABUNGA. In it, I said: ". . . the Greeks coined the term *barbarian,* which means 'bar-bar sayer' and really means 'those weird strangers whose language sounds like bar-bar-bar'." I'm not sure if this can be traced to one university's Latin teacher who trained many high school Latin teachers, but it would be interesting to see how many degrees of separation there are.

The mistake your Latin teacher made was to confuse the roots of the two words. *Barba* is Latin for 'beard', whereas the Greek word is not "barba (root) + inflection/derivative ending," but rather *bárbaros,* which breaks down into "bar + bar + inflection/derivative ending" The Latin *barbarus* was borrowed from Greek *bárbaros,* in both the sense of 'stranger' and 'uncouth person'. Latin usually borrows from Greek, by the way, not the other way round; but I misspoke when I used the word "coined," because ultimately, both Greek *bárbaros* and Sanskrit *barbara* 'stammering, non-Aryan' stem from Indo-European **barbar-*, which is of onomatopoeic origin, mimicking the sound of foreigners' speech. Both *bárbaros* and *barbarus* can act as adjectives or nouns; in English, we derive the adjective *barbarous* and the noun **barbarian** from Latin. Enter the confusion with *barba*.

Liddell & Scott's *Greek-English Lexicon* notes that originally, *hoi bárbaroi* referred to all non-Greek-speaking peoples, but specifically Medes and Persians. When the Romans adopted the term, it referred to anyone who was not Roman or Greek. In an interesting closing of the circle, the equivalent word was used by the Jewish writer(s) of the second book of the Maccabees to refer to Greeks.

The negative connotation was clear from the beginning and cemented after the Persian Wars, when *bárbaros* was used to mean 'uncouth', 'rude', and even 'brutal'. Foreign people—their behavior, their language, even their gods— were called **barbarian.** Nowadays, we use **barbarian** and *barbaric* most often to decry behavior that is brutal. The core term has proven to have great staying power, surviving with its meanings practically intact from ancient times to the present—the occasional bearded Latin speaker notwithstanding.

~*WRN*

bellwether

CHARLES E. JONES WROTE: Newscasters often refer to *bellwether stocks*. Since a **bellwether** was originally the lead sheep in a flock, upon whose neck was placed a bell, I wonder if the term was applied to stocks to draw an analogy between stock traders and sheep. Sheep not only follow each other but are also very skittish. Could we replace economists with sheep farmers?

Yes, originally, a **bellwether** was a belled wether (castrated ram) who led a flock of sheep—oxymoronic but true. Since the 1400s **bellwether** has also meant 'a chief or leader'. Because it often refers to a ringleader, or person who leads a mob, mutiny, or conspiracy, *The Oxford English Dictionary* notes that **bellwether** in this sense is usually contemptuous.

The more recent meaning of **bellwether** is 'a person or thing that shows the existence or direction of a trend'. For example, California is often seen as a **bellwether** for national trends. (Or is it now Florida?) Unlike the derogatory 'ringleader' sense, this usage doesn't show contempt for the leader.

Though investors and sheep may be skittish, **bellwether** doesn't imply this—its meaning has to do with the leader and not the followers. The term is commonly used in the financial world, but the fact is that most of us are followers of one trend or another, not just the sheep who've lost money in dot.com stocks. A *bellwether security* is a stock or bond that indicates the direction of the market or the economy. For example, U.S. Treasury bond yields tend to predict where the bond market is headed. *Bellwether stocks* are owned in large part by institutional investors who trade in large volume, so their prices reflect where the market will be a few weeks later. Stock indexes, such as the Nasdaq composite, are **bellwethers.** A *bellwether industry,* such as retailing, can predict economic trends. Yahoo! and Amazon.com have been referred to as the Internet's **bellwethers.** Intel and Microsoft are high-tech **bellwethers.**

Bellwether is used in politics to mean 'a district that has historically voted for the winner in a national election', implying that the winner there will be the national winner. In politics **bellwether** also means 'a candidate whose nomination is intended to split the vote or conceal another's candidacy', though the more common term for this is *stalking-horse.*

$\sim$*CGB*

bouncing baby

RICH RODEK WROTE: I just learned that a friend recently had a **bouncing baby** boy, but it is my experience that babies really don't bounce well. Where did this phrase come from?

How about a "bouncing swaggering puppy" (Goldsmith) or a "bouncing but well-disposed young woman" (Waugh)? In these examples, as in most cases, the adjective **bouncing** is used in the meaning 'vigorous' that harks back to the earliest meaning of the verb *bounce.*

The origins of *bounce* aren't entirely clear, but its primary meaning was 'to hit something or someone so hard as to rebound'. As early as 1387 the expression *beat and bounce* was known; it was still being used in the 16th century, as in this example from Spenser's *Faerie Queene* (1590, 1596): "And wilfully him throwing on the gras / Did beat and bounse his head and brest full sore." The expression was also used to describe knocking on doors, and *bounse/bounce* occurred alone (without *beat*) as well. It seems that *bounce* was preferred to *beat* or *knock* when the connotation of bounding movement was desired.

The 16th century saw two other meanings emerge, that of 'bragging or blustering' and of 'bounding or throwing yourself around like a ball'. People who *bounced* in the sense of 'bragging' did so with enough gusto to frighten or bully other people; the verb is also used in the sense of 'giving someone a good scolding'. As far as the sense of 'vigorous movement' goes, there's usually a connotation of heavy things being banged about or of people jumping with loud thumps; bouncing wasn't something that a light object or person did. Porpoises and fish bounce in the water; a cannon ball bounces down a set of stairs. If you think about it, bouncing a baby on your knee can start to hurt after a while too.

All these 16th-century meanings are more or less concurrent in development, and you can also find uses of the 'bounding movement' meaning extending to more lightweight things, including the expected *bouncing* balls, from this time period. However, the meaning that we know as the most common one today didn't really become prominent until the 19th century.

So your **bouncing baby** boy is a vigorous child who's likely to bound around and make a lot of noise. The implication is that the child is healthy, as opposed to a weak baby who doesn't move much. The expression has probably lasted because it alliterates so nicely; Thomas Fuller used it in his 1662 *The History of the Worthies of England:* ". . . Elmeby . . . where this bouncing babe Bonner was born."

~*WRN*

broad

BETH PARADA WROTE: I occasionally hear the word **broad** still used to refer to women, and I'm always offended, but it occurred to me that I had no idea what the origins of the term were. Was **broad** always a derogatory usage, or am I just over-sensitive?

I'm amazed you still hear this word, since it's definitely on the wane in current use. Still, if you do hear it, it's likely to mean one of three things:

1. The user is in a time warp and still probably says "my old lady" instead of "my wife" or "my mother."

2. The user is calling the woman in question a prostitute.

3. The user is consciously using the word to be derogatory or for effect.

Believe it or not, the 'woman' meaning of **broad** may come from an 18th-century slang use of the word to mean 'playing card'. How that meaning sprang up is uncertain, as is when and why **broad** also came to mean 'an entrance ticket or transportation ticket'. The origin of the 'ticket' meaning is in American circus slang, but it's only speculative to say that entrance tickets looked like playing cards in the era when this usage arose (1912 is the earliest citation).

What we have to connect women with tickets is a definition of **broad** in Jackson and Hellyer's 1914 *A Vocabulary of Criminal Slang, with Some Examples of Common Usages*. It's worth quoting in full:

> Noun, Current amongst genteel grafters chiefly. A female confederate; a female companion, a woman of loose morals. Broad is derived from the far-fetched metaphor of 'meal ticket', signifying a female provider for a pimp, from the fanciful correspondence of a meal ticket to a railroad or other ticket.

Those genteel grafters weren't the only ones using the term, and it became widespread in gangster-speak and then spread to "uneducated" youth, then (as slang usually does) to more mainstream youth trying to sound cool. The original meaning implied a woman who, if not a prostitute, was at least of loose moral character. The connection to prostitution was close enough that we get a false etymology from 1926 saying that **broad** is derived from *bawd,* and this exchange from Raymond Chandler's 1934 magazine piece "Finger Man":

"I saw plenty wrong with your broad's manners."

"She's not a broad."

However, the general use to mean 'woman' spread fairly quickly too; in *Guys and Dolls* (1932), one character says, "He refers to Miss Perry as a broad, meaning no harm whatever, for this is the way many of the boys speak of the dolls." This use was never really approved of, and the women's movement drove in the final coffin nails, so that it's rare to find a use of **broad** after 1975 that simply means 'woman'. So I think you're pretty safe in taking offense if you're called a **broad**—unless, of course, you practice the oldest profession.

~*WRN*

buck naked

DEAN MOORE WROTE: Couldn't find this one in the archives or *The Oxford English Dictionary.* Do you know the origin of the term **buck naked?**

You just never know from which direction inspiration will strike. I was stretched out in front of the tube last night, tortilla chips in hand, watching the Gore/Bush debate. Well, OK, listening. I was making a thorough examination of the inside of my eyelids, if you must know, when a sentence from George W. distracted me from my labor. "I believe they've moved that sign, 'The Buck Stops Here', from the Oval Office desk to 'The Buck Stops Here' on the Lincoln bedroom." I sat up. What *is* it that you pass when you pass the *buck?* Is it a good old George Washington dollar bill *buck?* Or is it another meaning of *buck* altogether? What *are* the other meanings of *buck* anyway? And, more important, was that a *pun* I just heard from Dubya? It was enough to send me to the books.

The Oxford English Dictionary attributes the main sense of *buck* as 'the male of various animals' to two Old English words, *buc* 'male deer' and *bucca* 'he-goat'. From there, only minor metaphorical leaps are needed to get you to most of the other noun and adjectival senses of *buck.* So, *buckskin* shortened to *buck* refers to the skin of a deer, and from there to shoes made out of the skin. Extensions of the 'male' part of the meaning of *buck* yielded in the 1700s a slang term for a 'spirited young man', and by the mid 1800s, offensive terms for a Native American or black man. By the 1870s, *buck* was short for the military slang term *buck private,* for a soldier of the lowest rank, one 'having no status other than being male'. It is conceivable (but, unfortunately, not provable) that our slang term for a dollar also derived from the 'male deer' *buck,* taking an indirect route via *buckskins,* which were traded as a form of money on the frontier.

The *buck* that "Stops Here" (referring to responsibility or blame that is usually passed on to someone else, but which, since Harry Truman's time, supposedly stops at the president's desk) is indisputably a poker slang term dating from the late 1800s, for a marker designating the position of the dealer. After each hand, the *buck* (originally a *buckhorn* knife, but later any small article serving the purpose) is passed on to the next player who is to deal. The responsibility associated with the dealer position lay in the amount of money the dealer was required to put in the pot when his or her turn came. A pretty neat trick of Bush's, I'd say—from money anted up by the *buck* holder to *bucks* taken by the same.

Which brings me to your question. **Buck naked,** slang for 'completely naked', came on the scene in the late 1920s, and the qualified **buck-ass naked** a bit later. It's one of those terms that is most often accompanied by the irritating phrases "of obscure orig." or "origin unk." Given the preceding array of choices, one might hazard that the *buck* in **buck naked** refers to the color of *buckskin,* along the lines of *buff,* as in "in the buff." But, while we're conjecturing, I might propose another possible etymology. Around the same time that

buck naked was making its debut, so was another slang term, *bucket,* for 'buttocks, rump'. Shorten *bucket* to *buck,* and you've got a term for 'ass-naked', which makes sense in a very, erm, transparent way.

~HL

bunch

BFWCT WROTE: I'm having trouble finding out the original use of the word **bunch.** If you have any information that might be helpful, it would be greatly appreciated.

Bunch can have a sweetness to it, as in "a bunch of daisies." Or it can have a sly, satirical edge to it, as in "a bunch of idiots." It emerges from the mouth with a consistent freshness and power; it has tremendous vigor and punch, partly from that terminating *-ch.*

"Of uncertain origin" is the phrase often affixed to **bunch,** making it yet another etymological orphan. It first appeared in print in English in the 14th century. We (Americans far more than the British) use this word today to mean a group of things that are alike—grapes, carrots, etc. We also use it to mean any kind of group, as in a **bunch** of money. **Bunch** has been coupled memorably with the phrase *honeybunch* and has been appropriated for the world of botany in the names *bunchberry* and *bunch grass.* Here, the word refers to clusters of berries and flowers, respectively.

Way down on the list of contemporary definitions is that of 'lump' or 'protuberance', yet a particular variation of that was its first meaning in the English language. Back then, **bunch** meant a 'hump on the back', either of an animal or a person. The first citation in *The Oxford English Dictionary* is from 1325, and this is from John de Trevisa's 1398 translation of *Bartholomeus De proprietabus rerum:* "A camell of Arabia hath two bonches in the back."

The *OED* seems to think that the word's origin is "probably onomatopoeic." The first citation for **bunch** as a verb in the *OED* is from 1362—some forty years later than the noun's appearance—where it meant to 'strike, thump'. Both the *American Heritage Dictionary* and *The Barnhart Dictionary of Etymology* disagree with the *OED* as to the word's etymology. *Barnhart* says that **bunch** entered the printed language in 1350 as *bunche,* meaning 'a little bundle', and that it's borrowed from the Old French *bonge,* which meant 'bundle'. This in turn emerged from the Flemish *bondje,* 'little bundle'.

Here's an etymological aside via Shakespeare. Until *Richard III* (1594), when you wanted to describe someone who, like Richard, had a back with a large hump, you called him *bunch-backed.* The term *hunchback* first appears in English in the play, and some scholars believe it was a misprint of *bunchback.*

$\sim$RG

can and may

JAN RAHM WROTE: In a lot of the things I read, **may** is used where I would use **can.** For example, "If you are interested, you may call us at [phone number]." Since **may** means 'permitted to' and **can** means 'able to', I think **can** would be the correct word. Or am I being too picky?

When I was a child, I used to ask my grandmother, "Can I have a cinnamon roll?" She would always answer, "You surely may." She was insisting on the distinction between the use of **can** for ability and **may** for permission.

As you might suspect, the distinction cannot be put so starkly. For one thing, the slippery slope that leads to the use of **can** for permission starts with its use to indicate possibility, as in "You can probably still catch her if you hurry." And for another, people rarely object to the use of the negatives "cannot/can't" for "no, you may not": "I'm sorry, but you can't go in there." So why object to the use of **can** in positive constructions? And while we're at it, there are dialects of English, Scots being one of them, that rarely use **may** for permission. All of which points to the fact that **can** has been gradually taking over the territory of **may** ever since it became an auxiliary verb.

Your question lands smack in the middle of this turf war: if the "speaker" (customer service representative? advertising copy?) means "it is possible for you to call us," then **can** is the more usual choice. If the permission given is along the lines of "there's nothing stopping you from calling us," then **can** is also preferred. (Example: "You can use the mouse or the keyboard, whichever you prefer.") However, if "you have our permission to call us" is meant, then **may** is still preferred, mainly because it sounds more polite and formal in positive constructions, and more insistent in negative ones ("Mother, may I?" "No, you may not!"). The more grammar-y reason behind it is that, at least in positive constructions, **may** is still preferred for representing the extreme end of the idea of permission, that of granting.

My favorite discussion of this issue is in *Merriam Web-*

ster's Dictionary of English Usage. Its editor (in reality, the author), E. Ward Gilman, notes that famous language mavens from Samuel Johnson to Bill Bryson insist that **can** should not be used to indicate possibility; then he proceeds to find examples of those very writers using **can** in precisely that way. He also has a good crop of examples of **can** being used for permission. And here's my favorite bit:

> The **can/may** distinction is a traditional part of the American school curriculum. The fact that the distinction is largely ignored by people once out of school is also a tradition.

> ∼*WRN*

chauvinist

MARK SHERRILL WROTE: One day recently, I stumbled upon the history of the word **chauvinist** in the *OED*. Since then, it has bothered me every time I hear the word used as synonymous with *sexist*. I recognize that this usage could jibe with the orginal meaning, but I suspect the interesting history of the term is getting overtaken. Any validity to my concerns, or am I being cantankerous?

The Oxford English Dictionary states that **chauvinist** comes from one Nicolas Chauvin, a rabidly patriotic member of Napoleon's army; it was then later applied to the veterans of the Napoleonic wars who were mocked for their unswerving loyalty to Napoleon long after his fall. However, some other sources say that the existence of an actual Mr. Chauvin is dubious, and that because most of the aging veterans were bald—*chauve* in French—they became known as *chauvins*.

Whatever the true origin, what's undisputed is that a Chauvin became a vaudeville character, and so the term *chauvinisme* came to mean 'blind and belligerent patriotism'. By the 1870s, English had borrowed the term in this meaning.

The broadening of *chauvinism* to include any sort of biased belief in the superiority of a particular race, creed, or cause emerged much later, in the mid-20th century. Both this meaning and the earlier meaning also took on the form **chauvinist,** and both forms are most often used with an adjective modifier to describe the kind of chauvinism or **chauvinist** being talked about. Seattleites are regional **chauvinists** because they decry the "Californication" of the Puget Sound area. New Yorkers are cultural **chauvinists** because they think the universe revolves around them. And the French still are famously French **chauvinists.**

The terms *male chauvinism* and *male chauvinist* emerged along with the women's movement in the late 1960s. The term *sexist* was coined concurrently (in 1965) on the analogy of *racist.* Now, in the same way that you don't have to be a male to be sexist, you also do not have to be a male to be a male chauvinist: you simply have to believe in the superiority of males, and be vocal about it. The misconception that male chauvinists are only males, however, is so pervasive that it seems redundant to say *male chauvinist* when **chauvinist** is being used alone so frequently as a synonym.

In fact, I think we're witnessing a meaning shift. I couldn't find any recent instances of **chauvinist** being used alone without a modifier in any sense other than that of 'sexist'. In every case, if cultural or national or any other kind of chauvinism was meant, the type of chauvinism was identified. You have to suspect that Bobby Riggs would have been pleased that his brand of chauvinism has become the definitive sort.

~*WRN*

clicks-and-mortar

JOE DISTEFANO WROTE: Lately I've been running across the word **click-and-mortar** used to describe the e-commerce operations of "traditional" retailers. I'm trying to find out if it was coined recently.

Click-and-mortar (or **clicks-and-mortar**) is a term that turns up frequently in a wide range of publications, sometimes written without the two hyphens. It's based on the earlier term *brick-and-mortar* (or *bricks-and-mortar*), which dates back to the mid-1800s in reference to a building or structure that has a durable physical presence. In the 1990s, the term *brick-and-mortar* began to be used to distinguish physical buildings or businesses from those located online or in cyberspace.

The first use of the term **clicks-and-mortar** was probably in July of 1999, at Industry Standard's Internet Summit conference. "The future of the Internet will not be about the physical world versus cyberspace, but about integrating the best of the two in what Schwab dubs 'clicks and mortar', said Charles Schwab co-CEO David S. Pottruck . . . Pottruck defined 'clicks and mortar' as knitting together the best of what is available in physical distribution with the best of the web world . . . He defined 'mortar' as being about more than store-fronts, manufacturing and distribution—it's about people" (*PR Newswire,* July 19, 1999).

Usually, **clicks-and-mortar** refers to a business that has traditional stores and offices as well as a Web site. But some **click-and-mortar** plans involve interactive Internet kiosks conveniently located in a store. Shoppers can view and order merchandise located in a different store, or can browse through the merchandise online instead of walking around the store. This trend has been called the *Webification* of stores.

Click-and-mortar businesses have been called *multichannel retailers.* As an executive from (the retailer) J. Crew observed: ". . . the best merchants will need to control all their channels to integrate data about how the same people shop in stores, catalogues and Internet sites" (*Washington Post,* 1999).

~*CGB*

clique (kleek or klik) and claque (klak)

BLYTHE WALKER WROTE: I'm curious about the difference between **clique** and **claque.** Don't they mean they same thing?

They don't. I've often gotten them confused myself, though. One reason is that they both refer to groups with a distinct, and not always congenial, point of view. Not to mention that they share every letter but one.

A **claque** is a group of people hired to applaud a performer. The word comes from the onomatopoeic French verb *claquer,* which the *Nouveau Petit Larousse* defines as 'to make a noise, speaking of the teeth or a whip'. It cites the example: "Ses dents claquaient de peur" 'his teeth rattled in fear'. *Larousse* also says the word can mean 'to applaud by striking the hands'. Eventually, **claque** came to refer to a group of people who were paid to strike those hands together. It was borrowed into English in the early 19th century, and the practice of hiring a claque was at its height in that century. It has taken on a negative connotation, too, because through the years claques have been paid to boo performers as well.

Claque has of course been connected to any kind of theatrical event where applause—or booing—is involved, but whenever I hear the word **claque,** I think of opera. I spoke with William Madison, associate editor of *Opera News,* about this, asking him how prevalent claques are in the American opera world. "It's diminished considerably," he said. "It was never as big in the United States as it was in Europe; it was never as big in Europe as it was in Italy; and it was never as big in Italy as it was in Milan, at La Scala." I asked him if these people were actually paid. "Oh, yes," he said. "It was a form of extortion. Before a singer made his or her debut at La Scala, he or she would receive a visit from the head of the claque, palm outstretched. That was protection money, so they wouldn't boo during your performance."

A **clique,** on the other hand, is a small, exclusive group of people—both in the sense of 'difficult to join' and of 'excluding others'. It seems to be from the Old French verb *cliquer,* 'to click', but how it got to its present meaning is not clear. *The Oxford English Dictionary* says that **clique** may have derived from **claque,** and *The Barnhart Dictionary of Etymology* says at one time the two words meant the same thing. *Claques* seem to be disappearing, but I don't think *cliques* ever will.

～RG

coach

Anonymous wrote: Do sports **coaches** and **coach** seats have anything in common other than their spelling?

Yes, in fact they do: the town of Kocs (pronounced just like "coach") in Hungary, where a type of very large four-wheeled carriage came into use in the 15th century.

These *kocsi szecker*—'Kocs wagons' that could hold a number of passengers, both inside and out—became popular fairly quickly across Europe. By the 16th century, you weren't a true aristocrat if you didn't have your own coach, and nearly every European language had adopted, and sometimes shortened, the adjective *kocsi* as a noun.

Coaches were popular because they were the fastest means at the time for a fair number of people to all get where they were going at once. By the 17th century they were being used as *stagecoaches*—conveyances that made established stops at each stage of a journey—and were used for transporting mail. *Hackney coaches* further democratized the use of these vehicles; with the advent of motorized vehicles, carrying even larger numbers of people became possible, and the coach's transition from a conveyance of royalty to a form of public transport was complete. In England, single-decker buses that travel between towns are still called **coaches.**

In the United States, meanwhile, the word **coach** began in the 1830s to be used to refer to railroad cars, especially to first-class passenger cars to distinguish them from sleepers. Sometime between about 1910 and 1930, the association with first-class compartments was lost, replaced by the idea of a *coach car* being any one where a large number of people sit. And of course, if a lot of people sit there, it's not exclusive. By the late 1940s, *coach seats* on a plane were the cheap seats.

And what does all this have to do with people in jogging outfits with whistles around their necks?

Blame the imaginative Oxford students of early Victorian England. That fastest-to-date of vehicles, the impressive **coach,** seemed a fitting metaphor for the university tutor who could carry a student along in such a way that he was sure to pass his exams. Both noun and verb soon left the cloistered colleges of Oxford and entered the general informal language, still frequently in quotation marks around 1850, and usually unmarked by the 1870s: "The superb Cuff himself, at whose condescension Dobbin could only blush and wonder, helped him on with his Latin verses; 'coached' him in play-hours . . ."(Thackeray, *Vanity Fair,* 1847–48).

This reference to "play-hours" doesn't refer to sports, but rather to Cuff's using out-of-classroom time to tutor Dobbin. However, by the 1860s, the concept of tutelage was extended to sports, first with boat racing and later with any kind of sport. So there you have it: from a Hungarian people-mover, to a one-man crash course, to a red-faced sideline presence. Evolution, yes—but progress?

~WRN

coast

PILAR MCADAM WROTE: It just struck me that the noun **coast,** as in *coastline,* seems very different from the verb **coast,** as in 'to move along (often downhill) without applying anything but an initial force, like on a sled'. Did these two words start out separately and converge? Or is there some common meaning?

Here is an early use of the noun **coast** that goes back to the root meaning of the word: "Syr Beaumayns smote hym thorou the cost of the body" (Malory, *Le Morte d'Arthur,* 1485). **Coast** comes from the Latin word *costa,* which means 'rib, flank, or side' and also gives us such words as *intercostal* and *cutlet* (through French *côtelette* 'little rib'). The Indo-European root is **kost-,* 'bone'. Until about 1800, **coast** could be used for the side of the body of a person or of an animal or of anything at all: "Otherwise the rays would not be refracted towards that coast rather than any other coast" (Newton, *Opticks,* 1704).

The other meaning of the noun **coast** in Middle English was the one that is now familiar to us: 'the side of the land' or 'the seashore'. It was used in this sense either with another noun, such as *land* or *sea* or *water,* or alone. From the 14th through the 17th centuries, **coast** could also mean 'a region': "While I abroad Through all the coasts of dark destruction seek Deliverance for us all" (Milton, *Paradise Lost,* 1667).

The verb **coast** originated in Middle English, where it had a multitude of senses including 'to go or move by the side of' a person or place or 'to travel by the coast of' a body of water or 'to approach' a place or person or 'to feel one's way'. All of these meanings have been either obsolete or very rare since the end of the 18th century.

French *côte* means 'rib, coast, shore'—and 'hill or slope'. There are not many examples of this meaning of **coast** in English, and the few I found are American. This sense of the noun is, however, the source of our modern verb meaning 'to slide on a sled down an icy hillside'. The meaning is implied in an American citation from 1775 and attested in the United States in the first half of the 19th century. From the sled on the icy hill, the sense was transferred to a bicycle. After the bicycle came the automobile.

By 1934, the *Dictionary of American Slang* by M. Weseen had the following entry: "Coast home, coast in . . . to win easily." **Coast** is, of course, now used alone in a figurative sense to mean 'to proceed with little or no effort': "After coasting through the late 1990s with older style and technology, they're struggling to stem losses in dollars and market share" (*USA Today*). It's been a long time since this meaning has been considered slang.

~GSM

cockamamie (COCK-uh-may-mee)

GUY HAAS WROTE: I've heard lots of **cockamamie** ideas, but lately I've been hearing a radio talk show host (with a Ph.D. no less) rendering the word as "cockamanie." Is it really a derivative of "decalcomania"? And is "cockamanie" a regional variant?

Of all the 'ridiculous or absurd' things, **cockamamie** is indeed a corruption of *decalcomania* (dee-kal-kuh-MAY-nee-uh).

There's one citation from Arthur Kober's *Parm Me* (1945) that spells the noun as *cockamanie,* but the usual form of both the adjective and the noun is **cockamamie.**

The French word *décalquer* means 'to transfer a tracing'. In the early 1860s, a craze for this method of decorating glass and porcelain jumped the channel from France to England. This craze was called *décalcomanie,* and there are citations of both the French spelling and the Anglicized *decalcomania* from that period. By the early 1950s, this form was abbreviated to *decal* and referred to the reverse transfer itself, including the fake tattoos that kids rub onto their skin and the AAA membership signs in car windows.

But whence **cockamamie?** Robert Chapman's 1986 *New Dictionary of American Slang* says it's "from New York City dialect." In the earliest citation, from Sidney Kingsley's 1935 play *Dead End,* the playwright uses **cockamamie** in the sense of 'a crazy or ridiculous person': "Haf an hour wid dat cockamamee yuh'd be dead!" Gerald Green, in *To Brooklyn with Love,* uses the same meaning when he re-creates 1930s Brooklyn slang. There's another indication of the Brooklyn connection, this time using **cockamamie** to mean 'decal', in a *New York Times* editor's gloss of Shelley Winters's use of the word to describe the movies she was in: "This word, translated from the Brooklynese, is the authorized pronunciation of decalcomania. Anyone there who calls a cockamamie a decalcomania is stared at."

It's certainly not uncommon for the pronunciation of words to be modified significantly (oh, OK, butchered) when they are borrowed into a language. The fancy linguistic description for what has happened to the pronunciation of *decalcomania* is a combination of elision (dropping of *de-* and

-l-), assimiliation (*kako-* becomes *kaka-; -mani*[*e/a*] becomes *-mamie*), and analogy (after such compounds as *cock-a-hoop, cock-a-dandy,* and even *cock-a-doodle-do*).

What's unclear is whether *decalcomania* came to be associated with ridiculous things or people before, during, or after the pronunciation transformation. We might look to the meanings of *cock-eyed, poppycock,* and *mania* and view it as guilt by association; or perhaps it was the fact that a **cockamamie** was a picture in reverse and either looked ridiculous on its own or could result in a ridiculous picture if transferred unskillfully. Chapman notes that decalcomanias were given away in candy boxes and gum packets, and that children used them for "antic self-decoration." (Translation: made themselves look ridiculous.)

⁓*WRN*

codger

S.C. Dixon wrote: Any ideas on the origin of **codger** when referring to an old person, particularly an old man?

In current American and British usage, **codger** is usually preceded by "old" and means 'an eccentric man, especially one who is old'. The word first appeared in Britain in the 18th century: "Old Cojer must not smoke that I have any concern" (Murphy, *Apprentice,* 1756) and "My Lord's servants call you an old out-of-fashion'd Codger" (Garrick, *Bon Ton,* 1775). **Codger** was also used in the 19th century to simply mean 'fellow' or 'chap'. In Dickens's *Nicholas Nickleby* (1838-39), Squeers says to Ralph, "I haven't been drinking YOUR health, my codger."

Glossaries of various dialects in Britain give a slightly different meaning: 'a miser; a stingy old fellow' (Sussex, 1875, and South Warwickshire, 1876); 'a dirty, mean old man' (Lincolnshire, 1877); 'a tramp; a mean pedlar; a term of contempt' (Cornwall, 1880).

But where did it come from? The 'poor peddler' sense points to a possible connection with *cadger,* a word that goes back to the 15th century. The modern verb *cadge* means 'to beg' or 'to get by imposing on another's generosity'. A *cadge* was initially an itinerant dealer who collected butter and eggs from remote farms for sale in town and also supplied those farms with goods from the shops. By the 19th century, the term was used for someone who hawked his wares in the streets and then for someone who went about begging or making his living in a disreputable way.

If **codger** is indeed a variant of *cadger,* we have an explanation for the pejorative sense of the word in the 19th century, but it's still not clear why it came to refer to an old man.

In 17th-century falconry, a *cadge* was a frame on which hawks were carried to the field. This is probably a variant of *cage* and might have resulted from confusion with the verb *cadge* meaning 'to carry about'. A *cadger* in falconry was the man who carried the cadge. A falconry Web site says that most cadgers were old falconers, and that's how **codger** came to be used for an old man. The problem is that the first citation for the falconry sense of *cadger* is from 1834 while the 'old man' sense of **codger** first appeared at least sixty years earlier.

It seems more likely that **codger** is indeed a variant of *cadger* meaning 'a tramp'. The fact that we usually say "old codger" rather than just "codger" indicates that the sense of 'old' is not necessarily implicit in the word itself but rather a meaning that developed over a period of time, perhaps because so many tramps were indeed old men.

~GSM

cold turkey and talk turkey

LORRAINE BRYAN WROTE: I've heard the phrase **cold turkey** used as an adverb, as in "go (or quit) cold turkey." But the dictionary also lists it as a noun with two unfamiliar definitions: 'blunt language or procedure' and 'a cold, aloof person'. Another unfamiliar definition related to the adverb is 'the symptoms experienced by a person undergoing drug withdrawal'. I have three questions: What does the temperature of turkeys have to do with drug withdrawal, who uses **cold turkey** to refer to blunt language or an aloof person, and can I say I "get cold turkey" when I try to give up caffeine?

By 1930 **cold turkey** was in use as an adjective, adverb, and noun in all the senses you ask about. *Random House Historical Dictionary of American Slang* has a few cites for 'cold, aloof', but this is not a common usage. The adjective more frequently means 'blunt, frank, plain', as in this quote from the *Daily News:* "Stalin didn't like certain cold-turkey facts [George] Kennan reported about Russia." The corresponding adverb has the senses 'impromptu' or 'bluntly, outright'. Carl Sandburg wrote in 1922: "I'm going to talk cold turkey with booksellers about the hot gravy in the stories." The noun, meaning 'the plain truth, the basic facts; blunt language or action', is illustrated by the phrase *let's get down to cold turkey*—roughly equivalent to *let's get down to business.*

The more familiar meaning of the noun is 'abrupt and complete withdrawal from the use of an addictive substance'. This could be a narcotic such as heroin but may also be nicotine, caffeine, and even a habit or addiction of any kind. The noun can also refer to the symptoms of withdrawal, so yes, you can say "I get cold turkey . . ." The corresponding adverb, as in the phrase *go* (or *quit*) *cold turkey* probably comes from the earlier phrase *talk cold turkey* 'to speak bluntly', the connection being the abruptness and unpleasantness of drug withdrawal. *Talk cold turkey* is probably a variant of the much earlier phrase **talk turkey,** also meaning 'to speak plainly, directly, or bluntly, with the intent of accomplishing something'.

There are various stories about the origin of **talk turkey.** One version is that a white man was talking to a Native American about dividing the game from a hunt: "You take the crow (or buzzard) and I'll take the turkey, or I'll take the turkey and you take the crow (or buzzard)." The Native American realized the white man was not talking turkey—he was not telling the plain truth. Or **talk turkey** may derive from the hunter's practice of making a gobbling noise so that the stupid turkey answers him with a gobble and gives away its whereabouts.

It may be that **cold turkey** is not connected to **talk turkey,** the correct connection being that leftover cold turkey is simple and unadorned, like the blunt and plain truth. Or it's been suggested that the goose pimples appearing as a symptom of drug withdrawal resemble the skin of a plucked turkey.

~CGB

colonel

Lynn Hsu Xavier wrote: I have been wondering about the origin of the military title **colonel**. Where did the word come from and why is it pronounced (KUR-nel) instead of (COH-loh-nel)?

Colonel is a perfect illustration of how the spellings and pronunciations of some English words can come to diverge. The culprit, as is often the case, is the word's etymology. Oddly enough, English took this word from Middle French in two forms—*coronel* (borrowed around 1550) and *colonel* (borrowed in the early 1580s). Both of these French forms were derived from Italian *colonnello* 'little column', and were so named because such an officer traditionally led the first little column at the head of a regiment.

The spelling with *r* was the result of dissimilation, the process by which a speech sound tends to become different from a neighboring sound. This process can be seen in the word *purple,* where the letter *l* was originally an *r* in the Old English word *purpure.* The influence of dissimilation can be heard currently in the common English pronunciation of *February* as (FEB-yoo-er-ee), in which the first (r) sound, difficult to say so close to the following one, becomes a (y).

The form *coronel* prevailed until the middle of the 17th century, when it disappeared in writing but not in speech. The written form with middle *l,* a closer reflection of the Italian, was increasingly favored in literary works, both in England and in France. Pronunciations for both English forms, however, (kol-uh-NEL) or (KUL-nel) for one, and (kor-uh-NEL) or (KUR-nel) for the other, survived until the early 19th century, when the pronunciation (KUR-nul), from which the middle unstressed syllable had fallen away through SYNCOPE, came to predominate. This pronunciation, derived from *coronel*, is the one that has persisted, while the spelling **colonel** has become the written standard. Hence the confusion.

The lexicographer John Walker (1732-1807) is quoted in *The Oxford Dictionary of English Etymology* (1966) as saying about **colonel,** "This word is among those gross irregularities which must be given up as incorrigible."

~*EP*

compass

JOSH GRECHUS WROTE: How did **compass** come to mean both: a) 'a device for determining directions' and b) 'an instrument for drawing or describing circles that consists of two hinged, movable legs'?

Compass actually has even more meanings than the two you give. Among other things, it can mean 'circle or circumference' and 'limits' and 'range' and 'capability'. As a verb, **compass** can mean 'to go around or encircle' or 'to achieve' or 'to make curved' or 'to comprehend'. Shakespeare used **compass** in at least fourteen different senses.

The verb is first attested in the late 13th century in the sense 'to contrive': "To such ende yt was y-come as he hadde y-compaced in ys thoght." The first appearance of the noun was in the early 14th century in a religious epic called *Cursor Mundi,* where it already had a variety of meanings: 'circumscribed area' ("in this compass"), 'ingenuity' ("wit compas slei"), and 'an instrument for taking measurements and describing circles' ("craftily casten with a compass"). In *Sir Gawain and the Green Knight* (1340), it meant 'proper proportion'. In Chaucer and in *Piers Plowman,* **compass** had the additional meaning of 'anything circular in shape'. And, when Chaucer speaks of "the trine compas," he means 'the three realms' of earth, sea, and heaven.

English **compass** was borrowed from Old French *compas* 'measure' or 'circle' or 'pair of compasses'. The Old French verb *compasser* means 'to measure' or 'to divide equally'. The ultimate origin of **compass** appears to be Latin *com* 'with' and *passus* 'a step or pace', and the original sense had to do with measuring.

The origin of the name of the measuring device (also called *compasses* or *a pair of compasses*) seems clear enough. Since it was used to describe circles as well as to measure, it's likely that the 'circle' sense of **compass** comes from the name of the device. If you draw a circle with a **compass,** you are "compassing" a circle. The 'understanding' sense of the verb is easily derivable from the 'measuring' sense.

But how did this word come to be applied to the instrument used for determining direction? It is possible that the application of **compass** to this instrument came from the sense 'circle' or 'circuit', referring to the shape of the dial—"all the points of the compass" form a circle. The earliest citations for this meaning in *The Oxford English Dictionary* date from around 1520, so we can assume it was established in spoken usage before that time.

A final note: German *Kompass,* Dutch and Norwegian *kompas,* and Danish *compas* all refer to an instrument for finding direction. Spanish *compas* and Portuguese and Italian *compasso* refer to the device for describing circles. French *compas* can be either, but that's a fairly recent development. In Old French it meant only the drawing device. So the Germanic languages adopted one meaning of the word, and the Romance languages the other.

~*GSM*

corny and corn

TRACEY WICKERSHAM WROTE: While checking the *Variety* Web site for some obscure fact, I saw in their *Slanguage Dictionary* that they claim original coinage of the word **corny.** This is a household word in my family, and I'm curious whether *Variety* really did invent it. If so, how did it filter to Enumclaw, Washington?

Launched in 1905, *Variety* (the show-biz publication) has had a reputation for slinging slang. As explained on its Web site: "In part it was a device to fit long words into small headlines, but it was also to create a clubby feel among the paper's entertainment industry readers." It's not clear whether *Variety*'s editors actually created the words or just spread and popularized them. Besides **corny,** the entertainment-industry terms *deejay, flack, lay an egg,* and *turkey* are all attributed to *Variety*'s creative staff.

Corny (and also **corn**) was first used by jazz musicians and critics in the late 1920s. It was a contemptuous term referring to jazz that was considered old-fashioned or dated, that is, of early 1920s vintage. By the 1930s **corny** was being used in mainstream publications—the popularity of swing bands caused jazz slang to filter into general slang. The term came to describe not only jazz, but poetry, emotional outbursts, or anything felt to be trite, overly sentimental, unsophisticated, or expressive of old-fashioned values.

The origin of **corny** and **corn** is connected with a few other terms referring to rural folk: *off/on the cob,* meaning 'rustic; unsophisticated' and *corn-fed,* originally meaning 'fed on grain; well-fed, plump' and later meaning 'rustic; unsophisticated' (1924) and 'trite; overly sentimental' (1933). So the connection is probably that country music (such as polkas and square-dance music) was branded by urban folk as unsophisticated and trite, and just plain inferior. A variation of this connection with rural life was suggested by the writer Mari Sandoz in 1946: "In the later homesteading period of the High Plains, 1890 to around 1910, the joke book that came free to every home . . . was the seed catalog [which] featured a great variety of seed corn . . . interspersed with short jokes and riddles, sometimes even cartoons. The jokes were all timeworn and over-obvious and were called corn catalog jokes or corn jokes, and any quip or joke of that nature was called corny."

Stuart Flexner's *Dictionary of American Slang* documents widespread teenage use of the terms **corn** and **corny** after 1940. But today's teenagers would consider these terms to be as old-fashioned as their parents' music, even in Enumclaw, Washington.

~*CGB*

cotton to

JOHN WILTENMUTH WROTE: Growing up in the Deep South I used to frequently hear the expression "I don't much **cotton to** that. . . ." I rarely hear it anymore but was curious as to how it came about.

You may not hear **cotton to** very often because it has now become more stigmatized as a Southern U.S. regionalism. However, various meanings of the verb have long histories and used to be more widespread.

Other than in its original, trade-specific meaning, *cotton* as a verb has always been used in informal, mostly spoken locutions. Five hundred years ago, to "cotton" wool was to use friction to make it rise to a regular nap. If cloth "cottoned well," the result was satisfactory, especially if you were trying to get the nap of different pieces of fabric to work together.

By extension, the expression *to cotton well* developed its first figurative meaning of 'to agree; suit; fit or go well together'. This meaning is listed in *The Century Dictionary,* and both it and *The Oxford English Dictionary* note the 16th- and 17th-century expression "this gear cottons," meaning that a situation is favorable or likely to succeed.

From the idea of getting on well together came the senses of 'fraternizing' (*cotton up to*) and 'agreement with or strong liking for' (**cotton to**). You could **cotton to** a person, an idea, or even a drink; nowadays, you usually hear the expression in the negative, *don't cotton to,* and it's usually used in reference to a concept, activity, or type of behavior rather than to people or concrete things. The following excerpts from recent list server discussions show that the expression is still alive and well:

"And by all means forgive me if I don't cotton to the current PC wary way of thinking about the world these days, I have no patience for that rubbish."

"Don't be surprised if some of the locals don't cotton to having stray cows wander across the road."

"You don't cotton to the idea your remote ancestors lived in a tree and went 'Ook ook!'"

You may also have *cottoned on to* the fact that there is another sense, used with *on*, that means 'to figure out'; this is largely a 20th-century meaning. We have a citation in our files from *Time* magazine, 1957: "... Washington's Democratic Senator Henry ('Scoop') Jackson, who had cottoned on to what the scientists were up to while visiting the Livermore plant."

$\sim$*WRN*

coulrophobia (kool-ruh-FOH-bee-uh)

DON HAGEN WROTE: Is there a word for 'fear of clowns'?

Yes, there is a word for it, and if you don't suffer from it (as I don't) then you would be shocked (as I was) at the number of people who fear or hate clowns. There are entire organizations supporting these folks, so if you count yourself among that number of people who shudder every time Ronald McDonald advertises the *McSalad Shaker* (and not just because you feel salad shouldn't be served looking like a beverage), take heart. Even celebrities suffer (by all reports, Johnny Depp has a touch of it).

Coulrophobia is the name for 'an unnaturally strong fear of clowns'. You may also hear it called *clownophobia* informally. The word comes from the Greek words *kōlobathēron,* 'stilt', and *phobia,* 'fear', and was coined fairly recently, in the 1980s.

Why do we fear clowns? Well, it seems that almost everyone has a horror story from a circus or celebration (again, I somehow escaped, and had a wonderful time at my eighth birthday party, balloon animals and all). Movies, TV, and books (*IT, Poltergeist, Killer Clowns from Outer Space, Seinfeld* with George and Eddie, *Animaniacs,* etc.) haven't helped. Then there are the costumes, face paint, and the terrifying element of surprise. And, of course, a few bad-apple clowns or the occasional true psycho (like John Wayne Gacy) have given all of those **coulrophobics** occasion to say "I told you so." Add to this the darker origin of the clown (probably a descendant of the Devil character in medieval miracle plays) and you get some serious fear.

Related phobias include *automatonophobia,* 'fear of ventriloquist's dummies'; *pediophobia,* 'fear of dolls'; and *pupaphobia,* 'fear of puppets'.

As for **coulrophobia,** I think Jack Handy's Deep Thoughts put it best on *Saturday Night Live:* "To me, clowns aren't funny. In fact, they're kind of scary. I've wondered where this started, and I think it goes back to the time I went to the circus and a clown killed my dad."

A sad and scary story indeed.

~*HGB*

cowabunga

KARL KARBACH WROTE: What does the American Indian word **cowabunga** mean?

Of course, pedant that I am, I must point out that there is not one Native American language but, rather, hundreds of them. That out of the way, **cowabunga** is as Native American in origin as *The Muppet Show*'s Swedish Chef's mutterings are Swedish. They both, in different generations, made television viewers laugh, but they are also both the creations of white guys of European extraction.

Almost any baby boomer will tell you that the first time he or she heard **cowabunga** (as it is now spelled) was on *The Howdy Doody Show*. The program ran from 1947 to 1960; Eddie Kean, the show's main writer until 1954, invented Chief Thunderthud and Princess Summerfall Winterspring as characters. Chief Thunderthud was supposedly the founder of Doodyville and began sentences with the nonsense syllable *kawa*. Anything that was good was "kawagoopa"; anything that was bad was "kawabonga." No one really has explained why this word for 'bad' was adopted by surfers in the 1960s (or, for that matter, why the spelling changed). Perhaps they already used the adjective *bad* to mean 'excellent'—a usage from Black English that became more widespread as jazz became more mainstream. And perhaps, if they wanted to shout something while surfing, "bad" didn't have enough syllables to sound like a really good way to say "killer wave, man."

And as long as we're speculating, there is a precedent in the use of *Geronimo!* for daredevils borrowing a Native American (or Indian-sounding) word as an exclamation: the paratroopers of the 505th battalion at Fort Benning, Georgia, after seeing the 1939 movie *Geronimo,* decided that would be a great word to shout as they jumped from the plane.

At any rate, if there are any aging beach boys out there who remember that a certain surfer first yelled **cowabunga** on a certain beach, word sleuths everywhere would love to hear about it. The word certainly has staying power, being resurrected by the Teenage Mutant Ninja Turtles in the 1980s and by Bart Simpson in the 1990s.

As for Eddie Kean's fake Indian-speak, people have been mocking or mimicking other people's speech since the Greeks coined the term BARBARIAN, which means 'bar-bar sayer' and really means 'those weird strangers whose language sounds like bar-bar-bar'. The practice underscores stereotypes and can be a tool for perpetuating racism, and I suspect that the same boomers who loved Howdy Doody as children would cringe if they listened to it now.

When everyone accepts the ground rules, however, linguistic difference is still a rich source of humor, as *The Muppet Show*'s Swedish Chef proves.

~WRN

cozen (KUZ-in)

CLARK BROOKING WROTE: In an excerpt from Captain John Smith's *A Description of New England,* 1616, I found the word **couzen** used this way: "... deceive thy friends, by fair promises and dissimulation, in borrowing where thou never intendest to pay; offend the laws, surfeit with excess, burden thy country, abuse thyself, despair in want, and then couzen thy kindred, yea even thine own brother, and wish thy parents' death (I will not say damnation) to have their estates?" I have unsuccessfully sought a definition of **couzen.**

After his famous adventures in Jamestown, Virginia, Captain Smith explored the coast from Nova Scotia to Rhode Island and gave it the name "New England." His book, *A Description of New England,* was a bestseller in its time.

The word you're looking for means 'to cheat; deceive; trick'. Judging by the sources in which it first appears, it was probably originally vagabonds' cant.

You couldn't find the word because the modern spelling is **cozen.** Before about 1710, it was spelled in many different ways: *coson, cousson, cousen, cosen, couzen, cozen.* Its early spellings suggest a derivation from (dialectal) Old North French *coçonner* 'to resell', from *coçon* 'retailer'.

The development of the word was probably influenced by Middle French *cousin,* which, in addition to its literal meaning of 'cousin', meant 'a dupe'. And Middle French *cousiner* is defined in Cotgrave's (1611) French-English dictionary as 'to clayme kindred for advantage, or particular ends; as he, who to save charges in travelling, goes from house to house, as cosin to the owner of everie one'. So Middle French *cousiner* implied (falsely) claiming kinship and then obtaining certain advantages, or even deceiving or cheating, under this pretext of kinship. Of course, you could also deceive or cheat your real relatives.

There is more about the connection with English *cousin,* which, by the way, used to refer to any relative, not just the son or daughter of an uncle or aunt. *The Oxford English Dic-*

tionary records the phrase *call cousins,* meaning 'to claim kinship with', and also the phrase *make a cousin of,* meaning 'to deceive or cheat'. So both English and Middle French *cousin* once meant 'a gullible person; a dupe', and these phrases play on the words **cozen/cousin.** Even the noun *cozenage,* 'the act of cozening; trickery', was originally spelled *cousinage,* the primary meaning of which is 'relationship of cousins; kinship'. The verse of Samuel Rowlands (1600) illustrates this double meaning: "Brotherhood once in kindred bore the sway, But that dates out, and Coosnage hath the day."

~CGB

criminy (KRIM-i-nee)

DANIEL RITZ WROTE: I was surprised to learn that *Gadzooks* is from "God's hooks," and is a form of swearing as in "I swear on the nails of the cross. . . ." *Jeepers Creepers* also refers to Jesus Christ, as well as many other exclamations (Gee, Jeez, etc.). I have not found anything on **criminy.** Is this a real word, and if so, what is its origin?

Criminy, which has also been spelled *crimini* or *crimeny,* is indeed a real word. *The Oxford English Dictionary* says it's 'a vulgar exclamation of astonishment: now somewhat archaic' and that it might be related to Italian *crimine* 'crime'.

Whatever its origin, **criminy** is one of those mild, old-fashioned euphemisms for "Christ," like *crikey, cracky, cripes, Christmas, Christopher Columbus,* and *G. Rover Cripes.* **Criminy** goes back at least to the 17th century: "O crimine! Who's yonder?" (Otway, 1681). In 1865 E. C. Clayton wrote in *Cruel Fortune:* "Criminy!—Raymond tight. I am astonished." That gives you some idea of the mildness of the oath by the middle of the 19th century! The situation was more serious in a 1700 quotation cited in *Slang and its Analogues:* "Murder'd my brother! O crimini!"

A similar euphemism is *jiminy,* as in *Jiminy Criminy* or *Jiminy Cricket* (which did not originate with Walt Disney), also meaning 'Jesus Christ'. Scholars speculate that *jiminy,* which has been spelled *gemony, geeminy, jiminy,* and *gemini,* derived through Low German from *gemini,* which was a corruption of the Latin *Jesu Domine* 'Jesus Lord'. This also goes back to the 17th century. Dryden in 1672 wrote "O Gemini! is it you, sir?" Byron played with the words in 1816: "Crimini, jimini! Did you ever hear such a nimminy pimminy Story as Leigh Hunt's *Rimini?*" And we find the following in *The Adventures of Tom Sawyer* (1876): "'Oh, geeminy, it's him,' exclaimed both boys in a breath."

Many cultures have prohibitions against speaking the name of God, and the third of the Judeo-Christian Ten Commandments forbids "taking the name of the Lord in vain." So we have developed euphemisms to fill the need for words to express astonishment, anger, frustration, and the like. This resulted in the 16th and 17th centuries in expressions like *Odd's bodkins* ('God's dear body'), *Gadzooks, zounds* ('God's wounds'), *'struth,* and *'sblood,* which leave out the word *God.* The mild-sounding *drat* probably comes through the 17th-century *od rat it* from "God rot."

A number of euphemisms retain the initial sounds of the taboo words, like *jeepers creepers* for "Jesus Christ" and *golly* and *gosh* for "God." Sometimes another word is substituted

for the forbidden, and we get expressions like *for Pete's sake,*
for the love of Mike, and *for crying out loud,* all variations on
"for Christ's (or God's) sake."

~GSM

curmudgeon (kur-MUDG-en)

JOHN CURRY WROTE: I would like to know the
origin/derivation of the word **curmudgeon**. It's one of
my favorite words, and I even have it spelled phonetically
on my vanity plate. Two questions specifically: 1) Is it related to the epithet "cur" at the beginning of the word,
and 2) Does it always refer to older men?

Curmudgeon is one of those words for which dictionaries
say "origin unknown," but there have been a number of theories over the centuries, and we'll take a look at some of them.

Random House Webster's Unabridged Dictionary defines
curmudgeon as 'a bad-tempered, difficult, cantankerous person'. It is usually applied to a man, especially an older man,
but that doesn't seem to be inherent in the word. The earliest
citations contain the sense of 'avaricious', but that has now
been lost.

According to *The Oxford English Dictionary,* the first written evidence of **curmudgeon** is in Richard Stanyhurst's *Description of Ireland,* published in Holinshed's *Chronicles* in
1577: "Such a clownish Curmudgen."

In 1600, Philemon Holland translated Livy's *History of
Rome* and rendered the Latin word *frumentarius* ('corn
dealer') with the word *cornmudgin.* That led, for a while, to

the supposition that the etymology was *corn* plus either Old French *muchier* or *mucier,* 'to hide', or Middle English *muchen* or *michen,* 'to steal'. In other words, a **curmudgeon** was one who hoarded grain. This explanation appeared in various etymological dictionaries until the early part of the 20th century. At that point, someone realized that the first appearance of the word predated Holland's use of it in 1600 by about a quarter century, and that Holland was making a play on words.

If you look up **curmudgeon** in Samuel Johnson's 1755 *Dictionary of the English Language,* you will find the following in parentheses before the definition: "It is a vitious manner of pronouncing *coeur méchant,* Fr. an unknown correspondent." *Coeur* means 'heart', and *méchant* means 'bad'. Dr. Johnson had apparently lost track of who had given him this etymology, and the "Fr." stands for 'from'. However, a man named John Ash published a *New and Complete Dictionary of the English Language* in 1775 in which he took Dr. Johnson's "Fr." to mean 'French' and, knowing no French, provided the etymology "from Fr. coeur 'unknown', mechant 'correspondent'." An embarrassing lexicographical moment.

Without having any real evidence, I think it's likely that **curmudgeon** has some connection with *cur,* which came into English early in the 12th century and is related to Germanic verbs meaning 'to growl'. As for the second part of the word, the *Century Dictionary,* published in 1889, suggests as a possible source either of two Scottish words, *mudgeon* 'grimace' or *murgeon* 'mock or grumble'.

I'm glad to hear that you are carrying on the curmudgeonly tradition. You probably know about Harold L. Ickes, who was secretary of the interior under FDR. He was famous for his outspoken bluntness and in 1943 published his *Autobiography of a Curmudgeon.*

~GSM

cut the mustard

CHARLES MCNEILL WROTE: Can't **cut the mustard**? It's an old phrase, and I have often wondered about its origin. It certainly is not intuitive or self-explanatory. *Mustard,* as we generally think of it, is not difficult or challenging to "cut"—and that's not what we do with it, anyway.

The semantic origin of **cut the mustard** ('to reach a desired standard') is still debated. The only thing anyone can state with assurance is that the first citation dates from the turn of the 20th century: "So I looked around and found a proposition that exactly cut the mustard" (O. Henry, *Works,* 1902).

There are two schools of thought about the *mustard* in question. One school believes that we are talking about actual *mustard,* the stuff you put on hot dogs. The other school thinks this mysterious *mustard* is probably a variant pronunciation of *muster.*

My intuition tells me to throw my lot in with this second group. **Cut the mustard** and *pass (the) muster* are synonymous. *Mustard* and *muster* sound alike. Obviously it is the same word, right? I am in good company if I choose this explanation, but I can't shake the bad feeling I get when I look at the books and articles on my desk and see that not a single one has unearthed a citation for *cut the muster.* If this were really a variant pronunciation, there should be citations every-where.

If anyone out there finds this missing link, then we can close the book on the *mustard* vs. *muster* controversy. Until then, let's look at the ways people have stretched that poor condiment *mustard* to make it fill this void.

There are those who claim that the *mustard* here refers to the mustard seed, which is very small and has a hard shell. Thus, **cutting the mustard** is difficult to do. Those who succeed in **cutting the mustard** (seed) are winners.

Others point out that mustard plants grow as large as 12 feet, and must be cut down in order to harvest the seeds. I haven't found an argument that explains the semantic leap from this *cutting* to the 'achieve success' meaning.

Still others refer to the vinegar used in the making of mustard. The ground mustard seeds are a base, and the vinegar is an acetic acid. My knowledge of chemistry fails me here, but I trust the people who actually make *mustard* when they tell me that vinegar is needed to **cut the mustard** (powder).

Finally, there are those who point out a use of *mustard* that referred to smart or courageous people early in the 20th century. They argue that this is the *mustard* in question, but again, the semantic leap is a long one.

The truth is that each of these proposed etymologies has a logical or linguistic weakness. I wanted to vote for one here in my conclusion, but I'm afraid I can't find a single explanation that **cuts the mustard.**

$\sim$*HGB*

deadbeat and beatnik

MATT BULL WROTE: Do you know the origin of the term **deadbeat?** I had always assumed that it was derivative of the **beatnik** movement of the 1950s. But my grandfather, who grew up near Frank Lloyd Wright (and dated his daughter), tells me that the locals used to call Wright a **deadbeat.** And that was at least as early as the 1920s.

Your grandfather is correct. **Deadbeat** is older than Frank Lloyd Wright. In fact, it dates from the Civil War period.

In the middle of the 19th century, one of the meanings of the verb *beat* was 'to swindle or cheat': "Our noble commander [is] contriving some plan . . . for to beat / From us everything . . . fit for to eat" (Huntington, *Songs Whalemen Sang,* 1849).

During the American Civil War, *beat* was used in military slang as a noun to designate a soldier who shirked duty: "A 'beat' is one who plays sick, shirks guard duty, drills, roll call, etc., and is always missing in a fight" (Wightman, *To Fort Fisher,* 1863).

Deadbeats were those soldiers who shirked duty by faking an injury or illness: "The really sick and the habitual deadbeats, anxious to escape duty, are marched from each company by a sergeant to the Surgeon" (Galwey, *Valiant Hours,* 1862).

Of course, human nature continues to produce shirkers, with or without a war. So we still have **deadbeats** of all varieties today: *deadbeat parents, tax deadbeats, deadbeat dates, deadbeat musicians,* and so on.

Since you brought up the **beatniks,** I will add a few words about that etymology. **Beatnik** was coined by Herb Caen, a columnist for the *San Francisco Chronicle,* in 1958. He combined the word *beat,* as in the *Beat Generation,* and the suffix *-nik,* probably by analogy with *Sputnik.* Some sources claim that the *beat* in the *Beat Generation* reflects 'jazz rhythm'; others say it is shortened from *beatitude.* The original citation from Caen proves both theories false: "*Look* magazine . . . hosted a party . . . for 50 Beatniks, and by the time word got around . . . over 250 bearded cats and kits were on hand, slopping up Mike Cowles' free booze. They're only Beat, you know, when it comes to work" (Caen, *San Francisco Chronicle,* April 2, 1958). So, your guess was actually backward. **Deadbeats** weren't named after **beatniks;** rather, **beatniks** were named after the slacking, shirking **deadbeats** of the last 100 years.

~HGB

deadline

STEVE WROTE: The term **deadline** refers to a specific time when a project is to be completed, but if it literally means something like a line beyond which you die, I'm wondering what harsh practice inspired the term?

This has been a week of **deadlines** for me. I have been feeling *under the gun,* so to speak, but I am happy to report that no one will actually die, whether or not we make our **deadlines,** and furthermore, that the likelihood of the term coming from a tradition of executing procrastinators is slim-to-none.

Dead has a number of figurative senses, from 'muffled' to 'absolutely'. The *dead* in **deadline,** however, is fairly close to the literal meaning, 'deprived of life'. There are two possible origins for the use you are describing.

Deadline first appeared as an American coinage that referred to the line around a military prison beyond which soldiers were authorized to shoot escaping prisoners. According to Lossing's *History of the Civil War* (1868): "Seventeen feet from the inner stockade was the 'dead-line', over which no man could pass and live." This use is also found in Congressional records as early as 1864: "The 'dead line', beyond which the prisoners are not allowed to pass." The citations for this use dry up at the end of the 19th century. It is possible that some Civil War buff in the early 20th century said, "If I don't get this essay finished by five o'clock, I'm dead!" and then thought, "Wow! Just like those guys who got shot escaping from prison! This is like my 'deadline'."

The other possibility is that the meaning of **deadline** we know today comes from an early-20th-century printing term. In the years before the first citation of **deadline** referring to a point in time, there are citations for the meaning 'a guideline on the bed of a printing press beyond which text will not print': "Make certain that the type does not come outside of the dead-line on the press" (Henry, *Printing for School & Shop,* 1917). This origin for our expression looks even more promising because **deadline** in the time-limit sense was originally an American publishing term, indicating the time after which material would not make it into a newspaper or periodical: "Corinne Griffith [the silent-era actress] . . . is working on 'Deadline at Eleven', the newspaper play" (*Chicago Herald & Examiner,* 1920).

There is no evidence to support a firm conclusion that the time-limit **deadline** came from one or the other of these two older uses. I am leaning toward the second possible origin on the grounds that the semantic drift is more likely within a particular speech community (in this case, publishing). This decision is not in any way based on my hope (as the clock ticks up to five o'clock) that there never was and never will be a truly "harsh" consequence for a little missed **deadline**.

~HGB

dead ringer and doppelgänger

SYLVIA CHROST WROTE: I've heard that the origins of the phrase **dead ringer** are tied to being buried alive and the idea of a **doppelgänger** or double.

A **doppelgänger** is 'a ghostly double or counterpart of a living person'; in German it means 'double goer'. This spiritual being inhabits the works of German Romantic writers and is typically used to symbolize a character's internal conflict. It's also a literary device used in the horror fiction of English-language authors such as Oscar Wilde and Edgar Allan Poe. A **doppelgänger** is usually sinister and exists to haunt the living person.

Fear of being buried alive is also a common literary theme in 18th- and 19th-century literature, first in Germany and later elsewhere. (Poe's 1839 "The Fall of the House of Usher" is an American example.) This fear was not unfounded. Until the 20th century, medical signs of physical death were unreliable; there are real cases of people being buried prematurely. A popular but untrue explanation of **dead ringer** is connected to the practice of tying a rope with a bell to a buried person's wrist. If the person was indeed buried alive, the bell could be rung for help.

Outside of literature, **doppelgänger** is sometimes used to mean 'a (living or dead) person who closely resembles someone else'. **Dead ringer** has the same meaning, but it's not a literary term. For example, maybe your boyfriend is a **dead ringer** for Brad Pitt. In this use, the adjective *dead* means 'perfect, absolute, exact, utmost', in reference to death being the final stage. *Ringer* means 'a double or counterpart'; so **dead ringer** means 'an exact double'.

But *ringer* has other pejorative meanings dating from the late 1800s. The basic sense is 'an impostor or deceptive substitute unfairly entered into a contest'. It can be a superior horse entered in a race to substitute for a slower horse, usually under an alias. Also in sports, a *ringer* is a professional athlete deceptively substituted for an amateur. In gambling games, a *ringer* is a marked deck of cards, a loaded pair of dice, a dishonest dealer, or an expert card player posing as a novice. A counterfeit item can be called a *ringer*. Other related meanings are: 'an outsider; uninvited guest; intruder'.

The noun *ringer* comes from the verb *ring (in)*, in the early 1800s meaning 'to falsify, disguise, or alter' or 'to introduce or substitute fraudulently'. *Ring (in)* can also mean 'to join with others, usually in an intrusive way'. These uses are probably connected to the meaning 'to announce by ringing a bell'. There is also a probable association with the slang expression *ring the changes* 'to substitute counterfeit money in various ways', a pun on the standard sense 'to go through all the variations in ringing a peal of bells'. As an alternative origin for *ringer*, Thomas L. Clark's *The Dictionary of Gambling and Gaming* says it was originally a finger ring with a small flange used for palming cards.

~CGB

diaper

DON WILLMOTT WROTE: My friend just came to visit, and he brought his baby boy along. That, of course, got me thinking about **diapers.** My dictionary seems to suggest that there's more to **diapers** than Pampers. Meanwhile, the Anglophile in me wants to know if anyone in Britain uses the word **diaper,** or whether all **diapers** are "nappies" over there. Care to elaborate?

The most well-known meaning of **diaper** is, of course, 'a piece of cloth or other absorbent material folded and worn as underpants by a baby not yet toilet-trained'. That's actually a secondary and relatively recent meaning for the word. **Diaper** originally referred to a kind of cloth, and still does.

Diaper is an old English word that's been in print (or scroll) at least since 1300. *The Barnhart Dictionary of Etymology* traces the roots of **diaper** to the Medieval Greek word *díaspros,* which means 'very white' or 'pure white'. It is a melding of the prefex *dia-*, which means 'entirely' or 'very', and the word *áspros,* meaning 'white'.

If you're starting to think, "Well, that makes sense. Diapers are white, have been for decades," think again. *Áspros* made its way into Medieval (i.e., Byzantine) Greek by way of the Latin word *asper,* which means 'rough'. (The English word *asperity* has the same root.) It did not take on the meaning of 'white' until probably after 900 A.D.

How did *áspros* go from meaning 'rough' to meaning 'white'? *Barnhart* says, "The shift in meaning of Greek 'áspros' from rough to white occurred during the time of the Byzantine empire in referring to newly minted pieces of silver, with figures in relief." My conjecture is that the transitional key is in the patterns of fine cloth being made in Byzantium. If you look at the patterns of the fine linens of today, some of them have a bas-relief quality to them—like coins. Soon enough, *díaspros* evolved into the Old French word *diaspre,* which was, as *Fairchild's Dictionary of Textiles* says, 'originally a rich, costly silk fabric woven in a small diamond-shaped pattern. Uses: vestments, etc., in the Orient'.

Eventually, the word entered English and referred solely to a kind of rich cloth. In 1513, in a poem titled "St. Werburge," a dinner with **diaper** cloth is described: "The tables were couered with clothes of Dyaper Rychly enlarged with syluer and with golde." Through the ages the cloth became less and less fine and today refers to a rather low-quality fabric. Presumably, it was somewhere along in this transition that the cloth began to be used for babies' bottoms. The first recorded use of **diaper** as a protective garment for babies is in 1837 in the United States.

As to whether anyone in Britain uses the word **diaper,** the answer is no. Well, maybe Brits with American friends use **diaper** instead of *nappy.* (The derivation of *nappy* is fairly simple, by the way: it comes from *napkin*).

Now, I think I'll go get changed for dinner.

~*RG*

disk and disc

MARINA PADAKIS WROTE: Mavens, please explain the distinction between **disc** and **disk.** At work we have been using **disk** for computer-related items, and **disc** for non-computer items. But then we get into trouble with "CD" vs. "CD-ROM" (i.e., compact disc vs. compact disk-read only memory). Laser disk or disc? Video disc or disk? Help!

Chaos is the rule when **disk** meets **disc.** Everyone has his or her own standard, and while some experts feel very strongly that they have the answer, there is no consensus. So, the good news is that it is very difficult to be entirely wrong.

Most general publications have adopted the standard that **disk** is correct in all circumstances but allow that many people also use the variant **disc.** The *New York Times,* the *Wall Street Journal,* and Random House all adopt this stance.

The other major school of thought tends to be supported by technical writers and has been adopted as the style of *Wired, Emedia, IEEE Computer Magazine,* the *Optical Video Disc Association,* the *DVD Video Group,* and others. This orthographic standard makes the distinction between **disks,** which are 'magnetic media' like floppy disks or hard disks, and **discs,** which are 'optical media' (i.e., read with a laser) like audio compact discs or CD-ROMs. Even the techno-geeks hit the wall of disagreement if you ask about magneto-optical disks/discs. No one has all of the answers.

Further confusion is introduced by the orthographic preference in British English for **disc** over **disk** as a general rule, with the sole exception of floppies and hard disks, which are written **disk** because of the influence of American English. **Disk** and **disc** both come to English from the French *disque* (spelled with a *-que,* no less!), so there is no etymological reason to prefer one or the other.

In my personal writing I fall in with the techno-spelling standard, though not because I understand the difference between magnetic and optical storage. For me the round objects like audio CDs and CD-ROMs are **discs** and the rectangular things—or the ones that look rectangular from the outside—are **disks.**

My advice would be to write whichever comes naturally, but to stay consistent. If you can only do this by simplifying everything to **disk,** then count yourself in good company and wave the *Times* at anyone who picks on you. If you are comfortable with the optical-magnetic distinction, then use it. The techies will applaud you.

~HGB

Dixie

SEVERN E. S. MILLER WROTE: I have heard two completely plausible and contradictory derivations for **dixie.** One simply has it that **dixie** derives from the Mason-Dixon line. . . . The other explanation is that **dixie** derives from a denomination of French money used in what became the Louisiana Purchase. The dix-franc (or whatever) coin would have been used in that region of the South. If this were the case, maybe we could start referring to Canada as "Loonie."

Or Canadians could refer to the United States as "Buck."

Dixie Land first appeared in the text of the song "Jonny Roach" by the minstrel show songwriter and Northerner Daniel Emmett in 1859; in the same year he also wrote a song called "Dixie's Land." There are no print references before that.

The University of Chicago Press's 1936 *A Dictionary of American English on Historical Principles* lists three possible etymologies. One is from the New Orleans banknote that bore the French word for ten, *dix;* these were called "dixies," and so the name then came to be applied to the South. The editors give short shrift to this theory, and we can too: there just doesn't seem to be any evidence for it.

The editors also note that many people think it simply derived from the Mason-Dixon line, but then they say "the weight of the testimony seems to point to a different origin." That origin, they assert, is from a man by the name of **Dixie** who had a plantation on Manhattan Island and was forced to take his slaves and move south because of antislavery sentiment in the North. His slaves liked their old plantation, which had been called "Dixie land," better than the new one, and often pined for it.

Aside from the obvious problem that Mr. Dixie's slaves would have been singing "up North in Dixie," there's no evidence that the term **Dixie** was used by Southerners before Emmett's song was published. Rather, I think it is clear that Emmett's song helped to popularize a term that was already being used by Northerners to refer to the South. Indeed, in 1861, a *Confederate Reader* contributor called H. Hotze expressed his fear that this northern term would end up being used to refer to the South: "This tune of 'Dixie'. . . . we shall be fortunate if it does not impose its very name on our country. The word 'Dixie' is an abbreviation of 'Mason and Dixon's line'. . . . Years before I heard the tune I have heard negroes in the North use the word 'Dixie' in that sense. . . ."

And as Emmett told his biographer in 1872: "'Dixie's Land' is an old phrase applied to the Southern States . . . lying south of Mason and Dixon's line. In my traveling days amongst showmen, when we would start for a winter's season south, while speaking of the change, they would invariably ejaculate [sic] the stereotyped saying:—'Wish I was in Dixie's Land,' meaning the southern country."

That's as close to the horse's mouth as we can get, methinks.

∼WRN

dumbbell

LYNNE WASNER WROTE: I'm interested in bells and found myself thinking about the origin of **dumbbell.** Does it derive from an unrung (mute) bell or perhaps one without resonance, and hence the association to one's (lack of) mental brilliance? Or could it derive from the type of person known to lift **dumbbells?**

Yes, **dumbbells** have a connection with bells, specifically with *campanology,* the art of bell ringing. Sometime during the 8th century, church towers began to be built to contain hanging bells. As lofty towers or turrets were being built for these bells, the bells themselves got bigger and bigger. Large-sized bells allowed the inhabitants of the towns and hamlets to hear the bell ringing, even if they weren't near the church. Though at Canterbury in the Middle Ages there were 24 men required to ring one bell, in general, bells could not be too large because of the difficulty of ringing them. Not only were they difficult to ring, but bell ringing required a great deal of practice. So a device was invented, consisting of a heavy weight suspended from a rope, to be used by novice bell ringers to develop their strength and skill.

Later, a similar device was used by gentlemen wishing to develop their physique. The term **dumbbell** is first recorded in 1711 in Joseph Addison's writings in the *Spectator:* "I exercise myself an Hour every Morning upon a dumb Bell . . . My Landlady and her daughters . . . never come into my room to disturb me while I am ringing." Since these exercise devices had heavy weights instead of real bells, they were *dumb* in the sense 'silent or mute'. The type of **dumbbell** with which we are familiar—roundish weights connected by a graspable bar—was in use by the middle of the 18th century, but at that time it was often made of wood.

The earliest recorded sense of *dumb* is 'lacking the power of speech; mute; silent'. (This is now usually offensive when applied to people.) The later sense 'stupid or ignorant' dates from about 1756, probably influenced by the German word *dumm,* which has the same meaning. Although a connection is possible, there is no proof of analogy between the two meanings of **dumbbell:** an exercise device and a stupid person. The slang term **dumbbell,** in the sense 'a stupid person', came into English around 1918. In this use of the word, *dumb* means 'stupid or ignorant', and *bell* probably refers to the head. For example, *to ring someone's bell* is to hit someone very hard on the head.

~*CGB*

Easter

MYLES ZUCKERMAN WROTE: I am curious as to the origin of the name **Easter** for the spring holiday. Is it connected to the direction *East?*

East and **Easter** are related in that they have a common Indo-European root: **aus-* 'to shine'. From this we get *east* 'the direction of the sunrise'. Our word **Easter** comes from Old English *ēastre,* which, according to the Venerable Bede, derived from *Eostre,* the Teutonic goddess of the dawn. The Indo-European word **ausos-* meant 'dawn' or 'a goddess of the dawn', and the names of the Greek and Roman dawn goddesses *Eos* and *Aurora* come from the same root.

But what does an Anglo-Saxon dawn goddess have to do with **Easter?** Eostre's festival was celebrated at the vernal equinox, and the commemoration of Christ's resurrection had to be a spring feast because of the connection with the Jewish Passover. The early Christian missionaries to Britain seem to have been practical folk and found it easier to attach the most important feast of the new religion to an already-existing spring festival. The rabbits and the eggs are, of course, also vestiges of the pagan celebration of spring and fertility. And the sunrise service on **Easter** morning? At pre-Christian spring festivals, people danced to greet the sunrise, and there is an old belief that the sun rising on **Easter** morning dances in the heavens. The custom of lighting the "new fire" at the **Easter Even** service also has its origin in pre-Christian Celtic customs.

In many European languages (the exception is German *Oster*), the name for **Easter** comes from *pesaḥ*, the Hebrew word for 'Passover': Greek *páscha,* Latin *pascha,* French *Pâques,* Italian *Pasqua,* and Dutch *Pasen.* From the Old English period until the 17th century, both **Easter** and *Pasch* (pronounced "pask") were used interchangeably to mean 'Passover' and 'Easter'. In the *Peterborough Chronicle* of 1122 we find: "On this geare waes se king Heanri on Christes maessen on Norhtwic, and on Paxhes he waes on Norhtham-tune" (This year King Henry was in Norwich for Christmas and in Northampton for Easter). A 1563 homilist spoke of "Easter, a great, and solemne feast among the Jewes." **Easter** eventually won out for the name of the Christian holiday, though *Paschal* (PAS-kul) is still an adjective meaning 'Easter', as in "Paschal candle" and "Paschal lamb." In Scotland and the North of England, children hunt for "Pasch eggs."

~*GSM*

-ed, the vanishing suffix

A MAINE FAN WROTE: It seems to me that constructions like *ice tea, old-fashion, whip topping,* and even *bake potato* are becoming more common. These look just awful to me. . . . On the other hand, nobody says *iced cream.* Is there any reason for the difference?

I share your pain. Modifiers without the **-ed** are proliferating—in coffee shops, supermarket aisles, just everywhere. *Can soda, can milk,* and *butter roll* have replaced *canned soda, canned milk,* and *buttered roll.*

It was not always thus. In the 12th and 13th centuries, **-ed** was pronounced as a separate syllable, as it is now in words like *salted.* For example, in the romantic poem *Havelok the Dane* (c1290), in the line meaning 'Ubbe dubbed him [to] knight', written as "Vbbe dubbede him to knith," the second word was said as (DUB-ed).

By the 16th and 17th centuries, **-ed** was no longer pronounced separately unless appended to a root ending in a (d) or (t) sound, as in *landed* or *started.* Thus *dubbed* was (dubd) and *stopped* (stopt). Writers of this period often used shortened spellings, including contractions, to reflect this: "He dubd on saint Michaell the archangels daie thirtie knights" (*Holinshed Chronicles,* 1577-87). ". . . Dub'd by his Grace with the Sword of State" (1685). Today, **-ed** remains a separate syllable in a few words like some senses of *blessed* (BLES-id), the noun *beloved* (bi-LUV-id), and the adjective *learned* (LUR-nid) or in biblical verse and song: "(HAL-ow-ed) be thy name."

But why is **-ed** dropped altogether? Assimilation plays a role. That is, when (d) or (t) is followed immediately by (d) or (t), there is a powerful tendency for the adjacent sounds to blend into a single sound. Even in perfectly standard speech you rarely hear the (-t) sound of *iced* and the (t-) of *tea* in *iced tea* as separate and distinct; you hear *ice tea.* The analogous *ice coffee* is not far behind.

In addition, speakers of some dialects, as well as newcomers just beginning to learn English, may tend to reduce final consonant clusters. For example, *next* may be (neks) or (nek). Or they may omit final consonants entirely. If you don't say them, it's difficult to hear them. And if you don't hear them, you probably won't write them. You'd have to notice them through reading. No wonder those sounds drop out.

I suspect, though, that most existing spellings won't change in the near future, at least in standard writing. Even *ice tea,* a likely winner, hasn't quite made it yet. An online search of recent major newspapers has *iced tea* prevailing in print over *ice tea,* eight to one. *Ice cream,* on the other hand, has been spelled with *ice* almost since it began to delight our taste buds in the mid-18th century. But wait; *The Century Dictionary* (1889) includes a bracketed caution: "[*Strictly iced cream*]." There's a bit of history even there.

⁓EP

either and neither

STEWART AND LILLIAN MEIN WROTE: There are two ways of pronouncing the words **either** and **neither** (with the "ei" pronounced with "ie," like the "i" in *like* or like the "ee" in *queen.*) Which is the correct way, and when did people start pronouncing them the other way?

The simple answer to the first question is that both are correct. (Or should I say "**either** is correct"?) But there is more to your question than that. These words have an interesting history that provides a glimpse into the kinds of attitudes that can develop about language.

In 17th-century England, the prevailing pronunciation was (ay) as in *cake,* with an occasional alternative (eh), so that **either** and **neither** rhymed with *weather.* The (ay) vowel remains for these words in parts of present-day Ireland and Scotland.

By 1800, both (ee) as in *weed* and (ie) as in *wide* were in general use in England. From the 19th century on, (ie) came to predominate there, especially in Southern England.

In most of the United States, the (ee) pronunciation is the most frequent and has been from this country's birth. Compilers of early American dictionaries (e.g., John Walker, 1836; Noah Webster, 1838) did not show (ie) at all. It was not until the 19th century that (ie) was borrowed from British speech. In 1911, the *Century Dictionary* added (ie), and from the 1930s on, (ee, ie) has been the pattern in American dictionaries.

As a relatively recent British borrowing, (ie) is found most frequently in the parts of the United States that have maintained historical and cultural ties with England— namely, New England and parts of the eastern seaboard. It is also heard on radio and television.

But this alternate pronunciation, whatever its history and regional distribution, has become a source of controversy, even vituperation. In the minds of many Americans, it remains closely associated with British educated speech. And while for some people, that lends (ie) a certain cachet, for others, it is a symptom of snobbery. Fueling this thinking is a quote from Daniel Jones's *An English Pronouncing Dictionary* (1924), where (ie) and (ee) are said to be the pronunciations "most usually heard in the everyday speech of families of Southern English persons whose menfolk have been educated at the great public boarding schools." And one British usage manual (Kingsley Amis, 1998) finds the (ee) pronunciation "a trifle underbred."

In sum, on both sides of the Atlantic (ee) and (ie) are considered standard pronunciations, shown in dictionaries without cautionary labels. However, it is useful to realize that in this country, at least, there are people who will sharply criticize (ie) as an affectation, and a borrowed one at that, even if it is a pronunciation you grew up with, integral to your natural speech.

~EP

-en and -s/-es

DAVID SCHREIBER WROTE: I've read that the English language once formed plurals the same way as Dutch and German, by adding **-en** to a singular noun (as in *oxen*), but today most English plurals are formed by adding **-s/-es** to the end of a word. How and why did something so basic as forming plurals change in English?

It was probably a case of survival of the fittest. The trend in language is to conform the few exceptions to the pattern of the regular rule. The **-s/-es** plural is derived from the regular (*strong*) plural inflection in Old English. Over half of the nouns in Old English and many of the most common nouns fell into this category. Since it was the most frequently used plural form, it prevailed over the **-en** plural.

Specifically, the **-s/-es** plural comes from the Old English possessive singular and nominative-accusative plural forms of "a-stem" masculine nouns. The "a" was the sound with which the stem ended in Germanic. Actually, the nominative-accusative plural form was originally *-as,* but in Middle English it became **-es** and was shortened to **-s.**

In Old English, there were also nouns in the irregular (*weak*) declension, forming their plural by adding *-n* or *-an,* and later, **-en.** These are the "n-stems." The word *oxen* is the only survivor of this group, though Middle English had forms such as *handen* 'hands'.

Other irregular plurals were so-called double plurals— the **-en** was added to an already plural form. *Brethren, children,* and *kine* (a poetic word meaning 'cows') illustrate this category. Another group of irregular plurals were called *mutated* plurals; modern examples are *feet* and *teeth.* And some plurals did not change their form from singular to plural; a modern example is *sheep.*

In the 13th century, the **-en** plural was used in England's Southern dialects, and the **-es** plural in the North and Midlands. By the 14th century, the **-es** plural was considered the regular form, and many nouns from other declensions, as well as new nouns, went over to this category. The result was that English noun inflection was simplified.

∼CGB

epiphany

MARCUS P. HAGEN WROTE: I'm seeing references all over to people having an **epiphany** when they really mean that they received a "revelation." It seems the meaning of the word is being lost. Any comments?

The Christian Feast of the **Epiphany** is celebrated on the 6th of January, the twelfth day after Christmas and the day after Twelfth Night. It is usually regarded now as the commemoration of the visit of the Magi (or Wise Men) to the infant Jesus. Theologically, Epiphany actually celebrates three events: the visit of the Wise Men, the baptism of Jesus, and the miracle at the wedding feast at Cana. All of these events were manifestations to the Gentiles of Christ's divinity and that's what **epiphany** means. The Greek word *epipháneia* means 'appearance' or 'manifestation' and comes from the verb *epiphaínein* 'to show forth' or 'display'. In the world of ancient Greece, the word *epipháneia* denoted a manifestation of divine power or a deity's appearance to a worshiper. Herodotus used the adjectival form to mean 'suddenly coming into view' when speaking of the gods.

Epiphany came into English from Old French and is first attested in the 14th century: "The epyphany, when the kynges come wery to present hyre sone with myrre, gold, and encenz."

By the 17th century, **epiphany** was being used to refer to the appearance of any supernatural being. In 1840 De Quincey used the word in a more general sense: "There had been two manifestations or bright epiphanies of the Grecian intellect." However, this usage is rare.

The current secular sense of an **epiphany** as 'a revelation' seems to have originated with James Joyce. In *Stephen Hero,* the early version of *A Portrait of the Artist as a Young Man,* written in 1914, Stephen overhears a conversation "out of which he received an impression keen enough to affect his sensitiveness very severely." Joyce calls such a moment an **epiphany** and says that in it, "the soul of the commonest object . . . seems to us radiant." It is the moment of a sudden, intuitive flash of perception and insight, usually caused by something very simple and commonplace. Joyce was not, of course, the first person to have such experiences, but he was the first to call them **epiphanies;** he wrote about 70 short pieces that he called *Epiphanies.*

Poets, novelists, literary critics, philosophers, theologians, and psychotherapists have been writing about **epiphanies** for years. More recently, people from gossip columnists and pollsters to CEOs and athletes are having them. The sense of 'revelation' is true to the root meaning of the word, but I confess that I cringe when I read a sentence like this one: "The trouble with CEOs like Allaire and Armstrong, laudable as their now ice-clear view of reality may be, is that they didn't have their epiphanies until the market hit them with a sledgehammer" (*Fortune,* 2001). Or when I find a Web site for a restaurant and bar called "Club Epiphany."

$\sim$*GSM*

eponym (EPP-uh-nim) and eponymous (uh-PON-uh-mus)

JOYCE LOVELACE WROTE: What word describes proper nouns that have come to be words with their own meaning, such as *Scrooge, Pollyanna, Xerox, Scotch tape?*

Scrooge 'a miserly person' (from the miserly misanthrope in Dickens's *A Christmas Carol*) and *Pollyanna* 'a blindly optimistic person' (from the heroine of Eleanor Porter's novels) are examples of a common type of English word formation.

The linguistic term is **eponym,** 'a real or imaginary person from whom a word is derived'. An **eponym** is also 'a word derived from a person's name'. For example, *Seatlh,* an Indian chief, is the **eponym** of Seattle, and, conversely, Seattle is an **eponym** derived from *Seatlh.* Said yet another way, *Seatlh* is the **eponymous** Indian chief who gave Seattle its name. **Eponym** and **eponymous** are ultimately derived from a Greek adjective, literally meaning 'upon name'.

Dickens's novels are the source of other **eponyms.** *Pecksniffian* (from Seth Pecksniff in the novel *Martin Chuzzlewit*) describes someone who embodies the trait of 'hypocritically affecting benevolence or high moral principles'. Not only do literary characters spawn **eponyms,** but **eponymous** adjectives are derived from authors' names. For example, *Dickensian* describes eccentric characters, squalid conditions, plots full of coincidences, or humor mixed with pathos. If you're wondering why we say *Dickensian* and *Faulknerian* as opposed to *Kafkaesque* and *Byronic,* there is no hard-and-fast rule as to which suffix is correct. In fact we can say *Whitmanesque* or *Whitmanian* and *Voltairean* or *Voltairian.* And, as far as I know, there is no rhyme or reason as to why Whitman and Keats are **eponymous,** but Poe and Shelley are not; perhaps it's poetic justice.

Eponyms can be compound nouns (*Melba toast*), verbs (*lynch*), altered forms (*dunce*), suffixed forms (*galvanize*), or even blends (*gerrymander*). Sometimes they take the possessive form (*Alzheimer's disease*). Some **eponyms,** such as *boycott,* were originally capitalized, and others, such as *maverick,* were always lowercased. Some are still capitalized, such as *Pollyanna,* and others are written either way. Both *scrooge* and *Scrooge* would be correct.

The other terms you mention, *Xerox* and *Scotch tape,* are trademarked names, but they are not based on a person's name, as are the trademarks *Listerine* and *Levi's.* There is no linguistic term for a trademark that is so ubiquitous that it stands for the thing itself, as *Band-Aid* for 'adhesive bandage'. It's an example of *synecdoche,* the rhetorical device of substituting the particular for the general.

~*CGB*

eventide

RICH RODEK WROTE: One of my favorite recordings by the group Grey Eye Glances is named **Eventide.** How did this word, meaning 'evening', come about?

I've known the word **eventide** since childhood from the hymn "Abide with me, fast falls the eventide," so for me it's always had religious/poetic connotations. When I looked it up on the Internet, I found it's now used as the brand name for a multitude of products from figurines to sound equipment! In Britain, an "eventide home" is a home for the elderly.

Eventide goes back to Old English *æfen-tid* and is found as early as the 10th century. It was common in literature through the 19th century. In Genesis 24:63 in the 1611 King James Bible, "Isaac went out to meditate in the field at the eventide." It was also used figuratively in a 1578 prayer: "This life hath not one hour certain, whensoever the eventide thereof cometh."

Æfan 'evening' is found in *Beowulf,* as is *tīd* (pronounced with a long *i*). From the 8th century until the 19th, *tide* meant either 'an extent of time' ("There they alight . . . and rest their weary limbs a tide." Spenser, *Faerie Queene*, 1590), 'a point in the duration of a period of time or an occasion' ("But we will see it—joyful tide! Some day . . . the mountains will we cross." Wordsworth, 1805), or 'a favorable time or an opportunity' ("The foolish virgins lost their tide: the wise had much ado to gain it." M. Lawrence, 1657).

The seven canonical hours of the church were called *tides*. *Tide* has also been used for over a thousand years in combination with other words to denote a definite time in the course of a day (*noontide*) or a season of the year (*summertide*) or a festival of the church (*Eastertide*).

Tide didn't mean 'the periodic rise and fall of the waters of the ocean and its inlets' until at least the 14th century. The Middle Low German word *getîde* had the same meanings as Old and Middle English *tid* and *tide,* but it also referred to the tide of the ocean. Old English used *flōd* or *flōd and ebba* for the ocean tide. It's not certain whether English later adopted the Middle Low German word or whether a similar transference of meaning took place with the English word *tid.* There is no evidence for a borrowing, so it was probably a parallel development.

When Chaucer wrote, "For day to nyght it changeth as the tyde" in the "Man of Law's Tale" (1386), it is likely that he meant the time of the flood tide rather than the flood tide itself. By the middle of the 15th century, however, *tide* clearly meant 'the ebb and flow of the sea' though it also retained vestiges of its earlier meanings.

$\sim$*GSM*

☞ familiar (noun)

LIZ KEUFFER WROTE: I'm wondering about the term "my **familiar**." I've seen it in the title of the book *The Temple of My Familiar* by Alice Walker and recently came across it in reading *Jane Eyre*. What exactly is "my **familiar**"?

In the sense that both Walker and Brontë are using the term, a **familiar** is the noun form of the phrase *familiar spirit.*

The adjective **familiar** came into Middle English from Old French and was originally used to describe anything or anyone relating to one's family or household. You could even have a *familiar enemy*—an enemy within your own gates, well known to you. The adjective also had the meaning 'intimate', the meaning from which the now-predominant sense of 'well-known' stems. The idea of 'too intimate' still survives in some old-fashioned expressions such as *get familiar with someone,* as in "You can sit next to me, but don't you try to get familiar." Charlotte Brontë's Rochester, in his use of *familiarly,* seems to imply both of these meanings when he speaks of his past life: "Hiring a mistress is the next worse thing to buying a slave: both are often by nature, and always by position, inferior; and to live familiarly with inferiors is degrading."

In the expressions *familiar angel* or *familiar spirit/devil,* the adjective carried the sense of intimacy. A *familiar angel* was a guardian angel; a *familiar spirit* or devil was in league with a human or was possessing a human. Rochester says his wife is "prompted by her familiar to burn people in their beds at night, to stab them, to bite their flesh from their bones, and so on." This is clearly Linda Blair in *The Exorcist*, not Wendy the Good Little Witch.

In contrast, Alice Walker's **familiar** is more of a manifestation of a life force that is the thread that connects people and animals across five hundred years of spiritual interaction. This is closer to the idea of a "familiar angel," and certainly would be the one I'd pick, if the choice were offered!

~*WRN*

fascination

MICHAEL SCHWARTZ WROTE: I have been told that **fascination** comes from *fascia,* the original bundle of sticks surrounding an axe handle that was the sign of Imperial Rome. However, I have also been told that, prior to sticks and an axe, the original "fascia" were statues of erect phalluses. Is this true or a stretch of someone's overactive imagination?

Actually, **fascination** does not come from *fascia*. There are several different words involved here.

Let's start with *fascia,* which is 'a band or bandage'. It is related to *fascis* 'a bundle or packet'. The plural *fascēs* was the name for the bundle of sticks with an axe projecting from it that was carried before the chief Roman magistrates as a symbol of power: the sticks for whipping, the axe for execution. The *fascēs* was the symbol of the *Fascist* government in Italy, which purported to be returning to the virtues of ancient Rome. The Indo-European source of *fascia* and *fascēs* is **bhasko-* 'gathering, bundle'. *Fasces* in English usually refers to the Roman emblem, but some authors have used it to mean 'a bundle'. Here's Melville in *Moby Dick* (1851): "With a frigate's anchors for my bridle-bitts and fasces of harpoons for spurs, would I could mount that whale and leap the topmost skies. . . ."

Fascinate, which came into English at the end of the 16th century with the meaning 'to bewitch', derived, by way of French *fasciner*, from Latin *fascināre* 'to bewitch or enchant'. It also meant 'to cast under a spell by a look' and was used especially to refer to the power of a serpent over its victim. The word lost the witchcraft connotation after the 17th century but continued to have the sense of 'charming and enchanting in a way that is difficult to resist'. Since the 19th century, the meaning of *fascinate* (like the meaning of *charm*) has weakened considerably. It now most commonly means 'to attract and hold a person's attention by some special quality'.

Now we come to the phallic connection. The Latin verb *fascināre* derives from the noun *fascinus,* meaning 'spell or witchcraft'. In early Rome, children were given phallic amulets to wear around their necks as charms to ward off evil spirits. As a result of this practice, *fascinus* came to mean 'penis', and there was a minor phallic deity named *Fascinus,* who was invoked to protect people against black magic, demons, and illness.

Etymologists disagree about the origin of *fascinus.* It's possible that it was borrowed from Greek *baskanos,* 'sorcerer'; if that's true, it comes from the Indo-European root **bho-* meaning 'speak'. What is certain is that *fascinus* meant 'spell' before it meant 'penis' and that the god Fascinus was a fairly late development. In any event, the Roman magistrates did not walk the streets preceded by attendants carrying statues of erect phalluses.

~GSM

fiasco (fe-AS-ko)

LUIGI AMORESE WROTE: The word **fiasco** in Italian means 'bottle or flask'. Can you explain how this word evolved into meaning 'a complete failure'?

In some English-language dictionaries, the first definition of **fiasco** is given as 'a flask or bottle'. But most give the popular meaning we all know—'a failure, a complete mess'. **Fiasco**'s origins are closely allied to those of *flask,* and the two words join at one point in their histories: both words can be traced to the Medieval Latin word *flascō* 'a small keg intended to carry wine'.

In Italian, the first meaning of the word is 'bottle', which was its earliest meaning as well. In the early 19th century, when **fiasco** began to be used to mean 'a failure' in Italian, it referred to a *theatrical* failure. It was always used with the verb *fare,* 'to make'. To bomb on the Italian stage or in the Italian opera house was to *fare fiasco,* 'to make a bottle'. The expression is still used in Italy today but, as in English, no longer refers solely to failures in the theater. I came across this at an Italian Web site devoted to the soccer games between England and Italy: "gli inglesi hanno sempre fatto fiasco in Italia," *fatto* being the past participle of *fare* 'to make'. This means: 'The English have always been a dismal failure [made a bottle] in Italy.' The Italians also use **fiasco** today in the same way as we do—by itself, without the verb 'to make'. A line from *Cara Megghi,* a sort of Italian *Dear Abby,* asks: "La tua vita sentimentale e' un fiasco?" 'Is your love life a disaster'?

According to the *Dizionario Etimologico Italiano,* the expression passed from Italian into French in 1835 as *faire fiasco.* And this is how it came into the English language. *The Oxford English Dictionary* says the first recorded use of **fiasco** meaning 'failure' in English was in 1855. However, I found a citation in the February 1, 1845, issue of *Punch.* Even at this early date they put a uniquely British turn to it. Under the headline "Alarming Failure," the article begins, "The eclipse of the moon, on Sunday week last, was what the *Post* would say, a 'fiasco'. In London it was regularly hissed at an early part of the evening."

But why is "making a bottle" equated with failure? *The Barnhart Dictionary of Etymology* offers a tantalizing suggestion: "The sense development is unknown, but one of many explanations refers to the alleged practice of Venetian glassmakers setting aside imperfect glass to make a common bottle or flask." That sounds very plausible to me. In other words, the Venetian glassmakers were probably engaged in crafting something much more difficult than a mere wine bottle, but if they made a mistake, they could always convert the error into a **fiasco.**

~*RG*

five by five

BOB NOWACKI WROTE: I've heard the term **five by five** in various movies and TV shows. It seems to mean something like 'OK'. *Random House Webster's Unabridged Dictionary* lists it only as a term from the 1930s meaning 'short and fat', but I hardly think Buffy's buddy Faith would characterize herself that way. Any updates you can share on the meaning of this term?

Absolutely. As a fellow *Buffy the Vampire Slayer* fan, I make it my business to keep up with the lingo (and that's no small task).

First, let me say that the 'fat' meaning of **five by five** is the older, well-known one. It comes (quite obviously) from the idea that a person "five feet tall and five feet wide," as the song "Mister Five by Five" claims, is a "mellow old fat" and a "real hep cat" (Don Raye and Gene DePaul, 1942).

The meaning we are talking about today, though, can be found in the *Random House Historical Dictionary of American Slang.*

Back to *Buffy,* where **five by five** is the trademark expression of Faith, the slayer-gone-bad character. In a recent episode, Faith claims to be **five by five** and ready for payback. Payback for what? That's a long story. So, two of Buffy's friends are helping her keep watch and one imitates Faith.

Willow (imitating Faith): Ooh, check me out. I'm wicked cool. I'm five by five.
Tara: Five by five? Five what by five what?
Willow: See, that's the thing. No one knows.

Ah, but Willow—we do.

Five by five is a radio communications expression that means 'loud and clear'. One of the fives represents the S units of reception strength. The other five is a rating of the signal clarity. **Five by five** is a good, clear signal. The radio use of this expression goes back to the 1950s: " 'All right, testing, one-two-three-four . . .' 'Five by five, Mr. Holloran!' " (Hunter, *Blackboard Jungle,* 1954).

The more metaphorical meaning that Faith uses wasn't recorded until the 1980s: " 'I hope everything's all right.' 'Yeah, everything is five by five' " (Eilert, *Self & Country,* 1983). That also seems to be the meaning used by Ferro, the drop ship captain in the movie *Aliens,* who says, "We're in the pipe, five by five" (1986). This use is primarily military, so it's a mystery where Faith, Sunnydale's best bad-girl, picked it up.

⌇HGB

floozy

BETH LEVY WROTE: A few days ago, I went for a flu shot. When the nurse . . . asked if I had any questions, I asked about the likelihood of my experiencing any symptoms of the flu after receiving the immunization. She responded, "You might find yourself feeling a little **floozy**. . . ."

I woke up the next day with no runny nose, headache, or muscle aches. I did, however, have an urge to expose far more than my upper arm . . . I began to wonder if being a **floozy** simply involves embracing a specific style of dress—à la stereotypical prostitute . . . Or maybe the term has more to do with a person's overall behavior and/or lifestyle. Anyway, where did this term come from and what has it come to mean in today's usage?

The question is, Beth, are you a **floozy** (a.k.a. *floozie, floosie, floosy, floogy, flugie, flusie, fluzie, faloosie*) by virtue of a predilection for leopard-print camisoles, a penchant for dancing on tables in nightclubs, and/or a career as a sex worker? In its current usage, the definition of **floozy,** exemplified by our own *Random House Webster's College Dictionary,* would indicate that the answer is all of the above. 'A gaudily dressed, usu. promiscuous woman, esp. a prostitute' pretty much sums it up. But as is so often the case when you dig deep into a word's past, this is far from the end of the tawdry tale on **floozy.** The real dirt on **floozy** is that it has relatively innocuous origins and that its current disreputable incarnation can be viewed as a reflection of an excess of mid-20th-century moralizing, with more than a tinge of the old double-standard.

The earliest sense of **floozy,** circa the late 19th or early 20th century, is that of 'a girl or young woman'. This sense most likely stems from a variety of words rooted in *floss,* a dialectal variant of which is *floose.* Attestations recorded from the 1700s on have *floss* as referring to the silky filament surrounding the cocoon of the silk worm, and by the mid-18th century to anything silky, downy, or fluffy. By the late 1800s, the adjectival sense of *flossy* (or *flossie*) had taken on the two distinct colloquial meanings of 'fancy, showy, stylish', and 'impertinent, saucy', as well as 'a young woman' in its noun form.

A quick check of the *Random House Historical Dictionary of American Slang* shows that, very early on, the noun sense of **floozy** as 'a young woman to whom attention is paid' (1911) vied with that of 'a questionable female character' (1914). The 'girl' sense stuck around at least until 1945, when you could say "You're off the beam because you got a sugar report from a flugie" and be perfectly understood as meaning "You are confused because you received a love letter from a girl." But starting around the end of World War II, this sense was almost completely supplanted by the derogative 'promiscuous' sense. This definition from the 1960 edition of the *Dictionary of American Slang* bears printing in full: 'an undisciplined, promiscuous, flirtatious, irresponsible girl or woman, esp. a cynical, calculating one who is only concerned with having a good time or living off the generosity of men; a cheap or loose girl or woman'. It was apparently just a short, high-heeled, step from enjoying sex (being an 'enthusiastic amateur', according to Partridge's definition of **floozy** in his *Dictionary of Slang and Unconventional English*) to being a prostitute, at least for women.

~*HL*

-ful

LES ALDRIDGE WROTE: General Mills and the American Cancer Society have a program called "Spoonfuls of Hope." Has *spoonfuls* become acceptable? I was always taught that it should be *spoonsful*.

Not only is *spoonfuls* acceptable, it is the only plural shown in most major dictionaries. One desk dictionary adds *spoonsful* as a kind of also-ran, and our Random House Webster's dictionaries acknowledge its existence in usage notes at the entry for **-ful.** In short, nouns ending in **-ful** regularly form their plurals by adding *-s* at the end, not internally.

As with so many aspects of English, present-day confusion is the product of historical change. Old English followed a pattern established in Teutonic languages in which a noun was followed by the adjective *full,* as in "a cup full of mead," to express the notion of a quantity that would fill a receptacle. When the noun and the adjective were separate, the noun was the only element that could be pluralized. The transition from two words to one apparently began in Middle English (ME), but examples showing how the combined form was pluralized are hard to come by. According to *The Oxford English Dictionary,* "owing to the practice of using the sing. of a noun of quantity instead of the pl. after a numeral, there is seldom any evidence to show whether the ME antecedent of a word like *dishful* is to be regarded as a syntactical combination or as a single word." As the evolutionary process continued, these forms were no longer viewed as a combination of noun and adjective, but simply as a noun. Constructs like "He that hath seene an egges shell full of dew . . ." (William Fulke, *A Goodly Gallerye,* 1563) became constructs like "A theatrefull of people" (George Moore, *A Mummer's Wife,* 1884), and eventually the attached word *full* became the suffix **-ful,** as in *spoonful.* Hence, "Spoonfuls of Hope."

Unfortunately, some teachers perpetuate language mythology. Even the *Merriam-Webster English Usage Dictionary,* renowned for its objectivity, speculates that "Somewhere, sometime, there seem to have been teachers who were convinced that internal pluralization was more proper or more elegant." One source for confusion is the fact that other compounds do form their plurals internally. They range from terms like *mothers-in-law* to compounds in which the addition is neither a phrase (like *in-law*) nor a suffix (like **-ful**) but a preposition, like *by* or *on*. Typical examples are *passersby* and *hangers-on*. In addition, when referring to an actual container that happens to be full, we can still use the two-word phrase: "We received two baskets full of fruit—a large basket of apples and a small basket of apricots." But normally, and quite properly, singular **-ful** becomes plural **-fuls.**

~*EP*

galoot (guh-LOOT)

CHRISTINE YOUNG WROTE: I'm looking for a definition and origin of the word **galoot,** as in "You're a big galoot." In an attempt to define it ourselves, friends and I tried to pick characters who would seemingly be **galoots.** It was determined that Brutus of Popeye fame was more a *lummox* than a **galoot.**

Actually, sailor-men weren't a bad direction to go with this word. From its first citation, early in the 19th century, **galoot** was a nautical word. "Some 'Gilute' let go the . . . sheets before hauling down on the chewlines" (Abbey, *Before the Mast,* 1859).

Galoot was a name for soldiers as well as sailors. In the United States, **galoot** was usually applied to young, awkward soldiers. The term gained popularity during the Civil War as it was applied to new recruits. In 1867, it was featured in

Smyth's *Sailor's Word Book:* "Galoot . . . a soubriquet for the young or 'green' marine." While it often referred to oafish or clumsy men, it could also just mean 'a guy or fellow', as in W. S. Kelly's *Lariats:* "All the local 'galoots' assembled on Wilson's ranch to see him off" (1905).

The origin of the word is (surprise!) a mystery. Some claim that it comes from Krio, an English-based Creole in Sierra Leone, but the authoritative Krio-English Dictionary edited by Fyle and Jones (1980) traces the Krio *galut,* meaning 'a large, heavy person', to English, leaving us with a dubious chicken or egg etymology.

Today **galoot** isn't used as much as it used to be. It can still refer to any unpleasant Brutus figure.

(Imagined dialogue #1):
Brutus: (as he throws Popeye across the room) Arghhh.
Popeye: Whoa! That big galoot has (mumble, mumble) taken Olive (mumble, mumble). I should eat me spinach (mumble, mumble).

It is also now used as a fond, teasing nickname, something Olive would call Popeye as she dangles from a crumbling precipice:

(Imagined dialogue #2):
Olive: Popeye, eat yer spinach already and come save me, ya old galoot!
Popeye: Galoot did you say? Well, (mumble, mumble) I yam what I yam.

$\sim$*HGB*

gay

MARY ELLEN MALAGUE WROTE: I'm wondering when **gay** became the term for the homosexual community. Why was this word chosen? Any history you can provide will be appreciated!

The 'homosexual' sense of **gay** was most likely derived from the meaning 'happy, carefree, hedonistic', the primary senses of the word in the early part of the 20th century. Homosexuals were stereotyped as having these personality traits. Another possible source is the slang term *gaycat* 'a boy, often one involved in pederasty, who acts as a lookout for tramps or criminals'. A third (and certainly plausible) source is the British sense 'living by prostitution', extended to refer to male homosexual prostitutes, and later, to male homosexuals.

An article by Ronald Butters of Duke University concludes that purported examples of the 'homosexual' meaning before the early 1940s have been "misconstrued from a later 20th-century perspective, . . . even though that meaning in all likelihood was not the intent of those who wrote or spoke the word."

A *Random House Webster's Historical Dictionary of American Slang* citation is ambiguous: "They were . . . gay, they learned little things that are things in being gay . . ." (Gertrude Stein, 1922). Even the 1938 movie *Bringing Up Baby* is not clear evidence for the meaning 'homosexual'. In one scene, Katharine Hepburn takes away Cary Grant's clothes, and he has to dress in her negligee. When another character asks Grant why he is wearing such clothes, he ad-libs: "Because I

Word Lore • 103

just went ga-a-ay all of a sudden." This could have been a double-entendre, but it would have been risky for Grant to identify himself as a homosexual. Professor Butters interprets Grant's use of **gay** to mean 'unruly, wacky, reckless', an obsolete slang sense.

The phrase *Gay Nineties* was coined in 1925 and would not have taken hold if **gay** also meant 'homosexual'. The same is true of the title of the 1934 movie *The Gay Divorcée.*

Most evidence shows that the 'homosexual' sense of **gay** was not established until the late 1930s or early 1940s, and even then, it was known only to homosexual, bohemian, or artistic subcultures. By the 1950s, the meaning 'homosexual' was known to the general public, but it was considered slang. In the 1960s it was used in the heterosexual community, coinciding with the gay-rights movement. By the 1970s it was the preferred term of self-reference for most homosexuals.

~CGB

ghetto

ANDREW HUBSCH WROTE: A friend and I were talking about the Warsaw **ghetto** during World War II and speculated on the origin of the word. I've heard there was an area of Venice called *Gheto,* to which the Jews were confined, but I also thought the word might originate from the Latin *iactare* 'to throw'. Any information?

Actually, the commonly accepted theory for the origin of **ghetto** involves both of your ideas. The Venetian word **ghetto** means 'a foundry for artillery' and comes from the verb *ghettare* 'to throw', which comes from the Vulgar Latin **jectāre*. **Ghetto** as the walled and gated area in which Jews were required to live was first used for a section of Venice in 1516, and scholars believe that the word comes from an iron foundry in the neighborhood. Jews were forcibly segregated from the 13th century on in some areas, but the word **ghetto** wasn't used until the 16th century.

Other theories for the origin of **ghetto** involve either Italian *Egitto* from Latin *Aegyptus* 'Egypt' or Italian *borghetto* 'a small section of a town' from *borgo* 'town'. Although the spellings are similar, the pronunciations are very different, so the connection is quite a stretch, and these theories are generally discounted. A derivation from Hebrew *chatsor* 'enclosure' has also been proposed, but there is no evidence for this.

The first appearance of **ghetto** in English was in 1611: "The place where the whole fraternity of the Jews dwelleth together, which is called the Ghetto" and "Walking in the Court of the Ghetto, I casually met with a Jewish Rabbin that spake good Latin" (Thomas Coryat, *Coryats Crudities*).

It wasn't until the end of the 19th century (after the ghettos for Jews in European cities had been abolished) that **ghetto** came to be used for a crowded and poor section of a city in which members of a minority group live. Israel Zangwill wrote in *Children of the Ghetto* in 1892: "The particular Ghetto that is the dark background upon which our pictures will be cast is of voluntary formation." In 1908 Jack London wrote in *Martin Eden:* "They dismounted and plunged off to the right into the heart of the working-class ghetto."

Ghetto began to be used as a verb meaning 'to put in a ghetto' in the 1930s: "Jews, who are ghettoed under the racial legislation" (London *Times* 1936). More recently, an article in the *Austin American-Statesman* notes that "The last decades have been described as a time when the country split between 'gated or ghettoed'" (January 2000). And, in a rather startling extension of meaning, here's a writer for the *Jerusalem Post:* "I would probably feel just as generous toward ancient situation comedies if they were appropriately ghettoed onto a single cable channel . . ." (June 2000).

~*GSM*

give your eyeteeth for

K. A. BORISKIN WROTE: Today I heard someone say that they didn't want to buy something that "cost their **eyeteeth.**" I've also heard people say they'd "give their **eyeteeth**" for something. How did a person's canines come to represent something of great or prohibitive value?

The *eyeteeth*—also called *cuspids, canines,* and *dog teeth*—are the four pointed teeth next to the incisors (front teeth) on either side of both jaws. They are called *eyeteeth* because they sit directly under the eye. Formerly, *eyeteeth* referred solely to the upper canines, but the word has come to include the lower canines as well. (They are called *dog teeth* and *canines* because they are especially pronounced in dogs. The word *cuspid* comes from a Latin word meaning 'point'.) Mammals use their *eyeteeth* mainly for tearing food.

The word *eyetooth*, which is of English origin, first appears in print in 1580. However, it was a while before it was used as the building block for various expressions. In fact, **to**

give one's eyeteeth for something was the last expression to come into use. It is first recorded in Somerset Maugham's *Cakes and Ale,* published in 1930: "He'd give his eye-teeth to have written a book half as good." Before that, expressions using *eyeteeth* related more to becoming an adult, and to acquiring the power and authority that comes with maturation. *To cut one's eyeteeth,* for example, 'to acquire wisdom and become worldly', first appeared in the 19th century. The *Encyclopedia of Word and Phrase Origins* says this expression derives from the fact that "the permanent set [of canines] is acquired when a child is passing into young adulthood. It is usually said in the negative, as in 'he hasn't cut his eyeteeth yet'." In the 1700s, *eyeteeth* referred mostly to the cuspids of dogs, and so, the *Encyclopedia of Word and Phrase Origins* speculates, "the phrase may have been suggested by the fact that fighting dogs were considered dangerous to handle when they developed their eyeteeth."

There's more. To *draw one's eyeteeth* means 'to take the conceit out of one'. To *have one's eyeteeth* means 'to be wide awake'. (Thomas Dyche, in the 1740 edition of his *A New General English Dictionary* defines *eye-teeth* as 'quickness or sharpness of understanding and parts'.)

As to how a person's canines came to represent something of great or prohibitive value, I found little to chew on. However, for a carnivorous animal to lose its *eyeteeth* would be a disaster. You could say, for nonhuman mammals at least, these meat-ripping teeth are a matter of life and death. So, applying this metaphorically to humans, to give them away is a very great sacrifice indeed.

$\sim$*RG*

glamour

The English word GRAMMAR originally meant 'learning', including magic and astrology. In 18th-century Scotland, *grammar* became *glamer* or **glamour** by a process called "dissimilation," in which a sound that is the same as a neighboring sound becomes different from that sound. Other examples of this are *purple* from Old English *purpure* and *pilgrim* from Latin *peregrīnus.*

The only sense of *grammar* that carried over to **glamour** was the one involving magic, witchcraft, and enchantment. Allan Ramsay wrote in 1721: "When devils, wizards or jugglers deceive the sight, they are said to cast glamour o'er the eyes of the spectator." Robert Burns wrote in "Captain Grose's Peregrin" (1789): "Ye gipsy-gang that deal in glamor, / And you deep read in hell's black grammar, / Warlocks and witches." It was Sir Walter Scott who introduced **glamour** into general literary usage, writing in "The Last Minstrel" (1805): "It had much of glamour might, could make a ladye seem a knight." **Glamour** soon spread from Scotland to England. Tennyson wrote in *Idylls of the King* in 1859: ". . . that maiden in the tale, Whom Gwydian made by glamour out of flowers." *Casting the glamour* over someone was the same as casting a spell. In "The Lovers' Litany," Kipling spoke of "Glamour, wine, and witchery."

In the course of the 19th century, the meaning of **glamour** began to shift away from 'witchcraft', but it still meant 'enchantment'. When Mr. Rochester says, "The glamour of inexperience is over your eyes . . . and you see it through a charmed medium" (Charlotte Brontë, *Jane Eyre,* 1847), he means 'a delusive or alluring charm'. In Willa Cather's *My Án-tonia* (1918), Frances says, "I expect I know the country girls better than you do. You always put a kind of glamour over them. The trouble with you, Jim, is that you're a romantic."

Glamour as 'the quality of fascinating or alluring by a combination of charm and good looks' is of American origin and is first attested in the 1930s in the expressions *glamour guy, glamour girl,* and *glamour boy.* A related '30s word is *glammy:* "The glammiest of the glamour girls—Tallulah Bankhead" (O.O. MacIntyre, *American Speech,* 1936). And there's *glam,* which is still in use: "The glamming of [beer] closely follows the upscaling of wine in America in the 1960s and '70s" (*New Republic,* 1993).

So much for warlocks and witches.

∼GSM

good-bye

LEE SUTHERLAND WROTE: I've heard that **goodbye** is a contraction of "God be with ye," and even that it was a slang word that came into wide use while being strongly frowned upon by upright Christian citizens. Is this true?

Yes, **good-bye** (or **goodbye/good-by**) is a contraction of "God be with ye (you)." The first use of a contracted form is recorded in a letter written by Gabriel Harvey in 1575: "To requite your gallonde of godbwyes, I regive you a pottle of howedyes." From the 16th to the 18th century, this contraction was spelled in many different ways: *godbwye, god b'uy, god buye, god b'wy.* The change from *god* to *good,* reflected in the modern spelling, was not fully established until the beginning of the 19th century, probably influenced by previously existing phrases such as *good day* and *good night.*

Another example of the change from *god* to *good* is *Good Friday,* originally written *god Friday,* and literally meaning 'holy or sacred Friday'. But why the change from *god* to *good?* Though derived from different Indo-European roots, the words *god/God* and *good* were usually spelled identically (as *god*) in Middle English, and so there was confusion and overlap between these two words. The spelling *good* first appeared about 1250, becoming the established spelling about 1450. Adding to the confusion was the obvious notion that God is good.

According to the century-old *Century Dictionary,* **good-bye** was "originally a pious form of valediction, used in its full significance, but now a mere conventional formula without meaning, used at parting." Actually, **good-bye** was a rather new English word at the time the Pilgrims sailed for America. According to Stuart Flexner, former editor-in-chief of Random House Dictionaries, "Slang is as old as English itself . . . American kids have been speaking a language of their own since they annoyed their Pilgrim parents at Plymouth Rock . . . It offended Puritan parents that their Pilgrim children took their traditional farewell—God be with you—and turned it into good-bye."

There are many other examples of the contraction of a phrase into a word. In fact the excerpt from Gabriel Harvey's letter quoted above has another familiar contraction: the form *howedye* (now spelled *howdy*) comes from the phrase "How do ye?" And in another of Harvey's letters, he writes: "Youre Latine Farewell is a goodly brave yonkerly piece of work, and goddilge yee, I am always marvellously beholding unto you, for your bountifull Titles." Here, *goddilge yee,* an obsolete expression of gratitude, is yet another example of a contraction, this one from the phrase "God yield (or reward) you."

~*CGB*

gremial (GREE-mee-ul)

ELLEN MURRAY THOMPSON WROTE: I've been reading a book by Patrick O'Brian which used the word **gremial.** I looked it up in my dictionary and could find no entry. I think the phrase O'Brian used it in went something like "He's not a gremial friend. I haven't known him long." I imagine it means 'close', but wondered if you might be able to find it in a dictionary.

Random House Webster's Unabridged Dictionary says that a **gremial** is 'a cloth placed on the lap of the bishop, as during the celebration of Mass or when he confers orders': "The scarf, the cross, the gremial, and the mitre of the bishop" (*Chronicles in the Annual Register,* 1811). This cloth, which is also called a "gremial veil," is usually of silk and decorated with gold lace. The original purpose was to prevent the bishop's vestments, which were presumably made of very costly and hard-to-clean fabric, from being soiled by his hands. Priests began using such "aprons" in the 13th century, but there is no evidence that they were called **gremials** until the 15th century.

That's not much help with "gremial friend," however. For that, we have to go back to the Latin root of the word, which is *gremium* and means 'a person's lap or bosom'. The Indo-European root has to do with 'gathering together'. It appears that the original sense of *gremium* referred to the lap or the bosom as a place in which something is put for safekeeping, especially a place where one holds a child. Therefore, your "gremial friend" is a friend you hold close—a 'bosom friend'.

If you happen to be reading something written in England between the 16th and 19th centuries, you might come across another, now obsolete, meaning of **gremial.** Scholars dwelling within the "bosom" of a university were called "gremial members" or "gremials": "That done they came all into the Quere [choir], and there helde the conuocation of the Uniuersite, being gremials" (Foxe, *Actes and Monuments of These Latter and Perillous Dayes,* 1563). There are numerous such references in the *Statutes of Cambridge:* "No gremial in the congregation of masters shall utter any words publicly except in Latin" (1855). A **gremial** member of a university or society was a full member rather than an honorary one.

The adjective **gremial** also referred to the internal affairs of a society: "It was the rule for the prior to be elected from among the inmates of the monastery; in other words, the election was to be 'gremial' " (Smith and Cheetham, *A Dictionary of Christian Antiquities,* 1880).

~*GSM*

grimoire (grim-WAHR) and grammar

ROB D. BARTLETT WROTE: I first heard the word **grimoire** referenced as a magical book (in *Dungeons and Dragons*). Every reference I've found says it is a book of magic, though the type of magic is quite varied from one definition to another. I read somewhere that it comes from Greek and that its roots are similar to **grammar** as a set of instructions. Is this correct, and is there a more specific/complete answer?

A **grimoire** is 'a magician's manual for invoking demons, etc.'. The word is first attested in English in the 19th century: "A witch with a Bible! It should be a grimoire." (Ainsworth, *Lancashire Witches,* 1849). **Grimoire** does indeed come ultimately from Greek, and it is related to **grammar,** but it has nothing to do with a set of instructions.

The Latin word *grammatica* comes from Greek *grammatikè téchnē* 'the art of letters'. (It's related to *graphein* 'to write'.) In classical antiquity, both the Latin and the Greek words referred to the methodical study of literature, including language and literary allusions, history, and criticism.

By the Middle Ages, *grammatica* had come to mean 'the knowledge or study of Latin', and that was extended to mean 'learning in general' because Latin was the language of scholars. Since the general populace didn't know Latin, all learning was regarded as mysterious and was popularly thought to include magic and astrology. As a result, Old French *gramaire* was sometimes used to refer to the occult sciences, and that's where we get **grimoire.**

Among the learned, **grammar** still referred to Latin. In

Shakespeare's *Titus Andronicus* (1590), Chiron says: "O, 'tis a verse in Horace; I know it well: I read it in the grammar long ago." By the 17th century, **grammar** came to be applied to other languages. Ben Jonson's *English Grammar* (1636) was the first reference to a grammar other than Latin.

The English word *gramarye* (pronounced GRAM-uh-ree) meant 'grammar' in the old sense of 'learning in general' in the 14th century. By the 15th century it had come to mean 'occult learning' or 'magic'. Sir Walter Scott used it in "The Last Minstrel" (1805): "Whate'er he did of gramarye was always done maliciously." It still has that meaning, in case you feel inclined to use it.

∼GSM

gruel, grueling, and gruesome

MAT MYSZEWSKI WROTE: I know that **gruel** is 'a thin, cooked cereal', that **grueling** means 'exhausting or arduous', and that **gruesome** means 'repugnant'. What, if any, is the connection between these words?

Gruel and **grueling** are definitely related, so we'll start with those two words. The Indo-European root **ghreu-* means 'to rub or grind', and that is the ultimate source of **gruel,** which is something that is 'finely ground'. **Gruel** came into English by way of Old French, but it's actually a Germanic word.

From **gruel** meaning 'fine flour or meal' in the early 14th century came the name for the thin liquid food made by boiling oatmeal or some similar substance with milk or water. Many of the early mentions of **gruel** are in medical treatises that recommended it as food for invalids because it was nourishing and easy to digest. A somewhat less healthful version is made by the witches in Act IV, Scene 1 of Shakespeare's *Macbeth* (1606): "Make the gruel thick, and slab [viscous]."

At the end of the 18th century, we find the colloquial expression "to have or get one's gruel" or "to take one's gruel", which meant 'to take one's medicine' or 'to be punished'. The expression probably comes from the fact that **gruel** was something given to the sick; if you "got your gruel," you weren't feeling very well, and if you "gave someone his gruel," you were causing him to feel unwell.

There's a story about the origin of "get one's gruel" that derives it from Catherine de' Medici's reputed habit of giving poison to her enemies in a drink of gruel. Unfortunately, the dates disprove this derivation.

Grueling meaning 'exhausting' or 'punishing', which dates from the middle of the 19th century, clearly comes from the colloquial sense of **gruel** as 'punishment'. **Grueling** has also been used as a noun to mean 'a defeat', especially in something athletic, as we might say that a team "takes a beating."

Now we come to **gruesome,** and things get a bit murky. Middle English had a verb *grue,* which appeared early in the 14th century and is still used in Scotland and the North of England. It means 'to shudder' or 'to feel terror or horror'. There is no evidence of it in either Old English or Old Norse, but it has cognates in German, Dutch, Danish, and Swedish. From this verb German gets *grausam* 'horrible or cruel' and English gets **gruesome.** The word is first attested in a glossary of 1570 where *growsome* is defined as 'horridus', but it was rare until the first quarter of the 19th century.

Is there a connection between **gruel** and **gruesome?** Some scholars believe that *grue* derives from the 'rubbing' or 'grating' sense of the **ghreu-* root—if something makes you shudder, it "rubs you the wrong way" or "grates" on you. It's certainly possible, but the link has been lost, so we can only speculate.

~*GSM*

gullible

ALICIA MURPHY WROTE: Where does the word **gullible** come from?

First, it doesn't have anything to do with seagulls. English gets that word *gull* from the Celtic languages: Welsh *gwylan* and Cornish *guilan.*

Gullible, meaning 'easily deceived or cheated; naive; credulous', first appeared in English in the 19th century. Carlyle wrote in 1825: "The king of quacks, the renowned Cagliostro, . . . harrowing up the souls of the curious and gullible of all ranks . . . by various thaumaturgic feats."

In Modern English, *gull* is both a verb meaning 'to deceive, trick, or cheat' and a noun meaning 'a person who is easily deceived or cheated'. So if you're *gulled,* you've been cheated. From *gull* comes not only **gullible,** but other words that we have now lost, such as *gullage, gullery, guller,* and *gullified.*

From the 14th to the 17th centuries, there was an adjective *gull* of Germanic origin meaning 'yellow or pale'. During approximately the same period, the noun *gull* meant 'an unfledged bird, especially a gosling'. Wycliffe used this noun in his translation of the Bible in 1382: "A nest of briddis . . . and the moder to the *gollis*. . . ." And Shakespeare used it in *Henry IV, Part I* (1597): "As that ungentle *gull* the cuckoo's bird, Useth the Sparrow." It's possible that the noun derived from the adjective since baby birds are pale and yellow.

The transition to *gull* in our modern sense is more problematic. An unfledged bird might be assumed to be easily deceived, so that's one possible origin. In that case, the verb came from the noun. The first recorded use of the noun was in 1594 when Nashe wrote: "Liues there anie such slowe ycebraind beefe-witted gull." (How's that for an insult?) Shakespeare used the noun *gull* the same year in *Richard III.*

The verb *gull* meaning 'to deceive' appeared in a satire called *The Hye Way to the Spyttel Hous,* published in the 1530s: "They . . . do but gull, and follow beggery. . . ." Fifty years later Shakespeare wrote in one of the sonnets: "That affable familiar ghost Which nightly gulls him with intelligence." So maybe the verb preceded the noun. In that case, it is likely that it came from another meaning of *gull,* common in the 16th and 17th centuries but now obsolete, 'to swallow or guzzle'. There was also a noun *gull,* probably of French origin, first found in the 15th century and meaning 'throat or gullet', from which we also get *gully.* If we take this etymological path, we assume that if you're **gullible,** you'll swallow anything.

~*GSM*

hobnob

MARNIE RUNDIKS WROTE: Okay, I hear the term **hob nob** (or is it **hob knob**?) used often, and I am not sure whether it is used correctly. Does it have a derogatory connotation? What is the etymology?

To **hobnob** means 'to associate on very friendly terms.' There's nothing derogatory about it. It does, in current usage, have a sense of 'associating with the rich and famous (or influential)'.

Hob and **nob** were originally *hab* and *nab* and probably came from the subjunctive forms of the Old English verbs *habban* 'to have' and *nabban* 'not to have'. "Habbe he, nabbe he" means 'whether he has or does not have'. Although there is a long gap in the written evidence for this phrase, it must have been part of the spoken language, for it reappeared in the 16th century as *hab or nab* or *habnab,* meaning 'hit or miss' or 'however it may turn out'. John Lyly wrote in *Euphues and His England* in 1580: "Philautus determined, hab, nab, to sende his letters."

Except in the dialects of Devonshire and West Somerset, where *hab or nab* is still common, the words changed to *hob* and *nob* by the end of the 16th century. The first written appearance of *hob, nob* meaning 'give or take' was in Shakespeare's *Twelfth Night* (1601), where Sir Toby Belch, who is trying to arrange a duel, says "His incensement at this moment is so implacable, that satisfaction can be none, but by pangs of death and sepulcher: Hob, nob is his word: giv't or take't."

By the 18th century, *hob or nob, hob a nob,* and *hob and*

nob referred to two people drinking to each other. To drink *hob or nob* or *hob a nob* meant 'to drink to each other alternately' or 'to take wine with each other with clinking of glasses'. **Hobnob** first appeared in various forms as a verb meaning 'to drink together' in the second half of the 18th century: "We hobbed and nobbed with . . . the celebrated bailiff of Chancery Lane" (Thackeray, *Paris Sketchbook*, 1840).

The loss of the alcohol connection and the shift to our modern meaning occurred in the first half of the 19th century. A Lady Grenville wrote in a letter in 1828, "It cannot be her interest to hob-and-nob with Lord Fitzwilliam." In 1879 George Macdonald wrote of a character in his novel *Paul Faber*, "He . . . hob-nobbed with Death and Corruption."

The 19th century also saw such words as *hob-nobber* and *hob-nobby* as well as the noun **hobnob** meaning either 'a drinking together' or 'a tête-à-tête'.

~*GSM*

Holy Grail

STEPHEN LESTAT WROTE: I would like to know the origin of the word **grail** as in **Holy Grail.**

A grail is a cup or chalice; but in point of fact I think the word hardly ever appears without being preceded by the word *Holy*. So, in a sense, there is only one grail—the **Holy Grail.** I know that the Knights of the Round Table quested endlessly after it. As did Monty Python. Not to mention Parsifal in Richard Wagner's opera of the same name. But why *were* they questing after it?

According to *The Oxford Dictionary of the Christian Church,* "The Grail itself is sometimes identified with the cup used by Christ in the Last Supper, and its effects upon those who see it are made to correspond closely with the effects of Holy Communion upon communicants." Joseph of Arimathea was supposed to have gathered the last drops of Christ's blood in the **Holy Grail** when He was dying on the Cross.

Legend has it this same Joseph of Arimathea brought the **Grail** to England, where it became lost. This is why we find Lancelot and other knights on a quest for the **Grail.** The legend of the **Holy Grail** first appeared in the early Middle Ages, not before. The word itself, *The Barnhart Dictionary of Etymology* tells us, comes from the "Medieval Latin *gradalis* 'a flat dish or shallow vessel', perhaps directly from Latin *crātēr* 'bowl', from Greek *krātēr* 'bowl', especially for mixing wine with water." It came into English via the Old French word *graal* and first appeared in print in English in 1330 as *greal.*

It is hard to overemphasize the importance of the **Holy Grail** in the literature of the Middle Ages. (It's also referred to as the *Saint Grail* and the *Sangrail.* Though it may not always be capitalized when alone, it inevitably is when coupled with *Holy.*) It first appears in Chrestien de Troyes's *Perceval* in the 12th century. Most famously, Thomas Malory's English prose version of the Arthurian legends, *Le Morte d'Arthur,* published in 1485, has Sir Lancelot searching in vain for the **Holy Grail.**

The **Grail** itself was symbolic of a sublime purity. It appeared as a vision to its pursuer; in paintings and drawings it is often depicted emanating beams of light. The *Dictionary of All Scriptures and Myths* sums it up: "Seen from different standpoints, the Grail became the emblem of moral purity, or of triumphant faith, or of soldierly heroism, or of a gracious charity; the radiance of it became the radiance of that ultimate perfection which allures those who struggle." So, in *Le Morte d'Arthur,* Lancelot gets a glimpse of the **Holy Grail** but cannot obtain it because of his sins. (Remember his affair with Queen Guinevere.) It is left to his son, Galahad, who is worthy, to find the **Grail.**

$\sim$*RG*

honky-tonk

TOM GARLOCK WROTE: Do you know the origin of the term **honky-tonk** in reference to a low class bar or saloon? Does it refer to the type of music played there? If so, what is **honky-tonk** music?

The beginnings of the word **honky-tonk** are American and lurk in low-class, raucous dance halls and bars. Although the word came into use before my time—around 1890—I still feel a kinship with the spirit of what it represents. The word can be used as a noun or an adjective, as in the Rolling Stones' "Honky Tonk Woman."

The derivation of **honky-tonk** is unknown, but it most likely comes from a rhyming duplication. The places where this sort of dancing, drinking, and hell-raising flourished probably sounded like one big *honk;* most likely, someone got in a rhyming mood one day, and the result stuck. In the eighth edition of *A Dictionary of Slang and Unconventional English,* Eric Partridge says that the phrase might be related to the New England dialect word, *honk,* which means 'to idle about'.

Honky-tonk eventually came to represent a kind of

music, too. I'm not sure anyone can strictly define what that is, but it seems to have its most resonant home in country-and-western music. Bob Wills, Lefty Frizell, Hank Williams, and George Jones have all been closely associated with **honky-tonk** music. Listen to them, and you'll have a good idea what **honky-tonk** is all about. Hank Williams even wrote a song called "Honky Tonk Blues." Probably the most famous **honky-tonk** song of all is J.D. Miller's "It Wasn't God Who Made Honky Tonk Angels." In it, you can hear these poignant lines:

> Too many times married men think they're still single.
> That has caused many a good girl to go wrong.

This is a mournful song, as opposed to Williams's jaunty melody, and it seems to me that, to a great degree, **honky-tonk** music has evolved into the kind of song that you associate with sitting alone on a barstool at three o'clock in the morning.

The phrase is also a verb, as in "I went **honky-tonking** last night."

There have been several movies made with **honky-tonk** in their titles. Clark Gable and Lana Turner starred in the 1941 MGM comedy *Honky Tonk*. In 1982, Clint Eastwood directed and starred in *Honkytonk Man*.

It's a great American phrase, I think.

$\sim$*RG*

hoodlum and hood

CELIA LAURENT WROTE: Apart from being a synonym for *hooligan*, I can find no other information on the origin of **hoodlum.** I have my own theory: **Hoodlums** don't like to be recognized for their deeds, so they pull **hoods** over their heads. The *-lum* part I get from *l'homme*, the French word for 'man'. Am I on the right track?

The term **hoodlum,** in the sense 'a young street ruffian, especially one belonging to a gang' is said to have originated in San Francisco about 1870. At this time there was a great deal of anti-Chinese sentiment—it was felt that Chinese immigrants were taking the jobs that would otherwise go to white boys. These boys became idle and rowdy and began to harass the Chinese laborers. The problem is described in "The City of the Golden Gate," an article by Samuel Williams appearing in an 1875 issue of *Scribner's Monthly:* "The Hoodlum is a distinctive San Francisco product . . . He drinks, gambles, steals, runs after lewd women, sets buildings on fire . . . One of his chief diversions, when he is in a more pleasant mood, . . . is stoning Chinamen . . . This sudden efflorescence of a sharply defined criminal class among boys—for the Hoodlum first appeared only three or four years ago—is somewhat alarming. . . ."

Though the term **hoodlum** is now standard English, it was originally slang. There are many theories as to its derivation—your "hooded man" theory is one of the more creative ones.

The most plausible theory was suggested in 1935 by Dr. J. T. Krumpelmann. Explaining that the Germans constituted the largest foreign-language group in San Francisco, he derives **hoodlum** from the German (Bavarian) dialectal term *Hudellump, Hodalump,* meaning 'ragamuffin, good-for-nothing'. But according to Charles Earle Funk (and other sources), **hoodlum** was the accidental coinage of a newspaper reporter. In a story about a gang of ruffians led by a fellow named Muldoon, the reporter spelled the name as Noodlum to avoid reprisals. The newspaper's compositor misinterpreted the name as Hoodlum. Alternatively, in Barrère and Leland's 1889 *Dictionary of Slang, Jargon, and Cant,* the term is traced to *hood lahnt,* meaning 'very lazy mandarin' in pidgin English. The theory that **hoodlum** is a mispronunciation of *hooligan* is the least credible, since **hoodlum** is recorded almost ten years earlier.

The term **hoodlum** was originally used to describe 'a misbehaved child, a loafer, or a rowdy street kid', but it came to refer to 'a small-time criminal, thug, or gangster'. The shortened form **hood** is first recorded about 1880, though it wasn't in common use until the late 1920s. Historically the double *o* in both **hood** and the first syllable of **hoodlum** have been pronounced as in *food* or *good.* Now the double *o* in **hoodlum** is more commonly pronounced as in *food,* and the double *o* in **hood** is almost always pronounced as in *good.*

$\sim$*CGB*

horns (cuckold's)

SID WAXMAN WROTE: Moses' horns was probably a mistranslation from the ancient Hebrew or Aramaic, but what about **cuckold's horns?**

Moses' horns does come from a mistranslation of the Hebrew in Exodus 34:29–30. The text describes Moses as he descended from Mount Sinai, with his face "shining." Not understanding this "shining" as 'sending forth beams of light', the Latin version used the other possible translation, 'sent forth horns'. Why they chose this translation is a mystery, but for hundreds of years the Bible mistakenly depicted Moses as *quod cornūta esset faciēs sua*.

Now, let's see about our expression *wearing horns* or *putting horns on* to describe a cuckolded husband. When most of us hear **"horns,"** we think about bulls, stags, rams, goats, antelope, unicorns, etc., right? Following this logic, some scholars suppose that this expression originated with bucks in the forest, battling for the right to mate with the doe(s). As a male was stabbed with the **horn** of his opponent ("horned"), he lost the fight and subsequently the female. While this scenario seems intuitive, there is no clear support for it in citations from the early use of the expression. The related expressions *wear the stag's crest* and *be made a stag* are later variants that probably came from the **horn** imagery.

Surprisingly, the majority vote lies with another (even more bizarre) explanation. I can only assume that the oft-cited etymology offered by Dunger in *Germania* (XXIX, 59) is very well supported (I was unable to find a copy of the original text). This explanation is based on a very old practice of cutting the spurs (the nail-like things on the back of a bird's leg) off a castrated rooster and engrafting them on the bird's comb (the fleshy red thing on the rooster's head). As flesh tends to do when it senses a foreign object, the skin on these combs grew around the spurs. Apparently this left the capons looking as if they had **horns.** Why any individual (much less entire cultures!) would do this to an animal is totally beyond me.

The castrated rooster image struck a chord in the public's concept of a cuckolded husband (especially in the period from the 15th century to the era of Shakespeare and Marlowe, when this phrase was tossed around liberally). My favorite harangue on the subject of women's infidelity is spouted by a suitably masculine and indignant Benedick in the first act of Shakespeare's *Much Ado About Nothing* (1598): "Pluck off the bull's horns and set them in my forehead: and let me be vilely painted; and in such great letters as they write, 'Here is good horse to hire,' let them signify under my sign,—'Here you may see Benedick the married man.'"

Our acquaintance with the image of the **cuckold's horns** is further bolstered by its continued productive existence as an image in other modern languages, like French (*faire porter des cornes*), Italian (*mettere le corna a*), and Spanish (*poner los cuernos a*).

~HGB

hot dog

MELANIE CHALMERS WROTE: My 16-year-old Chinese foreign-exchange student has asked me to explain why we call frankfurters **hot dogs.** My dictionary has no information on the etymology. Can you please help?

That's a **hot-dog** question.

Because I was familiar with the 1890s adjective **hot-dog,** meaning 'fabulous and exciting', I assumed that the name of the frankfurter must have come from some 19th-century Americans who knew a good thing when they saw it. I was wrong.

It turns out that the **dog** in **hot dog** really refers to canines. German immigrants in the 1860s called frankfurters *hündwurst* 'dog sausage' or *hündchen* 'small dog'. This may have quite innocently referred to the sausage's shape. However, some lexicographers connect *hündwurst,* and the English equivalent **hot dog,** to the dog-meat scandal of 1843, in which dog meat (and more) was found in New York meat-packaging plants. By the 1850s, cartoons and jokes abounded about the contents of New York's spiced sausage and other meats. Cartoons from the era show dachshunds being fed into one end of meat grinders and sausage coming out the other side. In the late 1850s, the minced meat used in sausage was referred to as *dog's paste.* The word *dog,* referring to this spiced sausage, is first recorded in the 1880s. **Hot dog** in this sense comes from college slang of the 1890s, according to the research of David Shulman, Barry Popik, and others.

You wouldn't think people would eat a food that took its name from such a disgusting source, and in 1913 the Coney Island Chamber of Commerce passed a resolution banning Coney Island vendors from calling their product a **hot dog.** For some reason, the fearless Americans kept eating the mysterious spiced sausage, and they kept calling it the **hot dog.** The Chamber of Commerce couldn't hold out forever; in 1939 Coney Island celebrated the 50th anniversary of the **hot dog** on a bun with Hot Dog Day.

～HGB

How's tricks?

PAUL KANE WROTE: A friend and I will sometimes greet each other by asking **How's tricks?**, but neither of us know where the phrase came from, nor do we have any idea what *tricks* is/are. Can you help us figure out what this catchy but mysterious greeting means?

Reading your question transported me straight to the 1930s Broadway of a Damon Runyon story, a world of dolls and dice, horse races and has-beens, and the hard-boiled slang of society's underbelly. A place where sugar is money, a duke is your hand, the jug is jail, being hot means having the coppers after you, and where you don't want to be on the business end of anything. A place where characters with names like Frankie Ferocious, Big False Face, and Ropes McGonnigle will as soon put the slug on you as greet you with a **How's tricks?** (or **How are tricks?**).

But if they did, I'd probably reply with a snappy, "Huh? Whaddya mean, tricks?" And that's when I realize that I better get my dukes on a dictionary quick or I'm going to be given the breeze faster than you can say "John Roscoe."

In *Random House Webster's Unabridged Dictionary,* I find no fewer than 16 senses for *trick* as a noun, all ultimately deriving from the Latin *trīcāre, trīcārī* 'to trifle, play tricks'. Besides its more common meanings, *trick* is also a term referring to the set of cards played and won in a round, a nautical term for a turn or spell at the wheel, and slang for both a prostitute's customer and a sexual transaction between prostitute and client. The nautical sense is quite old, with citations from the mid-1600s. Several books on underworld slang make it clear that, by the early 20th century, *trick* had entered various argots: in convict use, a *trick* was a prison term, in carnival and circus use, an outdoor show or performance, and among criminals, a professional act—a caper or a robbery.

Eric Partridge, in his *Dictionary of Slang and Unconventional English,* tentatively has **How's tricks?** deriving from either the nautical or the card game *trick.* Given these choices, I'd lean toward the nautical sense of 'a turn of duty', which at the same time that **How's tricks?** is first cited, was spawning similar meanings in other argots of the underworld. That the phrase was initially considered crude, even indecent, can be seen in this citation from 1924: " 'Well, Mrs. H., how's tricks?' His wife flushed slightly at the vulgarity of the phrase."

But I'm not convinced that's the whole story on **How's tricks?** The noun form of the Latin verb *trīcārī* is *trīcae,* meaning 'trifles, toys'. From at least the mid-16th century we have *trick* referring to 'a trinket, bauble, knick-knack'. Farmer's *Slang and its Analogues,* published in 1890, lists as current "Western American" slang a sense of *trick* meaning 'belongings, things, baggage'. For a phrase that is equivalent to "How's things?," it's not too far-fetched to think that it may have been influenced by this sense.

~*HL*

hustings

RICHARD THOMAS WROTE: I've visualized the **hustings** as fields with tree stumps in them, since campaigning politicians are said to be *on the hustings. The Oxford*

English Dictionary gives various definitions of **husting(s)** as being a council, assembly, or court of one sort or another. These don't seem to jibe with the American usage. The *OED* does allude to a confusion of **hustings** with *hoistings,* meaning 'a platform'. Perhaps our use of **hustings** is related to politicians having platforms?

In Anglo-Saxon times, a **husting** was an assembly or tribunal to which a king or other leader summoned retainers or guardsmen. It was also a judicial body that settled disputes between Scandinavian and English merchants. The Old English word was borrowed from a Scandinavian source, probably Old Norse *husthing,* a compound meaning 'house assembly'. (This assembly was held in a household, or inside a building, whereas other meetings might be held outside.) The change from *thing* to *ting* (like *nosthyrl/nostril*) probably took place before the word was borrowed into English. The English word *thing* survives in the sense 'a public meeting, court, or legislative assembly in Scandinavia'; the *Althing* is the parliament of Iceland.

As early as the 12th century, some English towns had a so-called *hustings court,* which decided minor civil suits and appeals from the rulings of sheriffs. It was also a court of record, as for the conveyance of property. In London this *hustings court* was traditionally held in The Guildhall, and the presiding mayor and aldermen sat on a raised platform, called a **husting.** The court still exists in London, though it doesn't have much power. The United States, especially the Midwest, also has a tradition of *hustings courts* that were set up temporarily in isolated areas. Even today, Richmond and other cities in Virginia have such courts, usually dealing with appeals from police courts.

The raised platform in The (London) Guildhall led to another sense of **hustings,** first recorded in 1719: 'a temporary platform on which candidates for Parliament stood when nominated and from which they addressed the electorate'. After 1872, when written ballots came into use, this meaning became obsolete.

From the historical references to 'a platform', **hustings** developed the more familiar sense 'any place from which campaign speeches are made'. **Hustings** also refers to 'the political activities involved in campaigning', or more generally, 'the campaign trail'. In these senses, **hustings** means the same as *stump,* though candidates don't necessarily speak from a raised platform or tree stump.

Some dictionaries label **hustings** as a British term, but it's fairly common in the United States. The plural **hustings** appeared in the mid-15th century and gradually became the usual form. It can be used with a singular or plural verb. Candidates may be *(out) on the hustings, take to the hustings, hit the hustings, take a day off from the hustings.* Some may even *set the hustings on fire,* though I haven't noticed this recently.

~*CGB*

-ic, -ical

KEN MOSHER WROTE: I've been wondering about the suffixes **-ic** and **-ical.** Often they seem redundant to me. I noticed, around the advent of Microsoft Windows, people started to refer to a *graphical user interface,* where previously I had always heard and used *graphic user interface.*

The suffix **-ic** forms adjectives from other parts of speech. It occurred originally in Greek and Latin loanwords (*metallic; poetic; archaic*) and, on this model, is used to mean 'having some characteristics of' (*sophomoric*); 'in the style of' (*Byronic*); and 'pertaining to a family of peoples or languages' (*Semitic*).

The suffix **-ical** is obviously a combination of *-ic* and *-al* and is used in forming adjectives from nouns (*rhetorical*). Originally it provided synonyms for adjectives ending in **-ic** (*poetic/poetical, geographic/geographical*). But some of these forms are now different in meaning (*classic/classical; economic/economical; historic/historical*). Some **-ical** forms, such as *tragical* and *majestical*, existed in older English but are now obsolete.

The New Fowler's Modern English Usage, Third Edition, states that more than half of this class of adjectives end only in **-ic**, and a quarter of such formations end only in **-ical.** The rest may end with either suffix. It may be that the **-ic** forms are more common in American English and the **-ical** forms in British English, but different copyediting styles may also be a factor. Also, some idiomatic phrases may require one or the other of these suffixes.

Adverbs formed from these adjectives almost always end in *-ically,* such as *musically.* An exception is the adverb *publicly*—we don't write *publically.*

In the term you mention—*graphical user interface*—*graphical* is used in the same sense as the word *graphic,* though *graphic* has several other senses. To my knowledge, it's always been *graphical* (not *graphic*) *user interface,* being invented in the 1970s and popularized by the Apple Macintosh in the 1980s.

~CGB

ill wind

POLLY GREEN WROTE: I have heard two different ways to use the phrase **an ill wind that blows no good:** (1) The situation must be very bad indeed since no one benefits from it, or (2) Every bad thing that happens benefits someone. Which is the proper usage?

On the basis of citations and experience, I pick number two. But your bewilderment is more than warranted by the ambiguity of this phrase. The confusion is compounded by multiple versions—with words dropped, changed, or reordered in idiosyncratic ways. Your first interpretation is a literal reading justified both by your wording and by a tendency for many of us to say, elliptically, nothing more than **Well, it's an ill wind. . . !** (*Ill* here means 'unfavorable; adverse', as in "ill fortune.")

The complete version is **It's an ill wind that blows no** (or **no one** or **nobody**) **good.** Commonly, it means that when someone loses, another usually profits. Early attestations suggest potential origins. For example, when we read from John Heywood's *Proverbs* (1562) that "It is an yll wynde that blowth no man to good," we can picture a sailing ship blown off course, but perhaps headed toward some paradisiacal island. Note that in early citations, it is the person who is blown toward the good fortune.

From the 18th century on, the image is turned around; good fortune is blown toward the person: "Tis an ill wind that dis na blaw Some body good" (Ramsay, 1714). Literature provides us with sufficient context to support the usual interpretation: "If he were not an idiot," said Monsieur Hochon, who had come in, "he would have married long ago and had children; and then you would have no chance at the property. It is an ill wind that blows no good" (Balzac's *Two Brothers,* translation by Katharine Prescott Wormeley).

That this is a dear and familiar cliché is borne out by a syntactic pun it has inspired. But here, too, we are haunted by confusion. This play on words is variously said to be about the clarinet, the French horn, or the oboe. It has been attributed to Duke Ellington, Ogden Nash, Sir Thomas Beacham, Danny Kaye, and Danny Kaye's wife, Sylvia Fine, who wrote the songs for all his movies. In truth, it was probably around before any of them. But whoever said it first, the words that ring in my ears were sung in 1947 by Danny Kaye in the movie *The Secret Life of Walter Mitty:* "And the oboe it is clearly understood / Is an ill wind that no one blows good."

~EP

incent and incentivize

JANET SLIFER WROTE: I've heard numerous mentions (at work) of **incent** used as the verb form of *incentive.* Is that acceptable? I haven't heard it elsewhere, and it doesn't appear in my dictionary.

Yes, **incent** is a real word, and it means 'to give incentives to; motivate'. But you're right, it's not in *Random House Webster's College Dictionary* or in other general dictionaries. And I couldn't find it in the ten or more business dictionaries I consulted. **Incent** is a back formation from *incentive*. A *back formation* is 'a word formed by dropping an actual or supposed prefix or suffix from an existing word'. A more familiar back formation is *enthuse,* from *enthusiasm.*

However, most dictionaries do include the similar verb **incentivize.** First recorded about 1970, it was not in common use until the 1980s. It's sometimes mentioned in usage guides that discuss the controversial *-ize* suffix in "jargony" words such as *prioritize, privatize,* and *finalize.*

The verb **incent** is used very often. In fact, it's much more common than **incentivize.** Obviously, it's found mostly in business contexts, but a teacher can conceivably "give smiley stickers to incent appropriate behavior, or to incent the students."

The earliest example I could find is in a 1981 issue of *Chemical Week:* ". . . we have to get the American industrial engine running again . . . If you set realistic performance targets with enough stretch in them, then you're trying to incent the participants on things that are within their control." And here's a recent example from the *Charleston Gazette:* "The way these business owners and managers see it, incentive compensation programs are likely to be used more and more . . . Unemployment is at all-time lows. . . . Companies have to find ways to incent their employees in a highly competitive environment."

Though **incent** has been widely used over the past 20 years, every so often I see evidence that people are hearing or seeing it for the first time. Our citation files hold this example from a 1997 article in the *Los Angeles Times:* "State Senate President Pro Tem Bill Lockyer's clunky new welfare reform verb—'to incent', meaning to motivate—is sure to incense grammarians." As for its acceptability, **incent** isn't even mentioned by grammarians who criticize other back formations such as *enthuse* and *burgle*. But because it's in the same category as these words, **incent** would probably be frowned upon as bureaucratic jargon.

~*CGB*

Indo-European

STAN GOLDSTEIN WROTE: The term **Indo-European** indicates, I believe, the source for all the European languages spoken today. It seems a far reach to me that the Germanic and Romance languages derive from Iranian and Indian. Could you clarify the term?

The Germanic and Romance languages don't derive from Iranian and Indian. Rather, they are all members of a large family of languages that derive from a common ancestor. The **Indo-European** family encompasses the following sub-families: Albanian, Armenian, Baltic (Latvian and Lithuanian), Celtic (Gaelic, Welsh, Breton), Germanic (English, German, Yiddish, Dutch, Danish, Icelandic, Norwegian, and Swedish), Hellenic (Greek), Indo-Iranian (Sanskrit, Persian, and the Indic languages such as Hindi, Kashmiri, and Punjabi), Italic (Latin and the Romance languages), Slavic (Russian, Polish, Bulgarian, Czech, etc.), and two extinct sub-families, Anatolian (or Hittite) and Tocharian (spoken in medieval Chinese Turkestan).

It was a British scholar named Sir William Jones who suggested in 1786 that Greek, Latin, and Sanskrit had common features, including vocabulary and grammar, that derived from "some common source, which, perhaps, no longer exists." We have no written evidence of this "common source," which scholars call **Proto-Indo-European** and which was probably spoken from sometime around 5000 B.C. to shortly after 2000 B.C. in an area in the northern part of eastern Europe. Since we know that Greek, Hittite, and Sanskrit were distinct languages by 1600 B.C., we can assume that the community of original speakers of **Proto-Indo-European** had broken up well before that and that their language had given way to its successors as the people migrated. Not all of the ancient languages have left written evidence, but from what we know of the modern languages, we can deduce the existence of "Common Celtic," "Common Germanic," "Common Italic," etc. In other words, the dozen or so early and modern Germanic languages derived from one common Germanic language; and the modern Romance languages and Latin derived from one common Italic language, both of which in turn derived from **Proto-Indo-European.**

We know this prehistoric language existed because of the words that are common to all or most of the **Indo-European** languages. Scholars have been able to reconstruct pieces of **Proto-Indo-European** and know quite a lot about it and therefore about the people who spoke it. The process of reconstructing a prehistoric language begins with words that are similar in a number of **Indo-European** languages. Such cognates provide evidence for the prehistoric word that was their common ancestor. (By the way, if you see a word with an asterisk (*) in front of it in an etymology, it's a reconstructed word. If it's followed by a hyphen, it's a root, and we assume that there were various suffixes added on for inflective purposes.)

The **Indo-European** root *deiwo- meant 'a deity, a god, a daylight god'. This was probably the name of the main **Indo-European** deity, originally the god of daylight, later the god of thunder and war. From this root came such words as Greek *dīos* and *Zeus;* Latin *deus* and *Jupiter* (from **Diu-pater* 'godfather'), as well as *diēs* 'day'; Sanskrit *devah* 'a god'; Old English *Tīw* 'the god of war and the sky'; Lithuanian *dievas* and Latvian *dievs* 'a god'; and Russian *divny* 'wonderful'. In addition to English *deity, divine,* and *diary,* which come from this root, we have *Tuesday* 'the day of Tiw'.

~GSM

☞ inflammable and flammable

KARL LAGNEMMA WROTE: Can you explain why **inflammable** has a similar meaning to **flammable?**

Inflammable and **flammable** both mean 'capable of being set on fire' or 'easily set on fire', so they're really the same, rather than similar, in meaning. This sense equivalence is confirmed by dictionaries, though some writers insist that **flammable** means 'combustible' and **inflammable** means 'explosive'.

Inflammable dates from the early 17th century. Originally its opposite was *noninflammable,* but now we use the easier term *nonflammable.*

In the word **inflammable,** the prefix *in-* functions as an intensive—it indicates increased emphasis or force. But because this prefix can also mean 'not', **inflammable** could mistakenly be interpreted as meaning 'not flammable'.

Though the adjective **flammable** was coined in 1813 in a translation of a Latin text, it was not commonly used until the early 20th century, when the scientific community, the fire-insurance industry, and, specifically, the National Fire Protection Association tried to revive the term as an official replacement for the ambiguous **inflammable.** After World War II, the British Standards Institution took up the campaign: "In order to avoid any possible ambiguity, it is the Institution's policy to encourage the use of the terms 'flammable' and 'non-flammable' rather than 'inflammable' and 'non-inflammable.' "

The campaign to revive **flammable** was successful in commercial and scientific contexts. But the general public was (and still is) resistant to the change, and so **inflammable** is still very much in use. **Inflammable** is more common in British English than in American English. It's also the word more usually used in nontechnical and figurative contexts: "The furor is a reminder that despite overall harmony, race has the potential to be an inflammable issue in Malaysia" (*Asiaweek,* 2000). Use of the literal and figurative meanings is shown in a headline in the (London) *Financial Times:* "Highly inflammable: Labour policymakers failed to foresee the speed and anger of the public's response to high petrol prices."

~*CGB*

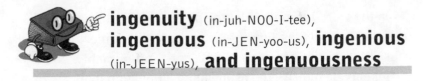

ingenuity (in-juh-NOO-I-tee), ingenuous (in-JEN-yoo-us), ingenious (in-JEEN-yus), and ingenuousness

PILAR McADAM WROTE: It's just occurred to me that the word **ingenuity** doesn't quite make sense. It looks like it's derived from the adjective **ingenuous,** which means 'simple or naive'. But its usage isn't related to that; it's really used more like a form of **ingenious,** meaning 'clever or inventive in a creative way'. Is the 'naive' term related to the application of "genius," or have they just grown together over time?

Ingenious and **ingenuous** are two words that always appear on lists of "words commonly confused," and the spellings are so similar that it's easy to understand why. Your definitions are correct.

English **ingenious** came through French *ingénieux* from Latin *ingeniōsus,* 'having good natural abilities' or 'clever', early in the 15th century. The earliest meaning of **ingenious** in English was 'intelligent or talented'. By the 16th century, it had also come to mean 'skillful' or 'clever at contriving things' or, in reference to an object, 'cleverly made'—all of which are modern meanings.

Ingenious also had the meaning of 'befitting a well-born person' or 'liberal' as in "the liberal arts": "A course of Learning, and ingenious studies" (Shakespeare, *Taming of the Shrew,* 1596). And here we get into the confusion with **ingenuous.**

Ingenuous first appeared late in the 16th century. Ben Jonson seems to have been the first to use it in the modern sense of 'open', 'frank', or 'honest': "Tell me, ingenuously, dost thou affect my sister Bridget, as thou pretend'st?" (*Every Man in His Humor*, 1598). **Ingenuous** comes from the Latin word *ingenuus,* which means 'native' or 'freeborn' or 'noble' or 'honest'. The assumption was apparently that a man who was of free birth was more likely to be honorable. There are examples of the 'noble' meaning of **ingenuous** in English in the 17th century, but it died out sometime in the 1700s, and the meaning shifted from 'open or frank' to 'innocently open or frank' and then to 'innocent'. (If you're innocent, it's easier to be honest.)

There is clear evidence in the citations in *The Oxford English Dictionary* that writers in the 17th and 18th centuries confused **ingenious** and **ingenuous.** As we saw above, Shakespeare used **ingenious** in the sense of 'befitting the well-born' in *Taming of the Shrew.* And he used **ingenuous** to mean 'talented' in *Love's Labor's Lost*: "If their sons be ingenuous, they shall want no instruction." In 1680, a preacher by the name of William Beveridge spoke of an "ingenious confession"—one assumes he meant 'open and honest'. The confusion was apparently cleared up (at least in theory) by about 1800, and the words have had separate meanings since then.

Now on to **ingenuity,** which is first attested at the end of the 16th century. It probably came from Italian, and its initial meaning was 'the condition of being free-born'. It came to mean 'nobility of character' and then 'honesty or sincerity'.

At the same time, however, as a result of the confusion between **ingenious** and **ingenuous, ingenuity** meant 'intelligence' or 'wisdom' and then 'skill or cleverness' and 'skillfulness of design'. A man named Robert Baker, writing a random collection of comments on what he regarded as misuses of English in 1770, said: "It is a considerable Blemish in our Language, that the Word **ingenuity** has two Senses; for hereby it often becomes unintelligible." He suggested the word "ingeniety" as the noun for **ingenious** and wanted **ingenuity** to be applied only to the sense related to **ingenuous.** Alas, he was too late. **Ingenuity** is a characteristic of an **ingenious** person, and **ingenuousness** is a characteristic of an **ingenuous** person.

~GSM

☞ iota (eye-OH-tuh) **and jot**

OWL WROTE: Do you know the etymology of **iota,** as in "not one iota of difference"? . . . Some dictionaries say [the meaning comes from the fact that] **iota** is the smallest letter in the Greek alphabet. However, someone once told me that the expression derives from a medieval debate within the Christian Church over some fine point, where the presence or absence of the letter **iota** in some word made a semantic difference. The latter sounds more interesting, but is there any truth to it?

Your source was probably referring to the first Council of Nicaea (325), at which there was a controversy over the expression of the relationship between Father and Son (God and Christ): one group wanted to use the word *homooúsion* 'of the same substance'; the other group said it should be *homoioúsion* 'of like substance'. The distinction is between *homós* and *hómois*. The first group won, and *homooúsion* (without the **iota**) was the word that was used in the formulation of the Nicene Creed.

However, I haven't found any citations indicating that this controversy has anything to do with the meaning of **iota,** which is the smallest letter in the Greek alphabet and is used figuratively in English to mean 'the least, or a very small, particle or quantity'.

Iota came into English from Latin and was first pronounced "jota" and then "jote" (both with a long *o*).

In the 1611 King James Bible, Matthew 5:18 reads as follows: "Till heaven and earth pass, one jot or one tittle shall in no wise pass from the law, till all be fulfilled." The Greek word that is translated 'jot' is **iōta,** so Jesus is saying that not the smallest letter of the law will be lost. Since the Greek letter **iōta** corresponds to the Hebrew *yod,* which is the smallest letter in that alphabet, the original reference in the Bible was probably to the Hebrew letter. William Tyndale translated this passage "one iott [pronounced as one syllable] or one tytle" in 1526. In his 1382 translation of the Bible from Latin, John Wycliffe used the phrase "oon i or titil," and his gloss explains that *i* is the smallest letter.

Iota and **jot** were used interchangeably: "Shall we lose, or sleightly pass by, any iota or tittle of the Booke of God?" (Daniel Featly, 1636). In Shakespeare's *Othello,* Iago says, "I see this hath a little dash'd your spirits," and Othello replies, "Not a jot, not a jot."

By the way, our verb **jot** meaning 'to write down quickly', which came into standard English from Scottish in the 18th century, probably meant originally 'to set down in the briefest form'.

~*GSM*

iterate and reiterate

ZEB LANDSMAN WROTE: Iterate and **reiterate** seem to mean the same thing. Are they used differently?

They do effectively mean the same thing—'to do or say something again; repeat'—but English speakers don't like it when synonyms really are synonymous, nor do we like repetition when there are so many synonyms to choose from, so now in fact they are generally used in different ways.

We're all so accustomed to the use of the prefix *re-* to mean 'again' that many of us have assumed that, somewhere along the line, English speakers forgot that **iterate** already meant 'do/say something again' and added a redundant prefix to it in error, the way some people have done with *irregardless*. In fact, the culprits are Latin speakers themselves: the verbs *iterāre* and *reiterāre* were both used. I can't prove it, but I imagine some Latin speaker once tacked *re-* onto *iterāre* in much the same way that English speakers often say "Will you repeat that again?"

Nowadays, **iterate** tends to be used for repeated actions, especially in mathematical functions, and **reiterate** is far more common (it must just sound right to us) and tends to be used for things one says, especially when repeated, um, over and over again. However, this is very fluid, and many literary writers—or just plain pretentious ones—use **iterate** to refer to spoken or written repetitions.

I also suspect that some who insist on using **iterate** regret the very existence of **reiterate** and wish people would be more careful in their distinctions. As I said, English speakers are like that: the tribes that inhabited the British Isles over the centuries were an acquisitive lot, and divisions of meanings often arose because whoever was attacking the islands that week brought their Old Norse or Norman French or Spotted Grouse synonyms along with their armies.

> Conqueror: That scratchy thing you wear over your hose is a shirt.
> Conquered: But we call it a skirt.
> Conqueror: It is now a shirt.
> Conquered: Okay, we'll call the top part a shirt and the bottom part a skirt.

(This is my unattested, screenplay version.)

~WRN

It is raining

CRAIG SILVERSTEIN WROTE: In the expression **It is raining,** what's raining?

As one of our former presidents might say, I suppose that all depends on what *it* is. What comes to mind when most of us think of *it* is the familiar referential pronoun. We were probably all taught in elementary school that *it* stands for a previously mentioned noun—usually a thing or an animal—as in "Have you seen his new car? I like it" or "Have some soup; it's good for you." Actually, even these sentences are not so simple. If we look carefully at the first example, we can see that *it* really substitutes for the entire noun phrase "his new car" and not just the word "car." (If *it* were filling in for "car" alone, the sentence would have read, "I like his new it.") The second example is different. "Some soup" refers to a specific portion of soup, whereas the *it* in "it's good for you" probably refers to soup in general, giving us a slight shift in meaning. All this may seem like a small point, but realizing that *it* is not just a simple substitute for a noun makes it easier to account for such references as, "Where's the blue paperback mystery book I was reading a few minutes ago? Oh, here it is!"

This referential function is even broader. *It* can point, for example, to a paragraph or more of previous discourse, or to something about to be mentioned ("To those who lived through it, the tornado was a terrifying experience"), or to something that doesn't have to be mentioned because it is physically present ("Stop! You'll break it!"), or even to something merely implied or deliberately vague ("It all started with Adam and Eve." "How's it going?" "Cool it!").

But the *it* in **it is raining** is not this kind of referential *it*. It is not simply a convenient substitute for a word or phrase. In *A Comprehensive Grammar of the English Language* (Quirk, Greenbaum, Leech, and Svartvik), the authors describe this *it* as "an 'empty' or 'prop' subject," a filler or place holder that fits neatly into the subject slot of a sentence. One of my professors used to refer to this *it* as a grammatical weather forecaster ("Baby it's cold outside!"), but *it* can also deal with time ("It's too late for mere apologies") and distance ("It's a long way to Tipperary"). *It* has little or no meaning of its own in sentences like this; according to Quirk and Greenbaum, *it* simply "refers quite generally to the time or place of the event or state in question."

But wait! I dimly remember a line from an old song: "It isn't raining rain, you know, it's raining vi-o-lets." Could *that* be what's raining? Or is it cats and dogs? No, even here the grammatical subject is still that indefinite, empty, prop *it*.

~*EP*

its and it's

CHRIS MOLANPHY WROTE: I was wondering if anyone, including you, kept track of what the most common grammatical mistake in the English language is. I would submit that substituting the contraction **it's** for the possessive **its** must be it. Seeing a phrase like "on it's own" in print makes me wince, but plenty of otherwise reputable publications let it go unchecked. Is it, as Casey Kasem would say, number one?

I'd guess that **it's** versus **its** is in the Top 20 on the Blooper Parade. Yes, the confusion occurs even in reputable publications: "For all it's faults, . . . this is a pretty interesting film" (*Cincinnati Post,* 1996). More commonly, **it's** is mistakenly used for the possessive, but I've seen many examples of **its** used for the contraction. I've even seen **its'** as an occasional odd variation. Analogously, the other possessive pronouns are sometimes mistakenly written as *her's, their's, our's, your's.* A related error is the confusion of *who's* and *whose.*

Contracted forms are not a modern convenience. *The Oxford English Dictionary* has a 1625 citation for the contraction **it's,** and the contraction *'tis* is attested a century earlier.

The original third person neuter possessive pronoun was *his,* which, to confuse matters, was also the masculine possessive pronoun: "Boston is two miles North-east from Rox-berry: His situation is very pleasant" (William Wood, *New England's Prospect,* 1634). The neuter *his* began to be replaced in the late 16th century, though it was in use until the late 17th century. By analogy with noun possessives (*boy's, girl's*), the new neuter possessive was originally written **it's,** and this form predominated throughout the 17th and early 18th centuries. There was great confusion between possessive **it's** and **its,** but in the mid-18th century, the form without the apostrophe began to predominate, finally prevailing in the 19th and early 20th centuries. As we know, the confusion never really went away, and possessive **it's** has come back with a vengeance.

Evidently the distinction between **its** and **it's** served to distinguish the possessive pronoun from the contraction. But *Reader's Digest Success with Words* points out that this distinction is not logical, ". . . since the same situation applies to nouns: *today's* can be the possessive of *today,* as in *today's weather,* or stand for *today is,* as in *Today's the day.* Logical or not, all modern usage guides consider it a mistake to confuse **its** and **it's.**

~*CGB*

-ize or -ise

DONNA SCHAER WROTE: My fifth graders and I are puzzling over an English spelling issue that frequently causes problems. Why is *realize* spelled the way it is and not *realise*? Why do we spell the word *prize* with a *z,* yet spell *surprise* with an *s?* There seem to be a number of words

whose endings of either **-ise** or **-ize** seem arbitrary. If, as
we surmise, the difference is American vs. English
spellings, why aren't all the *S*'s *Z*'s?

The difference is indeed between American and British
spellings, but as you've probably guessed, things aren't quite
as simple as that.

The suffix **-ize** has been around in English since the late
16th century. This is such a useful suffix for making verbs
from adjectives and nouns that it has become one of the most
common in English; we got it via French, which of course
uses the spelling **-ise.**

It orginally comes from the Greek infinitive verb ending
-dzein. As early as the 3rd century, Christians were taking
Greek words such as *baptídzein* and Latinizing the endings,
as in *baptizāre.* Originally, only Greek base words were Latinized in this way, but then the French began using the ending for Latin base words, as in *réaliser.*

Influenced by French, English speakers borrowed many
Latinized Greek words, such as *apologize,* which has always
been spelled with a *z.* They also picked up the suffix and have
used it to coin verbs ever since, from *fossilize* (18th century)
to *itemize* (19th century) to *computerize* (20th century).

The spelling of the suffix tended to be **-ize,** which makes
perfect sense considering the pronunciation and the spelling
of the Latin and Greek endings. However, because many of
these words were borrowed into English from French, the **-ise**
spelling was often seen. At some point during the vogue for
codification and standardization engendered by the Enlightenment, some bright spark in England decided that all words
with Latin bases should be spelled with **-ise,** and all words

with Greek bases could continue to be spelled with **-ize.** Thus Britons got saddled with having to memorize even more irregular spellings than we have to.

This idea never caught on in America, where **-ize** continued to be preferred. There is some dispute about the etymology of *analyze* so that some argue it really ought always to be spelled *analyse*, but otherwise Americans always spell this suffix with a *z*. As for words such as *prize, surmise, surprise,* and *revise,* these are not examples of a 'root + **-ize**' formation. You can look up the etymologies of individual "exceptions" to the **-ize** rule in any good dictionary.

~*WRN*

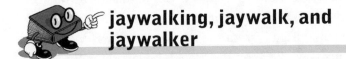 jaywalking, jaywalk, and jaywalker

J. TROUTMAN WROTE: Boston has recently announced yet another campaign against **jaywalking.** What is the origin of **jaywalking**?

Oddly enough, the term you ask about is probably connected with Boston, whose residents were said to favor the use of long words: "The Bostonian, supposedly sesquipedalian of speech, has reduced 'a pedestrian who crosses streets in disregard of traffic signals' to the compact 'jaywalker'" (*Harper's Magazine*, 1917). The verb **jaywalk** appeared in print a few years later than the noun. Both terms coincide with the appearance of automobiles on urban streets, so the offense of **jaywalking** did not refer to carelessly dodging a horse and carriage.

The history of the term is fairly clear. In the late 1880s, the word *jay* took on the slang meanings 'a gullible, naive fellow', and also 'an unsophisticated country fellow', both senses being derived from the habits of the much maligned *jaybird*. This 'country fellow' sense is the one used in George M. Cohan's 1906 "Forty-Five Minutes From Broadway":

> *If you want to see the real jay delegation,*
> *The place where the real rubens dwell,*
> *Just hop on a train at the Grand Central Station,*
> *Get off when they shout, 'New Rochelle!'* . . .
> *Oh, what a fine bunch of rubens!*
> *Oh, what a jay atmosphere!*
> *They have whiskers like hay,*
> *And imagine Broadway,*
> *Only forty-five minutes from here.*

The term **jaywalk** is said to refer to the likelihood that countrified *jays* and *rubens* (or *rubes*), being unfamiliar with traffic rules in the city, would cross the street in a heedless way. Or **jaywalk** may refer directly to the noisy, foolish, and aggressive habits of the bird. Either way, **jaywalk** is ultimately connected with this bird of ill-repute.

The term **jaywalker** may have been influenced by the earlier term *jayhawker* 'one of the antislavery guerrillas in Kansas and other border states before and during the Civil War'. These guerrillas used violent and aggressive tactics to keep slavery out of the region. Although **jaywalkers** have been called aggressive, city officials are equally aggressive against them—and not only in Boston.

~*CGB*

Jew's harp

ERIC KAHN WROTE: I know that a **Jew's harp** is an instrument played by the mouth and a finger, giving a twanging sound in hillbilly music, but how did it come to be called that? Is it derogatory?

This fairly ancient instrument is found in many cultures throughout the world, though none of its foreign names have anything to do with Jews. The European version is a small harp-shaped frame held between the teeth, with a projecting prong plucked to produce a twanging sound. Since the late 16th century, its English name was **Jew's harp,** but through the 19th century it was also called *Jew's trump* because it has a natural scale like that of a trumpet.

The name of the instrument is almost certainly connected with Jews, though there's no direct evidence to confirm this. *The Oxford English Dictionary* says it may have been made, sold, or sent to England by Jewish merchants, or may have been named to suggest the harps or trumpets of the Bible. Most sources discredit the theory that *Jew's trump* is an alteration of French *jeu trompe,* meaning 'play trumpet'. Also discredited is a connection with *gewgaw,* meaning 'something gaudy and useless', though this term may have originally referred to a musical instrument. The names *jaw's harp* (first recorded about 1880) and *juice harp* (dating from the 1940s) were either misinformed or politically correct alterations of *Jew's.*

Assuming the connection with Jews, the name is not necessarily an intended ethnic slur, as explained in *A Dictionary of Contemporary American Usage:* "Whether any derogation was originally intended is not known, but it is apparently believed that some might now be felt." Gordon Frazier, of the "Jew's Harp Guild," has said: "The way to combat the perception of the name 'Jew's harp' as a slur is not to try to change the language, but to improve the image of the instrument. We can do that by treating the Jew's harp as a legitimate musical instrument and encouraging others to do the same." Frazier is alluding to the fact that, especially in the United States, the instrument is sometimes considered inferior or unworthy (maybe suited only to hillbilly music)—an image problem shared by the harmonica (mouth harp) as used by folk musicians. But the instrument's varied history belies this conclusion. The **Jew's harp** has been used to heal the sick. Classical concertos have been written for it—as the *Century Dictionary* puts it: "The Jew's harp is capable of surprisingly sweet and elaborate effects." And a final claim for its usefulness: It was used by bachelors to serenade ladies in 19th-century Austria: "So popular was the custom and so discreet and persuasive the sound . . . that female virtue was endangered and instruments were repeatedly banned by the authorities," writes Anthony Baines in *Musical Instruments through the Ages*.

~CGB

jibe, gibe, and jive

MARK WICKENS WROTE: A common confusion is the use of **jive** for **jibe,** as in "His story doesn't jive with the facts." That should be **jibe,** right? Are the two words related at all?

Jibe means 'to be in harmony or accord; to agree'. The origin of this term is uncertain; it may be related to the similarly spelled **jibe** in the sense 'to shift a sail from one side to the other while sailing before the wind'. This sailing term was borrowed from a Dutch verb, and is also spelled *gybe,* especially in British English.

The accepted meanings of **jive** are 'to tease or bluff' or 'to dance to jazz or swing music'. The origin of this term is "obscure," a few degrees cloudier than "uncertain." Using **jive** as a variant of **jibe** in the meaning 'to agree' is usually considered an error or misspelling, though the "error" is so common that one college dictionary (not Random House) enters it without comment or warning label. The confusion between these two words is not new in the language. The journal *American Speech* records **jive** in a list of college slang from the 1940s: "Doesn't jive. Doesn't make sense." The *Dictionary of American Regional English* has many examples of the "error" from the 1950s through the 1960s. **Jibe** and **jive** are still commonly confused, as in this recent example from the *Washington Times:* "Their initial numbers just didn't jive, just didn't pass the initial smell test."

The general opinion on the **jibe/jive** issue is summed up in this quote from a 1980 issue of the *Daily News:* "Can you take seriously as a writer anyone who refers to 'the welfare roles of this country' and reports that everything a character said 'had jived with the facts'? Such a person may be taken seriously only as a symptom of decay in our language." (To protect the guilty, I won't divulge the writer's identity.)

A further confusion exists between the identically pronounced **jibe** and **gibe.** In the sense 'to mock or jeer', the preferred spelling is **gibe,** especially in formal writing, but **jibe** is an acceptable spelling variant. In the senses 'to agree' and 'to shift a sail to the other side', **gibe** is occasionally used instead of **jibe** but is usually considered an error.

Adding to the confusion is the fact that **gibe/jibe** in the sense 'to mock or jeer' is semantically similar to **jive** in the sense 'to tease or bluff'. So, error or not, these spelling and sense distinctions among **jibe, gibe,** and **jive** are very difficult to keep straight.

~CGB

jiggy

LYDIA MICKUNAS WROTE: What do you know about the word **jiggy?** It's used in . . . hip-hop lingo and has to do with . . . being really cool and having women, money, etc. But when I was a child, my father used this word like *antsy,* to mean 'excited or restless' (but in an annoying way). I think he only used the word when telling me to stop being so **jiggy.**

This slang term has been around at least since the 1930s. Originally it meant 'crazy', as in "He's gone completely jiggy." The senses your father knew, 'jittery; fidgety, restless; excitedly energetic', are still current today: "If I was too jiggy to hold the syringe, he'd shoot me up" (Radford & Crowley, *Drug Agent,* 1989).

But in the early 1990s, **jiggy** took on the new meanings 'wonderful, excellent, enjoyable, exciting, stylish', as in "Get yourself some jiggy gear." Actually, **jiggy** can refer to anything that's very cool, so it could also mean 'having women, money, etc.'.

Jiggy (and the phrase *get jiggy*) burst onto most people's radar in 1997-98, after the release of Will Smith's wildly popular rap song, "Gettin' Jiggy Wit It." A discussion of **jiggy** would not be complete without quoting some lyrics:

> *On your mark ready set let's go*
> *Dance floor pro I know you know*
> *I go psycho when my new joint hit*
> *Just can't sit*
> *Gotta get jiggy wit it*

In case you can't figure it out, the meaning of *get jiggy* is 'have fun, enjoy oneself totally'. More specifically, it means 'to lose one's inhibitions, especially when dancing or performing music', as in "Latin groovers get jiggy at the mercury-hot Conga Room on Wilshire Boulevard" (*Los Angeles Times*, 1998).

Slang has many ways to say the same thing. The phrase *get jiggy* (*with it*) is very close in meaning to an earlier (1970s) phrase *get down* (*with it*). What does *get* mean in these slang phrases? Connie Eble explains in her book *Slang and Sociability:* "Many (slang) phrases are built on verbs of generalized meaning such as do, get, make, and take. The verbs themselves contribute little to the specific referential meaning of expressions such as get a grip . . . get a life, . . . get down. . . ."

There's no agreement on the origin of **jiggy,** but it may be from *jig* 'dance' or *jiggle* 'move with short, quick jerks'. A less likely origin is the highly offensive term *jigaboo* 'a black person'.

~*CGB*

Jim Crow

JAN SCHAALE WROTE: We're wondering about the origin of **Jim Crow.** Was it a real person, or does the expression and usage originate from the Minstrel Show title?

Jim Crow is the discrimination against, or segregation of, black people in any of the myriad forms that it can take in this country of ours. Its original meaning was, disparagingly, 'a black person'. The expression has its origins in a song called "Jump Jim Crow" sung in blackface by one Thomas Dartmouth Rice in the early 19th century. Thomas Rice (1808–60) was not the first white man to appear in blackface, but he was the person to make this form of "entertainment" popular. In 1828, he caused a sensation in Louisville with "Jump Jim Crow." The song goes on for forty-four stanzas, all of them along the lines of the first verse:

> Come listen all you galls and boys
> I's jist from Tucky-hoe.
> I'm goin to sing a little song,
> My name's Jim Crow.
> Weel about and turn about and do jis so,
> Eb'ry time I weel about and jump Jim Crow.

The public took to this song and dance, and soon Rice was touring the United States and, later, England and Ireland. (There is some controversy as to whether he actually composed the song, or merely appropriated it.) Rice himself came to be known as "Jim Crow," and soon enough his cork-darkened grinning character became an archetype. By 1852, we have Harriet Beecher Stowe writing about Topsy in *Uncle Tom's Cabin*, "She was rather a funny specimen in the Jim Crow line." The phrase was being used to mean 'for blacks only' even earlier. *A Dictionary of Americanisms* cites an article in the 1842 *Liberator:* "It is this spirit that compels the colored man to ride in the 'Jim-Crow' car."

Thomas Rice died in poverty in New York, but his legacy lived on. His stereotypical portrayal of the singing, dancing, devil-may-care black person became the catchword for all the repressions inflicted upon African-Americans. The expression *Jim Crow law* refers to the antiblack laws passed to ensure that blacks stayed repressed. In the 1960s, the marchers and protesters in the Civil Rights movement were out to "kill Jim Crow." The movement was even called the *anti–Jim Crow* movement. In 1964, the unblinkingly honest singer Nina Simone composed her song "Old Jim Crow." This is part of the concluding verse, a good antidote to Thomas Rice:

> *Old Jim Crow*
> *You've been around too long*
> *Gotta work the devil*
> *'Til you're dead and gone.*
> *Old Jim Crow don't you know*
> *It's all over*
> *All over*
> *It's all over now.*

~*RG*

John Doe

RACHEL KAHAN WROTE: What's the origin of the term **John Doe?** Everyone in my family loves mysteries and police procedurals, and they asked me to find out. Even though I'm an editor and supposedly knowledgeable about the language, this one stumped me. Can you help salvage my reputation?

Both of our reputations are on the line, and this question isn't easy. **John Doe** had its beginnings in legal use. From the 15th century to the 19th, it was, in England, a legal fiction standing for the plaintiff in a dispute over title to real property. **Richard Roe** was the name given to the defendant. In order to avoid dealing with the rigid restrictions imposed on such matters in English common law, someone who wanted to regain possession of land from which he had been unjustly evicted would bring a different kind of action—an "ejectment" suit—in the name of **John Doe,** his fictional tenant.

Because this fictitious person couldn't deny anything that was said, the landowner was often able to oust the usurper and recover his land legally. Supposedly, the fictional defendant was a traveler who, while passing by, just happened to toss the mythical tenant off the property before going on his way. Chances for victory by the rightful owner were enhanced when the accused did not, for some reason, appear at the proceedings to defend himself. And the actual person who wrongfully had possession of the owner's land had no legal standing in the suit.

These suits were no longer necessary after the 1852 passage of the Common Law Procedure Act, which eased the previous restrictions. But by then the legal fictions had become conventionalized; they are now used frequently in both English and American law. Current use is looser, however. **John Doe,** *Jane Doe, Richard Roe, Jane Roe,* or—if need be— *Peter Poe,* are, according to *Random House Webster's Dictionary of the Law,* used in legal cases and documents, "either to conceal a person's identity, or because the person's real name is not known, or because it is not yet known whether the person exists" (James E. Clapp).

We can say, then, that the **John Doe** of early legal use was always fictitious; in current legal use he's more often a real person; and in extended metaphorical use, as 'an anonymous, average man', **John Doe** is a generic—once again not real.

Back to origins. *John* is easy enough to understand. It was the second most popular name in England even earlier than the 15th century (*William* took first place). *John* is still used as a generic (*John Barleycorn, John Q. Public,* etc.).

Doe is harder to track down. It is not in lists of early inheritable surnames in England. Nor was it one of the usual "bynames" in the Middle Ages—names you didn't inherit but acquired yourself. Bynames were derived from either a parent's name (*Peterson*), your location (*Underhill*), your occupation (*Smith*), or some nickname (*Wiseman*). Feverish research yields no *Doe*. I'm stumped! I can only speculate that *Doe* and *Roe* were convenient nonsense names, short and easy to remember. And they rhymed. On the other hand, there are a few putatively real *Doe*'s and *Roe*'s in modern phone books. Some of them are named "John" or "Richard" or "Jane." I wonder. . . .

~*EP*

josh

NAN TOMLINSON WROTE: Josh in the sense of 'kidding' or 'joking' may be related to the name Joshua, mayn't it? We know that the name Joshua is Hebrew and appears in the Bible. Neither of the two memorable biblical Joshuas was a joker. Any information to impart?

The two most important Joshuas in the Bible are Joshua ben Nun, who was a personal assistant to Moses, and Joshua ben Josedech, who was high priest at the restoration of the temple in 537 B.C. Joshua, with its diminutive **Josh,** became a popular name in English in the 18th and 19th centuries.

Josh meaning 'to banter or to make fun of' or, as a noun, 'good-natured banter', has nothing to do with the biblical Joshuas, though it might have to do with the name Joshua.

Random House Webster's Unabridged Dictionary says **josh** is "of obscure origin." *The Oxford English Dictionary* doesn't attempt an etymology but directs the reader to "Cf. Josh Billings, pseudonym of an American humorist." It's not clear whether it means Billings took his name from the verb or the other way about.

What is certain is that **josh** is of American origin. The earliest citation is from the *St. Louis Reveille* of 1845: "Look out in future, and if you must Josh, why, give a private one." *Saddle and Moccasin* by F. Francis (1887) contains a gloss: "He . . . liked nothing better than to . . . chin and josh [note, chat and joke] with them in his funereal fashion."

Josh Billings was the pseudonym of Henry Wheeler Shaw (1818–85); his collections of humorous writings didn't become well known until the 1860s, so we can discount him as a source for **josh.**

Another theory refers to a man named Josh Tatum, who was accused of passing "Racketeer Nickels" in Boston. Mr. Tatum was unable to either hear or speak, so he never actually said that what looked like five-dollar gold pieces were really gold-plated nickels—he just gave them to clerks and accepted whatever change was given him. No one was able to testify effectively against him, and he was allowed to go free. Since this happened (if it happened) in 1883, about forty years after **josh** meaning 'banter' appeared, we can also discount this theory.

According to the *Random House Historical Dictionary of American Slang,* the name **Josh** was regarded in mid-19th-century America as a typically rural name. A **Josh** was 'a country bumpkin' or 'a hick', a rustic who was rather slow and not too bright. Here's an 1863 quotation from Hearsill's *1491 Days:* "Luther says that the only thing he regrets in the affair is to be arrested by 'Joshes'." Lacking evidence of any other source, it seems likely to me that **josh** meaning 'to make fun of' has its origin in this use of the proper name. Joshes, then, were the ones who were joshed rather than the joshers.

～GSM

jumping the broom

JOSEPH DISTEFANO WROTE: Can you tell me how the phrase **jump over the broom** came to refer to getting married?

The phrase is most commonly **jump the broom.** The traditional act of **jumping the broom,** in which a couple jump together over a decorated broom that has been placed on the floor in front of them, is enjoying a resurgence in African-American wedding ceremonies.

In the antebellum South, slaves were often not allowed to marry, and so an alternative ceremony for marking a couple's commitment was adopted. Most historians and curators of African-American cultural collections agree that the tradition—at least as practiced by African-Americans—originated in the southern United States. However, that is not entirely accepted; there is still speculation about possible African ceremonial origins, one of which was for a bride to sweep the home of her mother-in-law on her wedding day.

Since wedding traditions differ so widely across Africa, I think the slavery-origin theory is more likely: slaves came from many tribes with quite divergent marriage traditions, and in researching this phrase, I discovered that the exact same ceremony is an ancient Celtic tradition. The link here is that many slave owners were Scots-Irish immigrants (or their descendants).

From the early days of Christianity in Ireland, rituals tended to blend the pagan with the Christian. An example of this was the handfasting ceremony, a commitment ceremony held when a priest was not available. Couples who just couldn't wait until the traveling priest turned up would ceremonially tie their wrists together, then join hands and jump over a broom to guarantee children. In Celtic tradition, the broom was a symbol of fertility; Beltane (May Day) festivities often included fertility rites such as broom-jumping or broom-riding. It seems possible that the idea of this type of unofficial but sincere marriage ceremony could have been adopted by early slaves at the suggestion of their Celtic masters. That the masters were party to these ceremonies is evidenced by one former slave's account of her own wedding quoted in Harriet Cole's *Jumping the Broom: The African-American Wedding Planner.*

Today, the ceremony can represent sweeping out the old and welcoming the new, or a jump into a new life, or (as it did for the Irish) the beginning of a new life in which domestic issues come to the fore. Some African-Americans reject it as a vestige of their slave past, and others embrace it as a unique cultural expression.

Linguistically, the term **jumping the broom** has not yet become synonymous with marriage in the way that "tying the knot" is. For more details about the modern ceremony itself, you can check out Harriet Cole's book.

$\sim$*WRN*

knave

S. AND L. MEIN WROTE: I was reading a book, and while a card game was being described I came across the word **knave.** Since the king, queen, and ace were already there, I guessed it to be the jack. Am I right, and where does this word come from?

Yes, the **knave** is the equivalent of the *jack* in reference to 'a playing card'. This sense of **knave** dates from the 1560s and is still the British term. The 'playing card' sense of *jack* is recorded about 100 years later and is the term used by Americans.

The term **knave** has a long history that predates the card game meaning. By about the year 1000, it meant 'a boy or a male servant' (from Old English *cnafa*), a sense recorded through the mid-1800s. (The related German *Knabe* retains this meaning of 'a boy' and similarly, French *garçon* means 'a boy' and 'a waiter'). But before 1200 **knave** took on its present English meaning of 'a rogue or scoundrel', probably because the original references were to a boy of the lower classes or to a servant of low status.

The playing card, which is the lowest court card, traditionally has a picture of a boy or a male servant of the king or queen. In the following rhyme, the **knave** is actually the head-servant but also a rogue or scoundrel:

> *The Queen of Hearts she made some tarts,*
> *All on a summer's day;*
> *The Knave of Hearts he stole those tarts,*
> *And took them quite away.*

So the term **knave** has undergone the linguistic process of *pejoration*, changing from a respectable to a less respectable meaning. Interestingly, the synonymous *jack,* a nickname for *John,* went through the same semantic change, originally meaning 'a lower-class person, commoner' and later, 'a rogue or scoundrel'. The archaic term *varlet* also had the two meanings of 'a servant or page' and 'a rogue or scoundrel' and is from the same source as the more familiar *valet.*

The term **knave** has been historically paired with *fool* or its synonyms, as in *Pepys Diary* (1658): "The veriest knave and bufflehead that ever he saw in his life." And here's an example from a recent edition of *Maclean's:* "No wonder the province's voters regard politicians as fools and knaves, necessary evils to be cajoled and ridiculed but never respected."

~*CGB*

legacy

CHARLES MCNEILL WROTE: I am curious about the origin of **legacy** as an adjective, as in the phrase "legacy software." Is this usage grammatically defensible? . . . the most common usage seems to be in computer-related matters; it suggests things that were once . . . standard but are now outdated.

We can almost print your query as today's column and leave it at that. But not quite. First, the grammar question. Notice that *grammar* is adjectival in "grammar question," and I bet you read it without a problem. *Grammar* looks like an adjective here, as does **legacy** in "legacy software," in that it modifies the following noun. We can more accurately call it an attributive, since it doesn't pass tests for true adjectives. For instance, you can't move it and say "My question is grammar." Nor is something "very grammar." Nouns are used attributively in English all the time: car doors, pencil sharpeners, book reviews—you get the idea. So "legacy software" can't be faulted for grammatical reasons.

But it's difficult to get used to a new way of using a word. When did you last use **legacy** in its original sense 'the office, function, or commission of a legate'? For the last few centuries, the basic meaning has been 'property passed down by will'. A **legacy** in this core sense is always good.

In an extended use, only a century or so newer, a **legacy** can be anything passed down, whether wonderful or horrible. From a recent obituary: "His commitment to social work and his focus on community organizing are a noble legacy that lives on in the countless social workers he taught and nurtured" (*New York Times*). In contrast, "Tragedies like the explosion in New Mexico last year that killed 12 people are part of the pipeline industry's legacy of spills and accidents, . . ." (*New York Times*).

Until recently, **legacy** in the computer world conformed to this general usage. The first citation of the attributive I have found appeared in the December 2, 1991, issue of *Info World:* "The announcements should give HP's installed base the capability to preserve legacy data while downsizing to PC-based networks." It was a reasonable extension; aging hardware, software, or data can be viewed as a **legacy** left behind by an earlier generation of technology.

But while some of us treasure our workhorse floppy drives, the computer industry is doing its best to make **legacy** entirely negative: **legacy** = old = bad = junk it and Buy New Stuff! New products incompatible with hardware you invested in a couple of years ago are touted as part of "the industry's move toward 'legacy-free' design, which banishes many accessories, such as floppy-disk drives or CD-ROMs, and ditches serial- and parallel-port connections for peripheral devices, such as printers, in favor of standardized universal serial bus (USB) connections" (*Austin American-*

Statesman, 2000). Think of the advantages: "When the time comes to upgrade a legacy-free desktop, you simply buy a new one. . . ." (*InfoWorld,* 2000). Yeah, right.

~*EP*

lieutenant

RICHARD WROTE: If COLONEL "is among those gross irregularities which must be given up as incorrigible . . . ," what do you . . . make of the British pronunciation of **lieutenant** as (lef-TEN-ant)—one tenant on the right and one on the left?

There does not appear to be a "rightenant," or even a wry tenant. But the word **lieutenant** came into Middle English from Middle French, sometime between 1325 and 1375, as a noun use of the adjective phrase *lieu tenant* 'place-holding'. The ultimate source of the British pronunciation (lef-TEN-unt), while not completely shrouded in mystery, remains uncertain. There are, however, a few clues.

In the time of Chaucer (c1340–1400), the distinction between the letters *u* and *v* did not yet exist in writing. Once they separated, people remained uncertain as to which sound each of these letters represented.

Another theory focuses on auditory rather than visual confusion. According to some scholars, the labial sound (w) at the end of French *lieu* (a sound made with the lips) was heard by speakers of English as either of two other labial sounds: (f) or (v). This theory has some merit if we consider that (w) is often accompanied by some degree of audible friction, a kind of blowing sound.

In any case, the pronunciations with (f) and (v) are reflected in various 14th-century English spellings of **lieutenant,** which included *leef-, leve-, lyff-* and later *lief-, live-, liev-,* and *luff-.* Other early forms reflected a (w) pronunciation, among them *lu-, lieu-, lyue-,* and *lew-.*

Even after the spelling of **lieutenant** settled, the (f) and (v) pronunciations remained, and variations of (lef-TEN-unt) are the usual British pronunciations today. In 1721, Dr. Isaac Watts, in his *The Art of Reading and Writing English,* complained that such terms are "pronounced in a very different Manner from what they are written, according to the Dialect or corrupt Speech that obtains in the several counties of England." He added that such pronunciations occur "especially among the Vulgar." John Walker, in the 1836 edition of his *A Critical Pronouncing Dictionary and Expositor of the English Language,* agreed, writing optimistically that "the regular sound, as if written *Lewtenant,* seems not so remote from the corruption as to make us lose all hope that it will in time be the actual pronunciation."

This did not happen in England, but it did happen here, largely because of the influence of Noah Webster—not only through his dictionaries but through his widely distributed *American Spelling Book* (1788), which sold more than 60 million copies. A passionate supporter of American linguistic independence, Webster almost single-handedly promulgated American pronunciations as well as American spellings.

∼*EP*

like

ROBIN MANDLEY WROTE: I was wondering if you knew the reason why **like** has recently become a replacement for *say, says, said.* For example, "She's like, 'I don't know.' "

This informal use of **like** goes back about 20 years, though parents are still noticing it in the speech of young people and thinking it's a recent development. The comments I hear are usually to the effect of "I wish it would go away." Its use has been extensively dissected by linguists, who conclude that it's mostly in the speech of middle-class American teenagers and college students, especially in cities, and is probably not used by anyone over the age of 40. Though many people perceive it as a female usage, it's actually used by both sexes about equally.

This particular use of **like** almost always follows a form of the verb *(to) be,* and it usually introduces a direct quote or paraphrase of what someone has said. But sometimes what follows *be like* is a subjective guess at what the person might have been thinking or feeling and can be translated as 'thinks or feels' rather than 'says'. Sometimes you can't tell whether the words have actually been spoken or are merely representing someone's thoughts: "When I saw the needle, I was like, uh-oh, I'm not doing this!"

Be like can follow a name or a first-, second-, or third-person pronoun. But the specific use of *it's like* is interesting—it usually reports a generally held opinion or someone's habitual style of speech: "It's like, 'Men are all jerks!' "

Articles in the journal *American Speech* (1990 and 1995)

discuss the functions of *be like:* to add emphasis; to introduce salient information; to involve a listener emotionally;
and to heighten the dramatic effect of a story. In fact, *be like*
often introduces an emotional outburst: "I'm like, 'Oh, my
God!' " And sometimes it introduces a dramatic facial expression or bodily gesture that substitutes for dialogue: "So I'm
like . . . [followed by rolling of eyes in disbelief]."

The verb *go/goes/went* is used in a similar way, before a
direct quote or paraphrase: "So he goes, let's have a beer."
Though this use of *go* has been in the language for about 50
years, it's gradually being edged out by **like.**

So why has **like** become a replacement for *say/says/said?*
It's linguistically innovative and versatile—it can report direct speech as well as inner thoughts, feelings, attitudes, and
states of mind. And since expression of feelings is a valued
cultural trend, use of *be like* isn't going to go away so easily.

$\sim$*CGB*

lo and behold

SPENCER A. NONYMOUS WROTE: In a letter . . . I started
to write **lo and behold** and realized that I was unsure of
the spelling. Is it **lo and behold** or **low and behold?** I
asked a few people, and we can't seem to agree.

It's definitely *lo,* an interjection meaning 'look! see! (frequently used in biblical expressions; now usually used as an
expression of surprise in the phrase **lo and behold**)'. Just to
confuse us, *low* was one of the many early spellings for that
interjection, in a list that also includes *lou, lowe,* and *loo.* But

that *low* is not the one that means the opposite of *high,* and the two words are not etymologically related. To confuse us further, we now have another *lo,* which does mean 'low', as in *lo-calorie.* No wonder people find English baffling.

Our *lo* of the day probably comes from Middle English *lo,* a shortened form of *loke,* in turn from Old English *lōca,* imperative of *lokan* 'to look'.

The phrase has been used in serious literature since at least the 1800s. To cite one example, "Lo and behold, there was something the matter with the great clock; and a workman on a pair of steps had taken its face off, and was poking instruments into the works. . ." (Dickens, *Dombey and Son,* 1848).

Lo alone is attested from around 1000. Perhaps its most well-known use, without *behold,* is from Alexander Pope's *Essay on Criticism* (1711), which begins with the familiar "Hope springs eternal in the human breast." The crucial lines are,

> *The soul, uneasy, and confined from home*
> *Rests and expatiates in a life to come.*
> *Lo, the poor Indian! whose untutored mind*
> *Sees God in clouds, or hears him in the wind . . .*

We can either assume a genuine error in interpreting Pope's lines or suppose that some early "politically incorrect" person found the phrase "Lo, the poor Indian" funny, because there has since been some limited use of *Lo* to mean 'Indian'! The cites are primarily facetious, as in R. P. T. Coffin's 1947 "He went to join Lo, the Poor Indian, on the Happy Hunting Grounds."

As for the phrase itself, **lo and behold,** what we have here is yet another example of common redundancy in English (see SPITTING IMAGE). This one would translate as "Look and look." I have checked with our younger Mavens to see if there is a current equivalent of **lo and behold,** redundant or not. They've come up with nothing so far, and we begin to suspect that today's twenty-somethings cannot be surprised.

~*EP*

lollygag

NATE SALTUS WROTE: I enjoy your site and check it every morning along with the NASA astronomy picture of the day. Yesterday, a co-worker was waiting on us at lunch and asked why we were still **lollygagging** around. So, I thought, I bet that's on the *WOTD,* but I don't see it. Did I miss it or is that one yet to be researched?

No, you didn't miss it.

I think most everyone's heard of this word. What's odd to me, though, is that *Random House Webster's Unabridged Dictionary* has *lallygag,* rather than **lollygag,** as the main entry. So does *The Oxford English Dictionary.* Do you know anyone who uses *lallygag?*

Lallygag isn't even in spell checker. I guess that means that if you use *lallygag* when you're word processing, you haven't misspelled it, since it doesn't exist.

Fortunately, the *Dictionary of American Regional English* and *Random House Historical Dictionary of American Slang (HDAS)* have **lollygag** as the main entry. Well, strictly speaking, *HDAS* says either is correct. What does that tell you? Where is Ira Gershwin when you need him?

As to the actual definition of the word, **lollygag** means 'to loaf' or just 'to pass the time idly'. **Lollygag** has a secondary meaning which is 'to kiss or neck'.

Lollygag is American born and bred. It made its first appearance in print in the 1860s. The indefatigable Evan Morris, known to his fans as *The Word Detective,* says the clue might be in *loll.* Morris says this "is a very old word originally meaning 'to droop or dangle'. We use 'loll' today to mean to relax or pass time idly, the sort of behavior that vacations are designed to encourage. There seems to be a plausible connection between this 'utterly relaxed' meaning of 'loll' and the 'wasting time' sense of **lollygag.**"

Notice we're speaking of *loll,* not *lall. Lall* means 'to make imperfect *l-* or *r*-sounds, or both, often substituting a *w*-like sound for *r* or *l* or a *y*-like sound for *l'. Lallying* doesn't sound very restful, does it?

According to the *Cassell Dictionary of Slang, loll* is also an old dialect word that means 'tongue'. That might elucidate the kissing part. To make things even sloppier, *The Barnhart Dictionary of Etymology* suggests the 'gag' in **lollygag** was employed for its sense of 'stuffing' or 'filling'. This leaves us with a vivid picture of a tongue being thrust down the throat.

This picture of tongue-thrusting is further supported by an 1868 tirade from an Iowa newspaper, the *Northern Vindicator,* writing of "the lascivious lolly-gagging lumps of licentiousness who disgrace the common decencies of life by their love-sick fawnings at our public dances."

This sounds vaguely familiar.

~*RG*

mack

TOM JENKINS WROTE: My daughter recently returned from college in Wyoming using the word **mack** as in: "She was going to 'mack' my boyfriend." This, she explained, meant outrageous flirtation, perhaps including some hugging and kissing, with intent to steal her guy. Apparently the meaning falls short of actual seduction. How new is this term, and how did it develop?

Mack has been used by college kids to mean 'hit on' or 'kiss' for only the last fifteen years or so, but the verb is a lot older than that.

The word **mack** goes all the way back to the Dutch word *makelaar* for 'a broker' and comes to us through the French *maquereau* for 'a pimp'. The word is seen in English as early as the 15th century: "Nighe his house dwellyed a maquerel or bawd" (Caxton, *Cato Magnus,* 1483). This use continued into the 18th century.

In the 19th century, the form **mack** appears with the meaning of 'a pimp' or 'to pimp', but the form did not become common until the 20th century: "Your broad . . . starts signifying about your not having a license to mack" (Wepman, *The Life,* 1964). During this period, the first references to **mack daddies,** or 'successful pimps', are found in African-American rhymed recitations.

Also during the 1960s, **mack** developed a second meaning of 'the sweet talk a pimp uses with prostitutes', as in: "The pimp . . . by his lively and persuasive rapping ('macking' is also used in this context) has acquired a stable of girls" (*Trans-action VI,* 1969).

Later, **mack** was extended to refer to any flirtatious talk with someone of the opposite sex: "I don't want you women to be macking with the brothers if they ain't tending to business" (Wolfe, *Radical Chic*, 1970). While this sense of **mack** was originally African-American slang, it was introduced to the mainstream in the 1980s and 1990s through rap music: "...think they be mackin' but they actin'/ Who they attractin' with that line?" (Notorious B.I.G., *Big Poppa,* 1995).

Since the mid 1990s, **mack** has been primarily college slang, used by teens and twenty-somethings to talk about flirting or kissing. It is often found in the construction *mack on,* probably by analogy with the phrase "hit on." **Mack** can still be used as a noun to refer to someone who is good at "hooking up" with members of the opposite sex, probably through truncation of *mack daddy,* which, these days, refers more often to smooth-talking teenage boys than it does to pimps.

~HGB

man alive

JESSE KRANK WROTE: All right, the day has come when I found myself using a phrase I used to make fun of my mom for using: **man alive.** ("Woman dead" I would reply.) I have heard it used elsewhere but still have never discovered its origins. So, where, when, and how did **man alive** originate?

Well, in fact, someone called Frances M. Whitcher beat you to it: " 'Woman alive,' says I, 'what be you dewin!' " (*The Widow*

Bedett Papers, 1856 or 1846–51, depending on whether you believe the bibliography or the main entry in the 1936 *A Dictionary of American English on Historical Principles* from the University of Chicago Press.)

I guessed, when I read your question, that **man alive** was contemporary with the emergence of *land alive, sakes alive, law sakes alive,* and simply *alive* as mild expletives in the early to mid-19th century. Wrong! In its fuller form, *any/all/each man alive,* it's attested as far back as 1230.

There's a nice citation from 1858 in *The Oxford English Dictionary* that shows how the transition from emphatic phrase to expletive probably happened: "There is no assignable cause; man alive cannot tell a reason why." (This is attributed to one Gen. P. Thompson—but oddly enough, I can't find him or his abbreviated work, *Audi. Alt. Part.,* listed in the bibliography. Not a good day for reliability from reference works!)

The first citation of the expletive use seems to be from J. B. Buckstone's *Presumptive Evidence,* either 1828 or 1829, again depending on which source you believe (are we detecting a pattern here?). I quite like the following one from Caroline M. Kirkland's 1839 *A New Home—Who'll Follow?:* "Man alive! What do you put yourself into such a plaguy passion for?"

The fact that Whitcher could say "woman alive" shows how productive *alive* can be when used in an emphatic way, especially in the expressions I noted above. Harriet Beecher Stowe uses it on its own in *Uncle Tom's Cabin* (1852): "Where alive is that gal?" My Montana-based grandparents always said "man a-livin'!" These days, none of these expressions is very frequent, with the exception of **man alive,** which feels a little old-fashioned, and deliberately euphemistic—in other words, mom-ish.

~WRN

man, woman, and human

JANE CARNALL WROTE: It is now accepted that **man** means 'male human being'. (At least I think it is: I haven't seen **man** being casually used for 'human' in ten years or more). But at what point, and why, did the confusion arise? If the origin of **human** is Latin *homō*, what is the origin of **man,** and of **woman?** And when was **man** first used as a substitute for 'human'? Or was it the other way around? Was the word **man** once ungendered, meaning 'female human or male human', and if so, what was the English word for 'male human' then?

When Old English was first recorded, **man** meant 'human', and this remained the primary sense of the word. But **man** in the sense 'male human' came into use a few hundred years later, so the twofold meaning of **man** has caused confusion for at least a thousand years.

Old English *wer* was the usual term for 'male human' (and also 'husband'); it survives in words such as *werewolf.* By about 1200, Middle English *were* (Old English *wer*) fell out of use and was replaced by **man.**

In early Old English, *wif* was the corresponding term for 'female human' (and also 'wife'); it survives in terms such as *midwife* and *old wives' tale.* There was also the term *wifman,* a compound of 'female human' and 'human'. Later, the spelling *wifman* was altered to *wimman* and *wumman;* the spelling **woman** first appeared about 1250.

Though the word **human** contains the word **man,** it has nothing to do with **man.** It's derived from Latin *humānus,* which is probably related to Latin *homō,* meaning 'human being', and (very rarely) 'male human'.

Use of **man** to mean 'human' has drastically declined in recent years, but no, it hasn't disappeared. Many people still use the term *mankind,* and we have fossilized expressions such as *man in the street.* However, there is progress: most people wouldn't use *spokesman* or *policeman* to refer to a **woman.**

~CGB

merry

BECKY CERVENKA WROTE: In reading an account of the history of Christmas cards, I was surprised to read that one of the first commercial Christmas cards used the "Merry Christmas" inscription with **merry** in the spiritual sense of 'blessed' (as in "merry old England"). Is this indeed true—**merry** means 'blessed'?

I have found no evidence that **merry** has ever meant 'blessed'.

King Alfred used *myrges* to mean 'causing pleasure or happiness' in his 9th-century translation of Boethius. The phrase "Merry England" first appeared in a 14th-century history, and **merry** meaning 'pleasant' was also applied in the

Middle Ages to such varied places as paradise, Jerusalem, and London. **Merry** meant 'pleasing to the ear' when referring to birdsong or to music, as in this line from Coverdale's translation of Psalm 81: "Bring hither the tabret, the merry harp with the lute." If the weather was **merry,** it was fine.

The modern senses of **merry**—'full of cheerfulness', 'joyous', and 'festive'—are also attested in the 14th century: "Mery was the menye & maden gret loye"—Many were merry and made great joy (*Destruction of Troy,* 1400). When we wish someone a "Merry Christmas," we are wishing them, as the British say, a "happy Christmas"—a joyful, festive holiday.

When Charles II was called the "Merry Monarch," it certainly wasn't a reference to his sanctity. In *A Child's History of England,* Dickens wrote: "There never were such profligate times in England as under Charles the Second" and then gives his readers "a general idea of some of the merry things that were done, in the merry days when this merry gentleman sat upon his merry throne, in merry England." (In *The Earl of Rochester's Verses for Which He Was Banished,* the Earl was less circumspect in speaking of his king: "His scepter and his prick are of a length, / And she may sway the one who plays with t'other.")

To *make merry* first meant to have a jolly time, but by the 18th century it came to mean also 'to make fun of': "The people made merry with this absurd and brutal statute" (Goldsmith, 1771).

Old English *myrige* or *mirige* meant 'pleasant, delightful, or agreeable', but the word derived from an Old Teutonic word **murgjo-* meaning 'short'. The Indo-European root is **mreghu-,* which also meant 'short' and from which we get a multitude of other words, some through Greek, some through Latin, some through French: *embrace, bracelet, abbreviate, breviary, brief, abridge, brassiere,* and *pretzel.* The Greek word *brakhíōn* is a comparative meaning 'shorter'; it also means 'the upper arm', which is shorter than the forearm, and that's how we get the arm-related words (a pretzel is in the shape of folded arms).

But how did we get from 'short' to 'pleasant'? It is possible that there was once a verb from this root meaning 'to shorten', perhaps 'to shorten time'. Something that shortens time is pleasant. Is this too much of a stretch? Try this: the German word *kurz* means 'short' and *Kurzweil* means 'pastime, amusement, or entertainment'. *Lang* means 'long' and *Langweile* means 'boredom'. Time passes quickly when you're having fun.

~*GSM*

mickey mouse

VIC TIDWELL WROTE: I was thinking of a term I often heard in the military: **mickey mouse.** (I assume that the lack of capitalization is appropriate since the term clearly never referred to the Disney character.) A person who was **mickey mouse** was a little crazy, or perhaps a little too much concerned for detailed rules and performance; too demanding. On the other hand, the term was also used in reference to an organization which, in the mind of the speaker, was less than 100 percent operationally effective. Do you have any background on the term, and is it (or was it) limited to military usage?

Your last question is the easiest to answer. No, **mickey mouse** (also found with caps **Mickey Mouse**) is not limited to military usage. There are, however, several meanings of **mickey mouse** that have been associated solely with the military, like the "Mickey Mouse ears" radio from the Vietnam War era, the bomb release mechanism in World War II fighter planes, or the World War II name "Mickey Mouse movie" for an instructional film about venereal disease: "a two minute Mickey Mouse would be added, a trailer of clinical shots showing diseased organs in full color"(W. Stevens, *Gunner 89,* 1966, reference to World War II).

The meanings to which you refer are all used and understood by civilians and military personnel alike. A **mickey mouse** person is usually timid or foolish: "There are many Mickey Mouses in office across the country, from both parties and at all levels of government" (*Business Week,* 1974). In Australia, **mickey mouse** refers to a cheap or unreliable product. In American and British English, **mickey mouse** is often used as an adjective for tedious or trivial activities: "The big reason that they don't have enough men [i.e., police officers] on the highways is because they're doing too much other Mickey Mouse" (*Kansas City Star,* 1974). A parallel use is indicated by students who use **mickey mouse** to describe blow-off courses or assignments: "The athletes . . . are encouraged to take specially-tailored mickey-mouse courses so as not to jeopardize their athletic standing" (Rapoport and Kirshbaum, *Is the Library Burning?,* 1969).

Poor Mickey Mouse! You would think that any word coming from the name of a beloved star of such animated classics as *Fantasia* and the inspiration for our childhood Mouseketeer clubs would be positive. But **mickey mouse** doesn't mean 'sweet' and 'lovable'; it means 'timid', 'foolish', 'tedious', 'pointless', 'nitpicking', or 'unreliable'. So our childhood friend Mickey is an example of the hazards of being small and cute—folks just won't take you seriously.

~HGB

mine and my

RICHARD T. WROTE: The question is: in certain oldish references—"The Battle Hymn of the Republic," among others—**mine** eyes have seen **mine** used where most of us would now use **my.** What's the story on this one?

Thou hast **my** respect and **mine** admiration for thy wit and thine intuition. **My, mine,** *thy,* and *thine,* in the previous sentence, are "possessive adjectives." This group also includes *your, his, her, their,* and *its.* Possessive adjectives belong to a larger group called "determiners," including the articles *a, an,* and *the.* Determiners precede nouns and noun phrases, which they limit or qualify in some way.

Mine has cognates in early Teutonic languages, like Old Frisian, Old Saxon, and Middle High German, and came into Old English before the 10th century. All of these forms derived from a Proto-Germanic adjective *minaz,* formed from the Gothic genitive *meina,* a form of the pronoun *me.* **My** is a reduced form of **mine;** in Early Middle English, both were used as first-person singular possessive adjectives meaning 'of or belonging to me' and were almost, but not quite, interchangeable.

From the 13th century through the 18th, the operating

principle for differentiating between them, at least in southern England, was that **mine** (or an alternate form, like *min, myn,* or *myne*) was used before a vowel sound or before *h,* especially weak or silent *h,* and **my** was used before consonants. Shakespeare exemplifies the principle: "Shall I not take mine ease in mine Inne" (*Henry IV, Part I,* 1597); "A Ministring Angell shall my Sister be" (*Hamlet,* 1602). **Mine** before *h* is seen in this citation from Chaucer: "Then seyde he thus myn hertes lady swete . . ." (1374).

The rule was not always followed, any more than grammatical rules are invariably adhered to in Modern English. For example, "I wyll that John myn sone haue myn seid place callyd Upwode Halle" (1467). In particular, **mine** was universally preferred in Scotland.

The reduced form **my** began to occur even before vowels as early as the 14th century and eventually replaced **mine** as the sole first-person singular possessive adjective, except in archaic or poetic contexts. Even there, the old rule generally holds, with **mine** before vowels or *h.* As noted, "Mine eyes have seen the glory . . ."

My and **mine,** *thy* and *thine,* and even *a* and *an,* share a parallel history and parallel historical functions. In Modern English, however, it is only with *a* and *an* that the preconsonantal vs. prevocalic distinction is retained (a banana; an apple).

$\sim$*EP*

misprision (mis-PRIZH-un)

T. GREEN WROTE: Occasionally the word **misprision** pops up in news accounts as the strange crime of the victim of a felony failing to report it. My dictionary traces **misprision** back to 'a mistake' in Old French before breaking it apart into Latin roots. How did we get from 'a mistake' to so weird a crime?

Let's summarize those Latin roots for those who don't have a copy of your dictionary.

Misprision came into English through Anglo-Norman, from Old French *mesprison* or *mesprision* 'mistake, error, wrong action or speech'. The Old French verb meaning 'to mistake' was *mesprendre* from *mes-* 'wrongly' and *prendre* 'take', which comes in turn from Latin *prehendere* 'to seize'. (Note that the English noun *mistake* comes from *mis-* plus Old English *tacan* 'to grasp'.)

The initial meaning of **misprision** in English was 'a neglect or violation of official duty by one in office'. In 1425 the Rolls of Parliament spoke of "such misprisions and defaultes of ye said Sherefs."

In the 16th century, there was a crime called *misprision of treason*. This was originally an offense that was related to treason but involved a lesser degree of guilt and was not a capital charge. Statutes were enacted stating that concealment of a person's knowledge of treasonable actions should be regarded as *misprision of treason,* and it wasn't long before *misprision of treason* was interpreted to mean 'concealment of one's knowledge of treasonable actions'. Treason was not the only action one could conceal knowledge of; "misprision of felonie or trespasse" appears in a 1579 book of legal terms.

Misprision eventually found its way into common popular usage. In 1662 we find "It was almost made an Heresie . . . for anyone to be seen in his company, and as a misprision of Heresie to give him a civil Salutation as he walked the Streets" (Peter Heylin's biography of Archbishop William Laud). In 1862 Thomas Trollope wrote in *Marietta:* "Guilty of misprision of flirting."

From the late 16th century to the middle of the 19th century, **misprision** was also commonly used in English to mean 'a mistake' or 'the mistaking of one thing or word for another'. Shakespeare used it this way in *Love's Labor's Lost* (1594): "A fever in your blood! why then incision Would let her out in Saucers, sweet misprision."

James E. Clapp notes in *Random House Webster's Dictionary of the Law* that, "absent some affirmative act to conceal the felony, it [*misprision of felony*] is not normally a crime in the United States."

~*GSM*

Miss, Mrs., Ms., and Mr.

CHARITY TERRY-LORENZO WROTE: One of my women's studies professors explained that the title **Mrs.** or *Missus* came from the possessive *Master's*. . . . I was hoping you could tell me if this is correct or not. If it's not correct, where does *Missus* as a title for a married woman originate? My dictionary tells me it comes from *Mistress,* but that it does not currently refer to a married woman—it means the "other" woman.

You're on the right track, but your professor got the genders confused!

The titles **Miss** and **Mrs.** are both abbreviations of the word *mistress*. The missis (or *the missus*) is a dialectal or informal term for one's wife, or the mistress (female head) of a household. The pronunciation (MISS-iz) reflects an altered pronunciation of *mistress*.

Mistress had many meanings in Middle English, some of which are still familiar: female head of a household, goddess, sweetheart, expert in some occupation, teacher, and governess. Basically, *mistress* referred to a woman who had expertise, power, and control. But it was also used as a title of courtesy when addressing an unmarried or married woman. The sense to which you refer, the 'other woman; the woman who occupies the place of wife' came into English about 1600.

The abbreviation or shortened form **miss** was first used in 1645 (in John Evelyn's *Diary*) to mean 'a concubine; a kept mistress'. About twenty years later, Samuel Pepys first used the term as a capitalized title before the name of a girl or unmarried woman. Around the same time, John Dryden first used **Miss** as a term of address. There are also examples in which it referred to a female baby.

The abbreviation **Mrs.** was first used in 1615 before the name of a married woman, as it is today. However, to confuse matters, it was also the abbreviation of *mistress* in all the many senses of that word, and it also distinguished an unmarried woman from a child: "Mrs. Veal was a maiden gentlewoman" (Daniel Defoe, *The History of Colonel Jack,* 1723).

The male equivalent of *mistress* was *master,* which meant, among other things, 'male head of a household'. In the 16th century, *master* changed to *mister,* and the abbreviation **Mr.** arose to identify a man but not his marital status.

So it appears that the uses of **Mr.** and **Mrs.** were somewhat parallel until the 19th century. At that time, **Mrs.** began to refer only to a married woman.

The abbreviation **Ms.** was first used as early as 1949, in Mario Pei's *The Story of Language*. It may be a blend of **Miss** and **Mrs.**

~CGB

mocha (MO-ka)

JOHN KYLE WROTE: My wife and I are in an argument about the term **mocha.** She thinks that mocha . . . is the result of adding coffee . . . to chocolate, and the term **mocha** signifies that the coffee has been added. I, on the other hand, understand that a *café mocha* is created by adding chocolate to a cup of coffee, and therefore the term **mocha** is more closely related to the chocolate, not the base element, the coffee. So, is **mocha** synonymous with coffee, chocolate, or both? Where did the term originate?

The word **mocha** comes from the city of Mocha, a port in southwestern Yemen on the Red Sea. It is a city that was intimately connected with coffee's early history. Most experts agree that the coffee tree came from the Ethiopian province of Kaffa—hence, *coffee.* But if Ethiopia was its birthplace, the city of Mocha made coffee famous.

From the 15th century onward, the Arabs—who held a strict monopoly on the trade—exported nearly all their coffee beans from the port of Mocha. Thus the name **Mocha** became synonymous with coffee. Most of the coffee exported from Mocha went to other Muslim countries, but in the late 17th century, Mocha coffee arrived in Europe. The first citation for the word is from the 1773 edition of the *Encyclopædia Britannica:* "The coffee ought to be of the best Mocco." Seventy-five years later, Nathaniel Hawthorne wrote in *The House of the Seven Gables:* "Requesting Phoebe to roast some real coffee, which she casually observed was the real Mocha. . . ."

In the 17th century, the Dutch got their hands on some seeds from the coffee tree—seeds which the Arab traders had guarded zealously. Soon enough, they were cultivating coffee in their colony of Indonesia, particularly on the island of Java. In the 19th century, Aden usurped Mocha as Yemen's main port. That, along with the fact that the Arabs no longer had an exclusive on the coffee trade, eventually pushed the city of Mocha into obscurity.

But what about **mocha** as in *café mocha? Café mocha* is made by mixing chocolate (either sweetened, ground chocolate or chocolate syrup) with one ounce of espresso. Steamed milk is then added to the mixture. So, why isn't the concoction called a *café chocolat?* According to *The Great Coffee Book,* "It is likely that most Europeans tasted coffee before chocolate. Therefore, when chocolate first appeared, they found it reminiscent of, or confused it with, the wild and fruity flavors of Yemini coffee." We have to remember that at that time chocolate was only drunk, not eaten. It was actually quite a bitter drink, and unsweetened.

I think it's clear how **mocha** came to mean 'coffee'. But I don't think it's clear how the word came to mean 'chocolate'.

I think we have one of those etymological puzzles on our hands. I'm sure the phrase *café mocha* made perfect sense at one time, but it doesn't today.

~*RG*

momentarily

FIONA POWELL WROTE: I am British living in the USA. This leads me down many strange verbal paths, as I often use words in a different way, or encounter new words for familiar objects. One of my most curious encounters has been with the word **momentarily.** To Americans, this word means 'in a moment'. To me as a Briton, this word means 'for a moment'. This has led to some riotous mix-ups! What was the original meaning of the word?

Oh, there are lots of "false friends" between British and American English—terms that you think should mean the same thing in both places, but don't. A few more:

—to *table* a motion in the United States is to put it aside, whereas in the United Kingdom it means to put it on the agenda;

—if you tell an American cook that his or her meal was "quite good," it's a compliment, although indicating a bit of surprise at the fact; the British cook would be hurt that it was only "quite" good instead of "rather" good;

—a play that is a *bomb* is a failure in the United States and a success in the United Kingdom.

As you pointed out in your longer e-mail to us, the sentence "the doctor will be with you momentarily" would be taken by a British English speaker to mean a very short consultation indeed. In fact, the meaning 'only for a moment' is the oldest, from the 16th century, and the meaning 'in a moment' is labeled "North American" in *The Oxford English Dictionary,* with a first citation from 1928. However, a sentence such as "Blake was momentarily distracted, and his car slid off the road" still reflects a common, recognized use in the United States—in fact, it is arguably still the most common.

Actually, I'm not quite convinced that the use of **momentarily** for 'in a moment' is entirely original to North America. There is another late-18th-century meaning, 'from moment to moment', that is recorded on both sides of the Atlantic in the 19th century. The treatment of this meaning in various dictionaries shows how fluid the meanings are. *The Oxford English Dictionary* chooses a clear example of 'from moment to moment' to illustrate its meaning: "The light was momentarily getting worse." However, *Merriam-Webster's Third International Dictionary* lumps together the meanings ('at any moment; from moment to moment') and cites the decidedly un-American, un-20th-century Charlotte Brontë: ". . . momentarily expected his coming." *The Century Dictionary* (1899) lists the definition "From moment to moment: as, he is momentarily expected" yet gives the extremely odd example sentence "Why endow the vegetable bird with wings, which nature has made momentarily dependent upon the soil?" (Why indeed? Leave those vegetable birds on the ground where God put 'em.)

Clearly, if major dictionaries couldn't decide how to separate the meanings, it should not be surprising that the idea of 'in a moment' developed from 'moment by moment'. It's also clear that, at least in its definition, *The Century Dictionary* recognized the 'imminent' sense of **momentarily** a good thirty years earlier than the first citation in *The Oxford English Dictionary.*

~WRN

moot

ARI X. WROTE: Does **moot** have two contradictory definitions?

Since you haven't specified which definitions you mean, I'm assuming something along the lines of 'debatable' and 'not worth debating'. These aren't quite opposite in meaning—'debatable' means 'doubtful' or 'open to debate' rather than 'worth debating'. But what you have noticed is that a 19th-century shift in the meaning of **moot** has now overtaken other senses as the main meaning.

Most of us are familiar by now with the expression "a moot point," meaning a point that's irrelevant and therefore not worth debating. Many things can be moot—arguments, discussions, topics, even actions: "We are only at the beginning of this stock market debate. Perhaps the markets will zoom up again, rendering the subject moot" (*International Herald Tribune*). There is also some evidence of people beginning to use **moot** as a substitute for *invalid:* "Plus, I could have canceled at any time, making the card moot" (*Albuquerque Journal*).

This sense of 'irrelevant' is an extension of a much older use of **moot** that is rooted in legal terminology, whence in fact the word originates. As an adjective referring to legal arguments and cases, **moot** means 'not actual; theoretical; hypothetical'. The Old English word *gemot* (pronounced "guh-MOAT") meant 'a meeting'; the Middle English *mot(e)* was a legal assembly in early England. The word **moot** came to refer to a legal debate or argument, as well as to the place where it happened. The more modern meanings of the word come from the practice of holding mock debates and trials for the benefit of law students; there are still *moot courts* today: "The space will allow us to . . . do things that we're now required to rent space to do. We'll have a conference room, a moot courtroom in the basement" (*Albany Times Union*).

The logic of the progression in meaning is this: an argument that has no legal standing because it is merely *for* practice has no value *in* practice, and is therefore ultimately irrelevant. However, the earlier sense of 'debatable' has still not completely disappeared, and that is probably why you noticed a difference in the main meanings. Whether the meaning should ever have shifted is a moot point!

By the way, *mute* is sometimes mistakenly used instead of **moot,** which has no (y) in its pronunciation.

~*WRN*

My bad!

Lou Howort wrote: I am a high school teacher in an inner-city public school in Manhattan. Lately I have been hearing many students saying **My bad!** if they make a mistake. I was wondering if you are aware of this term, and if it goes beyond the locality of New York City.

The exclamation **My bad!** is an apologetic way of saying "My fault! My mistake!". It's said to derive from the game of pick-up basketball, popular in the inner city. A player may say it when a foul is committed or when the ball goes out-of-bounds. Generally, black urban youth have filtered the language of professional sports through the street vernacular of hip-hop culture. If you're interested in other slang terms derived from pick-up basketball, take a look at *The Back-In-Your-Face Guide to Pick-Up Basketball* by Chuck Wielgus and Alexander Wolff. Other pick-up sports have produced pithy vocabulary. For example, **My bad!** has been compared to the volleyball term *I go!*, shorthand for "I got it!"

Some people nominated **My bad!** as a candidate for 1999 "Word of the Year," an end-of-the-year contest sponsored by the American Dialect Society. It was immediately pointed out that the phrase is over 20 years old. However, it was popularized by the 1995 cult movie *Clueless,* which was, incidentally, a gold mine of teenage slang.

My bad! is only one of the many clever interjections (or exclamations) common in the speech of young people in recent years. For example, the exclamation *Not!* is a way of saying that the previous statement is untrue: "That's a cute dress. Not!" Another exclamation that became popular in the 1990s is *As if!*, roughly meaning 'To the contrary; no way!'

The phrase **My bad!** is probably decreasing in use compared to its popularity in the mid-1990s. However, it's still current slang used in all parts of the country, not just New York City. It's used by young people and some adults in sports (even professional sports) and in many other non-sports contexts. It's even infiltrated cybertalk as a convenient shorthand expression.

~CGB

naughty, naught, and nought

SEVERN E. S. MILLER WROTE: I have been wondering about the relationship between **naughty** and **naught (nought).** Why does **naughty** mean 'naughty'?

Naught and **nought** both come from the Old English word *náwiht* or *nówiht* 'nothing'. Near the end of the 9th century, King Alfred translated the Latin word *nēquitia* 'worthlessness' or 'badness' with *náwiht,* so it must have acquired the sense of 'bad' by that time. He also used it as an adjective with the sense 'having no value, good for nothing', and it was an easy extension from 'worthless' to 'bad' or 'poor'. By the Middle English period, in addition to meaning 'nothing', **naught** and **nought** clearly meant 'bad' or 'of poor quality' and then, more strongly, 'morally bad', 'wicked', or 'evil'.

The first written evidence of **naughty** is in the allegorical and moral satire *Piers Plowman* (1377): "Alle maner of men . . . That nedy ben and naughty. . . ." Here **naughty** means 'having naught' or 'poor'. In the following centuries, the more common meanings of **naughty** as applied to actions or people were 'evil or immoral' or 'bad or improper'; when applied to things, it meant 'inferior or of bad quality', as "naughty wool" or "a piece of naughty land."

In Shakespeare's plays, **naught** can mean both 'worthless' and 'bad' or 'wicked'; **naughty** generally means 'bad' or 'wicked', with a stronger meaning than in 21st-century usage: "thy sister's naught" (*King Lear*, 1605); "So shines a good deed in a naughty world" (*Merchant of Venice*, 1595). In *Richard III* (1594), Shakespeare plays on the meaning: "Naught to do with Mistress Shore! I tell thee, fellow, he that doth naught with her, excepting one, Were best to do it secretly alone."

The translators of the King James Bible (1611) used **naughtiness** in James 1:21 to translate the Greek *kakía,* which means 'badness, evilness, or wickedness'. In the Old Testament, **naughty** is used to translate the Hebrew *beliyyaal* 'worthless' in Proverbs 6:12 and **naught** is used for Hebrew *ra* 'evil' in II Kings 2:19 and elsewhere. **Naught** and **naughty** were popular words in sermons in the 17th century. A clergyman named Sanderson spoke in 1656 of those who "from doing nothing proceed to doing naught," and a Mr. Barrow referred in 1677 to "a most vile flagitious man, a sorry and naughty governor as could be." **Naughty** was also used for wayward and disobedient children by the 17th century.

By the 19th century, the sense of **naughty** had been weakened, and it was no longer applied to adults except playfully and meant 'mischievous' when applied to children or 'mildly improper' when applied to actions or conduct. In 1861 a man named Finlay wrote of a woman who had "turned her attention to the naughty reading of the Greek classics." And in 1882 an article in the American *National Police Gazette* referred to "those naughty naughty parsons up and at it again." And, of course, at the end of the 19th century, we had the "naughty nineties."

~*GSM*

the new new thing

LAURA WILLIAMS WROTE: Did the *new new* phrase begin with the publication of Michael Lewis's *The New New Thing* in the fall of 1999? Or does it go back further than that?

The ubiquitous phrase **the new new thing** is really an "old old thing," because it was used by other writers well before publication of the book by Michael Lewis. In 1990 Russell Baker of the *New York Times* wrote about Earth Day: "The always ravenous media maw will insist upon it and public-relations people, who know how quickly we tire of yesterday's fantastic event, will create it for us: a brand new New Thing, rich in photo ops and feel-good potential."

You can choose to write this phrase in any of several ways: **The new new thing; the new, new thing; the new New Thing;** or **the new-new thing.** And the phrase has many other catchy spin-offs. For example, there is *the new new math, the new new man,* and *the new new standard. The new new religions* in Japan are those formed after the 19th century. There are the New Democrats, and then there are *the new New Democrats* who favor privatization of Social Security. In fashion there is *the new new look:* Did you know that pink is the new black but orange is *the new new black?*

Getting back to *The New New Thing* by Michael Lewis, it's about Silicon Valley and specifically about Jim Clark, the founder of Netscape (the Web-browser company), Silicon Graphics, and Healtheon. In looking for and finding **the new new thing,** Clark changed the way Americans think about business.

Author Lewis explained it this way in a 1999 article in the *New York Times:* "It's easier to say what the new new thing is not than to say what it is. It is not necessarily a new invention. It is not even, necessarily, a new idea—most everything has been considered by someone, at some point. The new new thing is a notion that's poised to be taken seriously. It's the idea that is moments from gaining general acceptance and, when it does, will change the world . . ."

Here's an example of the use of the phrase in describing *Survivor,* a program representing the trend of reality TV: "This is going to be a huge new-new thing. I think it says that we like kind of peeping in on the intimate lives of other people" (Fox News Network transcript, 2000).

The New New Thing by Michael Lewis, *The Right Stuff* by Tom Wolfe, and *Generation X* by Douglas Coupland are book titles that popularized existing phrases, but they don't represent the first use of these phrases. In contrast, *Catch-22* by Joseph Heller is a book title that does represent the first known use of a phrase.

~*CGB*

nice

MATT BULL WROTE: I've heard it said (can't remember where—probably high school English class) that the word **nice** used to mean 'foolish'. I've run across this connotation (I think) in Shakespeare. Are these two different words, or has the meaning changed?

You're absolutely right about 'foolish'. **Nice** can be traced back to the Latin word *nescius* 'ignorant', which is actually a combination of the prefix *ne* 'no' and the verb *scīre* 'know'—also the basis for the word *science*. In other words, if you were **nice,** you did 'not know'. You were ignorant or foolish. Just think of 'no-science'. *The Oxford English Dictionary* has an example from 1450: "They seiden he was a fool . . . and that they sien neuere so nise a man" (*The History of the Holy Grail*).

This word is incredibly confounding. A century after its first appearance in print in English around 1300, **nice** took on widely divergent meanings, including 'timid', 'fussy', 'dainty', and 'strange'. In Chaucer's *Romaunt of the Rose* (c1370) the word means 'wanton or lascivious': "Nyce she was, but she mente Noone harme ne slight in hir entente, But oonely lust & jolyte."

By the early 1500s, **nice** was being used to mean 'requiring great precision or accuracy'—nearly the opposite of its original meaning. (The **nice** we're overwhelmed with today, meaning 'agreeable', first appears in print in 1769.) This is why **nice** seems like two (or more) different words. In a sense, it is. The experts really have no idea why **nice** took on so many distinct meanings so quickly.

As for Shakespeare, he uses the word thirty-two times and, it appears, in thirty-two different ways.

Finally, I have always been an admirer of Samuel Johnson's accuracy with language, and he doesn't fail me here. He speaks of lying to Boswell in this example, employing **nice**'s meaning 'minute, fine, or subtle':

He [Johnson] would not allow his servant to say he was not at home when he really was. "A servant's strict regard for the truth must be weakened by such a practice. A philosopher may know that it is merely a form of denial; but few servants are such nice distinguishers. If I accustom a servant to tell a lie for me, have I not reason to apprehend that he will tell many lies for himself."

~*RG*

none

LARRY BLOCK WROTE: I am a new visitor to your site and I love it. In fact, I think it is truly peachy. In reviewing some of the entries for this year, I came upon [a sentence that begins] "Over the years the @ sign has had a few jobs, but none were. . . ." Shouldn't it have said "none was" or am I just being an old codger?

It's amazing how many of you write and ask if you're being "an old CODGER" or "an old fogie." Maybe there's some subliminal recognition there that language changes, even when you rue the fact!

In this case, however, we're not talking about language changing or standards slipping, but about something that has always been a fact in English. Strictly speaking, **none** has never been only a singular noun. It derives from the Old English *nan,* a blend of the negative *ne* 'not' and *an* 'one'. Old English was a heavily inflected language, much as German still is but Modern English is not; *nan* was inflected for case, gender, and plurality, and thus always had both singular and plural forms.

Across all levels of English usage, from academic writing to newspaper reporting to speech, people use a singular or plural verb with **none** according to the principles of what Quirk, Greenbaum, Leech, and Svartvik refer to as "notional agreement" (*A Comprehensive Grammar of the English Language,* 1985). Notional agreement refers to the way that verbs and pronouns are treated as singular or plural based on the user's concept of the singularity or plurality of their subjects or antecedents, regardless of what "ought" to be done according to strict rules of grammar.

Some examples might help here. If **none** as a subject refers to something that seems multiple by nature, a speaker will use a plural verb: "None of the guests have arrived yet" feels akin to "people haven't arrived yet." However, if the speaker wants to emphasize "not one," a singular verb tends to be used: "None of the guests has arrived yet! [Dammit!]" It's the underlying concept that dictates the verb: if I speak for my colleagues and say "Heather, none of us want you to go back to graduate school and leave us," underlying "none of us" is the concept of "we" rather than "not me, nor her, nor him, nor her, etc."

And consider this sentence: "I've gained weight, and none of my clothes fit me." **None** is clearly the subject of the verb *fit* in this sentence, but the word *clothes* is a plural noun that does not allow of the concept of more than one "cloth." You'd have to come out with the highly unnatural "Not one of my pieces of clothing fits me" to force the concept of **none** as "strictly for singular use only" to work in expressing that idea.

Aren't you glad there's now one less thing to worry about in your codgerage?

$\sim$*WRN*

nonplussed (non-PLUSST)

TIM BOGARDUS WROTE: What's going on with the word **nonplussed?** In the last year I've seen it used (everywhere from the *New York Times* to the *ESPN* Web site) to mean 'unimpressed' or 'indifferent', when, as far as I can tell, the only correct definition is 'confused' or 'perplexed'. . . . Has the usage of this word changed. . . ? Frankly, I'm **nonplussed.**

The correct meaning of **nonplussed** is 'utterly perplexed; completely puzzled'. It's derived from the Latin phrase *nōn plūs* 'not more, no further'—referring to a state in which nothing more can be done. To be **nonplussed** is to be at a total loss as to what to say or do. It's puzzling as to how **nonplussed** has come to mean 'undisturbed, unimpressed, indifferent'. The prefix *non-* means 'not, no', but *plussed* has no meaning in English. It's likely that the negative prefix makes one think the meaning must be 'not something' rather than 'utterly or completely something'. Or there may be an analogy with *unfazed,* a word with a similar meaning.

The correct meaning of **nonplussed** does prevail, although there are quite a few instances of the new meaning to which you refer. A few examples: "[Bill] Gates seemed nonplussed by the Net until late 1995. By 1996 he became a fanatic" (*ZDNet,* 1999). "Both authors are nonplussed by the notion of dog fashion shows. 'If you don't compromise the dog, what the hell?' Ms. Knapp said" (*New York Times,* 1999).

I must say I was utterly perplexed by the entry in the newest edition of *The New York Times Manual of Style and Usage:* "Nonplused does not mean fazed or unfazed. It means bewildered to the point of speechlessness." To me, it does (more or less) mean 'fazed' but does not mean 'unfazed'. Despite this confusion, perhaps the *New York Times* copyeditors should pay more attention to the basically sound advice in their usage book. The fact that this book takes on the topic shows that the meaning of **nonplussed** has indeed become an issue; the previous edition did not have an entry for this word.

Incidentally, the spelling **nonplussed** is more common than **nonplused,** at least in American English. The double *s* occurs because the second syllable is stressed.

~*CGB*

nuclear

PILAR MCADAM WROTE: I can't stand it when I hear people talking about (NOO-kyuh-ler) energy, as opposed to (NOO-klee-er). So many people make this error, and it seems to be spreading. Any clue how it originated (not to mention why it continues)?

Wow! "I can't stand it" says it all. This notorious mispronunciation of **nuclear** is without question the one most hated in the English-speaking world (at least in the United States), and the one most likely to inspire the listener to fury, ranting, tearing of hair, and gagging.

This is an extraordinary level of emotional involvement. After all, it's just a pronunciation, right? No one is hurting anyone. But these feelings exist precisely because (NOO-kyuh-ler) is an error that surfaces unexpectedly—not in the speech of the uneducated, but in the speech of the rich and famous, of people we want to respect, like doctors and lawyers, professors, even presidents of the United States, for heaven's sake! The most famous alleged perpetrator was Dwight Eisenhower. Jimmy Carter has his own unique variation: (NYOO-kee-er).

Two common forces underlie this error. The first is *metathesis,* a tendency to switch things—in this case, sounds. Confusion happens. Just listen to people trying to say *relevant* or *prevalent; cavalry* or *Calvary.* The (l) and (v) easily switch places as the speaker's eyes glaze over. Another example is *asterisk,* often pronounced (AS-tuh-riks). With **nuclear,** we actually have the sounds (y) and (l) switching in the final two syllables, more easily understood if we render them as (-kluh-**y**er), the correct one, and (-**k**yuh-ler), the unmentionable.

The second force—a powerful one—is *analogy.* A Wise Reader out there found only one other common word in English that ends in (-kluh-yer)—*cochlear.* Analogy with (-kyuh-ler) is another matter. Hundreds of such words bombard our ears: *molecular, spectacular, particular, vascular, muscular, circular, macular . . .* I could go on.

A third basis for this error—inherent human fallibility— leads us into dangerous territory. The fact is, not everyone sees words and hears sounds well—or listens—or cares. You can carefully say *tenet* in a conversation, only to have your interlocutor respond with *tenant,* out of indifference, perhaps, or pure habit.

Linguistic habits are hard to break. Sadly, the rest of us may just have to bear it. To stop (NOO-kyuh-ler) proliferation, we'll have to wait for a new source of energy that we can all pronounce.

~EP

often

DEX PACKARD WROTE: As I was growing up, I learned to pronounce this word with the *t* silent: (OFF-un). I hear more and more people saying (OFF-tun). Which is correct, or is it a regional dialect thing?

The pronunciation with (t) is not restricted by region; nor is it age-related—that is, it doesn't represent a pronunciation shift emerging as a new generation reaches adulthood. It does have an interesting history involving the passage of time, though.

Often ('frequently') was first attested in 1250 in *The Story of Genesis and Exodus* as a variant of the older term *ofte* (pronounced OFF-tuh) and the still older form *oft*, now chiefly literary. The development of **often** was probably influenced by Middle English *selden* 'seldom'. Chaucer used *ofte* before consonants and **often** before vowels. *Ofte* was replaced during the 16th century by *oft* when the (uh) sound represented by *e* at the ends of words ceased to be pronounced and the two words came to sound exactly alike.

In that same century, **often** became the term of choice in Standard English; the *t* was pronounced. One century later, the (t)-less pronunciation became predominant among the educated in North America and Great Britain, and the one with (t) became stigmatized.

Early dictionaries of English omitted any reference to (OFF-tun) until the mid 1970s, signaling either a lack of acceptance or insufficient frequency. During the 1970s and 80s, the pronunciation was noted enough among educated speakers to warrant its creeping quietly into major dictionaries—usually with a subtle cautionary label.

By the late 1990s, all major American dictionaries but one included (OFF-tun), side by side with (OFF-un), with no special label—an indication that many writers and educators now consider the pronunciation perfectly standard. However, J. C. Wells, editor of *Longman's Pronunciation Dictionary* (1989), conducted a poll among nearly 300 native speakers of British English. While his book shows both pronunciations as equal variants, 73 percent of those who answered his questionnaire preferred the one without (t).

Apparently, grains of salt are in order. The (t) pronunciation may now be standard, but its critics still thrive. Charles Elster, in his 1999 *The Big Book of Beastly Mispronunciations,* quotes several 20th-century writers on usage who have blasted it—among them H. W. Fowler, who said that it "is practiced by two oddly consorted classes—the academic speakers who affect a more precise enunciation than their neighbours . . . & the uneasy half-literates who like to prove that they can spell" (1926). Elster himself espouses the negative view, saying that "today the bad odor of class-conscious affectation still clings to it as persistently as ever," adding that the *t* is silent in analogous words like *soften, hasten,* and *listen.*

That last point is certainly true. But the extremely negative view of (OFF-tun) is a bit harsh. Those who don't say it may find it annoying, but those who do probably learned it as children. If they were truly snobbish, they'd drop the (t).

OK

DENNIS MOSLEY WROTE: I have heard that the term **OK** comes from a Revolutionary War hero who won a battle in upstate New York in a swamp whose name started with a K. His men called him "Old K." After the war this fellow ran for office, and a slogan of the day said, "It's Old K with me!" which became "It's **O.K.** with me!" Any truth to this?

It's a good story, but there's no truth to it. Over the past hundred years, there have been dozens of theories about the origin of the expression. Here's a sampling:

It comes from Greek *olla* 'all' plus *kalla* 'good'. It is a contraction of Scottish *och aye.* It comes from the West African language Wolof. It comes from the French *aux quais* 'at the quays', the place where French sailors arranged rendezvous with the ladies of the Colonies. It comes from *Old Keokuk,* the name of a Fox chief. It comes from German *Oberst Kommandant* 'Colonel in Command' and was used by some unspecified German officer to initial orders at the time of the Revolution. It comes from a Choctaw term, either *hoke* or *okeh,* meaning 'It is so'. One of the most enduring theories involves Andrew Jackson, who was a notoriously poor speller. It was said that he spelled "all correct" either "ole kurrek" or "oll korrect" or "orl kerrect" and abbreviated it **OK.** None of these theories can be supported with documented proof.

Now here's the truth (as we know it, until someone finds other evidence):

The explanation given by Professor Allen Walker Read of Columbia in a series of articles in *American Speech* in 1963 and 1964 is the one that is now accepted. He writes that the first appearance of **OK** in print was in the Boston *Morning Post* in March 1839: "He of the Journal . . . would have the 'contribution box,' et ceteras, o.k.—all correct—and cause the corks to fly, like sparks, upward." **OK** was taken from the first letters of a facetious phonetic spelling—'oll' or 'orl korrect'. Yes, I know this sounds far-fetched, but there's more evidence.

In 1838 *O.W.* for 'All Right' (Oll Wright) appeared in the Boston *Morning Post.* Americans seem to have been indulging in an orgy of abbreviations and deliberate misspellings at the time: *K.Y.* for 'No Yuse', *N.S.M.J.* for 'Nough Said Mong Jintlemen', and, my favorite, *O.K.K.B.W.P* for 'One Kind Kiss Before We Part', reported in New York in 1839. The fad apparently began in Boston in 1838; by the following year it had spread to New York and New Orleans.

That's the origin of **OK.** Its endurance after the end of the abbreviation fad is another story. In 1840 when Martin Van Buren, who was born in Kinderhook, New York, was running for president, his supporters formed a club. An ad in 1840 says, "The Democratic O.K. Club are hereby ordered to meet. . . ." The O.K. stood for 'Old Kinderhook'. (Whether Van Buren was called "Old Kinderhook" before the campaign is unknown.)

In 1919 H. L. Mencken wrote: "Dr. Woodrow Wilson is said

to use okeh in endorsing government papers." Wilson believed the Choctaw origin theory and insisted that was the correct spelling. Others in the 1920s evidently agreed because that spelling was popular. By 1929 we find the spelling **okay** as well as **OK** and **O.K.**

So there you have it: What is probably the most common American expression, one now known throughout the world and adopted into other languages, had its origin in the fortuitous combination of faddish word play and the need for a catchy campaign slogan.

~*GSM*

on or off the wagon

CASSIE MELVILLE WROTE: Could you please explain what the term being **off the wagon** is intended to mean in relation to drinking? And where it originates from?

This pair of metaphors—**on** and **off the wagon**—has been associated with battling the booze for around one hundred years. Here's the sequence: someone pledges to abstain from drinking alcoholic beverages, usually after a period of excessive drinking but sometimes for religious or other reasons. Having stopped, this person is **on the wagon.** If the person starts drinking again habitually, he or she has fallen **off the wagon.** In other words, a person must have been **on the wagon** for a time in order to be regarded as **off the wagon.**

The early forms were *on the water wagon* (or *cart*). Horse-drawn water carts didn't distribute drinking water. They were used during the late 19th century, especially during hot, dry summers, to wet down dusty roads. This was a period of active crusading; women—and a few men—campaigned fervently for Prohibition on a national scale. Members of such organizations as the Women's Christian Temperance Union (founded in 1874) and the Anti-Saloon League (formed in 1893) tried desperately to close down breweries and saloons, hoping to reduce domestic abuse by encouraging sobriety in husbands and fathers.

Many of the men who pledged to stop drinking asserted that no matter how much they longed for a strong drink, they would rather climb aboard a water cart to quench their thirst than break their vow. *I'm on the water cart* came to mean "No, thank you; I'm not drinking any more." As the metaphor became more popular, *wagon* overtook *cart* in the American idiom (*cart* is still used in England). The notion that you could easily fall **off the wagon** was recognized early on.

The *Encyclopedia of Word and Phrase Origins* claims that the earliest literary citation for "I'm on the water cart" occurs in "Alice Caldwell Rice's *Mrs. Wiggs of the Cabbage Patch* (1901), where the consumptive Mr. Dick says it to old Mrs. Wiggs." This antedates *The Oxford English Dictionary*'s earliest attestation, a 1904 definition from *American Dialect Notes,* 'to abstain from hard drinks'.

A search in Nexis reveals that both the "on" and "off" forms of the metaphor have been extended to such things as dieting, exercising, and even government spending sprees. In one bizarre citation, the metaphor refers to spates of serial killing! Apparently, one can go **on the wagon** with regard to any habitual activity or vice. Or vice versa.

~*EP*

ornery

GREGORY PAYNE WROTE: A word I am interested in is **ornery.** My understanding is that it is a corruption or derivative of *ordinary.* But to get from *ordinary* ('usual, common') to *ornery* ('stubborn, obstinate, mulish') seems a bit odd.

Ornery is a dialect use of *ordinary* and has also been spelled *awnry, o'nary, onery, onry, ornary,* and *ornry.* All of these spellings are written representations of the way people pronounced *ordinary.* What's interesting is that, instead of just remaining a dialect form of *ordinary,* **ornery** developed a meaning of its own and became a completely new standard English word.

It does seem like quite a stretch from 'usual or common' to 'stubborn' until we fill in the gap in the development of the meaning. The *Dictionary of American Regional English* gives several examples of **ornery** meaning 'ordinary' in the 19th century. Here's one from Pennsylvania: "When I condescend to unbuzzum myself . . . to folks of ornery intellect and caparisoned to me, I know very few people that ar'n't ornery as to brains . . ." (1838).

A Maryland farmer by the name of Brown wrote in his journal in 1816: "The Land is old, completely worn out, the farming extremely ornary in general." If something is "ordinary," it's 'nothing special', and from there it's an easy step to 'not very good'. **Ornery** developed the sense of 'low' or 'mean' or 'inferior' during the first half of the 19th century. Mark Twain used it this way in *Huckleberry Finn* (1884): "The more I studied about this the more my conscience went to grinding me, and the more wicked and low-down and ornery I got to feeling." Examples of **ornery** with an edge of contempt abound throughout the 19th and 20th centuries: "Southerner: You ornery fellow! do you pretend to call me to account for my language? Yankee: I did but drop a hint." (*Massachusetts Spy and Worcester County Advocate,* 1830).

By the middle of the 19th century, **ornery** also came to mean 'unpleasant and troublesome' and 'ill-tempered and cantankerous': "Good company betters the orneriest sort er weather" (Winthrop, *John Brent,* 1862). We find it applied in this way to animals (horses, mules, goats, cats, sheep, and mosquitoes) as well as to people and objects. The 'stubborn and obstinate' sense seems to be a further development of the 'troublesome and cantankerous' one. When someone or something isn't doing your bidding, it's natural to call him, her, or it "stubborn." The most common meaning of **ornery** today is 'disagreeable in disposition', combining the senses of 'ill-tempered' and 'obstinate'.

Journalists have long been fond of referring to both the public and legislators as **ornery:** "We are forced to spend all this money solely because mankind up to now is too ornery to organize international life on some more sensible basis" (*Baltimore Sun,* 1938).

~GSM

ourself/ourselves

J. MELIN WROTE: In some New Thought literature I've seen the word **ourself** used a great deal. Should it be **ourselves** in order to be correct grammatically?

Ourself has been criticized as ungrammatical and even absurd, on the basis of the fact that *our* is plural and *self* is singular. However, historically, the word *self* was plural as well as singular, and **ourself** was used in the same way as we now use **ourselves.** The form **ourself** probably arose by dropping the *-e(n)* endings of the Middle English plural forms *our selven, our selve, our selfe.* The "correct" form **ourselves** did not appear in print until the early 1500s.

Even after **ourselves** became the predominant form, **ourself** survived in "royal or editorial we" constructions, in which *we* is really *I:* "We have taken unto ourself such powers as may be necessary." **Ourself** is also used in a slightly different context, as when the subject is "us as individuals," or when the subject is one's own person or individuality considered as private and apart from others: "It is for ourself that we should strive for greater knowledge."

In Web searches I found that **ourself** is commonly used by business firms: "This is to introduce ourself as manufacturer and exporter of Laces, Braids . . ."

So it seems that **ourself,** though technically ill-formed, does sound right and does serve a purpose in certain contexts. However, most dictionaries and usage guides caution against its use.

Ourself is not the only "ill-formed" pronoun of this type. Though my spell checker doesn't allow *themself,* this form is commonly found in speech and writing and may refer to several people or to one person, especially if gender is not specified: "Did the witness perjure themself?" As an alternative to *themself,* the pronoun *theirself* is occasionally used, even by the best writers: "All they want to do is leave theirself a case for appeal" (Norman Mailer, *Executioner's Song*). And the plural *yourself* is occasionally found in informal contexts: "You guys ought to give yourself a day off for a job well done!" Those of you who cringe at the use of **ourself** and analogous forms will be glad to know that the form *usself* has fallen out of use.

~CGB

passing fair

EUGENE DILLENBURG WROTE: If you decide to tell the story of **passing fair,** please be sure to include that wonderful poem by Dorothy Parker. . . .

Indeed, yes—but first, a little history. Old English *faeger,* from which *fair* is derived, meant 'beautiful; pleasant'. This sense has remained in English, although it is no longer the most common meaning. As for the "passing" in **passing fair,** it is the same adverb discussed in PASSING STRANGE, with the same meaning: 'surpassingly; extremely'. **Passing fair,** then, started life meaning 'extremely beautiful'.

In modern writing, **passing fair** can still evoke our literary past, with 'dazzling beauty' expressed in deliberately dated language. From a 1999 Canadian newspaper: "Lowly commoners marrying princes of the blood is what fairy tales are all about (she a kitchen maid, but passing fair; he the highest in the land)."

In recent years, this traditional sense has been stifled by a perception that *passing* means 'passably'. There is also a strong association with barely "passing" grades. This was exemplified in a 1997 newspaper article quoting a previous interview in which Elizabeth Taylor, responding to praise of her looks, said, "Oh, I don't think I'm beautiful. I'm passing fair." This clearly reverses the meaning of *passing*, although *fair* is at least still 'pretty'.

A similar semantic reversal is seen with *fair*. The meaning 'neither good nor bad' has almost completely conquered 'beautiful': "To one whose French is only passing fair . . ." (*Chicago Tribune*, 1985).

Perhaps there is some kind of reciprocal negative influence between *passing* and *fair*, resulting in pejoration of the entire phrase, a change to a less respectable meaning. This kind of shift can cause confusion. If a woman is described these days as **passing fair,** is it a compliment?

Of course, ambiguity offers artistic virtues. I'll let you decipher multiple meanings from Dorothy Parker's *Roundel*.

> *She's passing fair; but so demure is she*
> *So quiet is her gown, so smooth her hair,*
> *That few there are who note her and agree*
> *She's passing fair.*
>
> . . .
>
> *Yet if the passing mark is minus D—*
> *She's passing fair.*

~*EP*

passing strange

CARL B. LIND WROTE: Passing strange seems to be used with increasing frequency (e.g., it was in a recent George Will column). What is the origin and specific meaning of this phrase?

This adverbial use of *passing* does not mean what you might expect. It is neither 'merely adequately' nor 'fleetingly', but 'surpassingly; exceedingly; very'. Something **passing strange** is very strange indeed.

The verb *pass* derives from the Latin noun *passus* 'step; stride; pace', having come into English in the 13th century from the Old French verb *passer* 'to step; walk; go'. While the original meaning in English was simply 'to go, proceed, move along', the more specific sense of 'to go by; move past; overtake'—now the primary meaning—existed from the beginning. By the late 14th century this sense had been extended to the abstract concept 'to go beyond the usual'. Accordingly, from the 14th century on, one of the meanings of *passing* was 'exceedingly, preeminently, extremely'.

Both adjectival and adverbial uses of the term in this sense were common through the 19th century. Shakespeare used adverbial *passing* liberally. We have, for example, "I am passing light in spirit." (*Henry IV, Part II*); "Yet are they passing cowardly." (*Coriolanus*); "I have a daughter that I love passing well." (*Hamlet*) As late as 1883, Howard Pyle wrote, "Little John had grown passing fond of good living through abiding at the Sheriff's house." *Surpassing* and *surpassingly* have now supplanted *passing* in this sense.

In fact, adverbial *passing* survives almost exclusively in two phrases—**passing strange** and PASSING FAIR. Current citations for the former include, from a recent issue of the *Wall Street Journal:* "We do find it puzzling, and passing strange, that France would . . . focus so much attention on the danger to them of a strong United States rather than the dangers that we and France together face from countries like Iraq."

One reason that **passing strange** has lingered in the imagination of English writers must be the memorable speech in Shakespeare's *Othello* in which Othello tells how he won Desdemona: "When I did speak of some distressful stroke, That my youth suffer'd, My story being done, She gave me for my pains a world of sighs: She swore, in faith, 'twas strange, 'twas passing strange, 'Twas pitiful, 'twas wondrous pitiful. . . ." These lines are quoted frequently outright and are also echoed in modern writing as "it's strange, passing strange. . . ."

With frozen expressions from the past, misunderstanding of a term like *passing* is influenced by common current senses. One finds the occasional quote suggesting that **passing strange** means moderately (rather than extremely) strange: "It's more than passing strange that a winner in two Republican primaries would have to encourage his fellow Republicans not to fear his campaign, as McCain has done" (*Houston Chronicle*). Errors like this often signal a new and contradictory meaning. That's what happened to PASSING FAIR, but that's a whole 'nother story.

~EP

piss and vinegar

JOSH GRECHUS WROTE: I'm curious about the origins of the term **piss 'n' vinegar.** Someone mentioned they thought I was acting this way today and said that was probably the Norwegian in her. Seems to me like a term that would have nothing to do with being Norwegian. Would you care to shed a little light on this interesting term?

Well, if being Norwegian means being 'full of youthful energy and vitality', then it could make you full of **piss and vinegar.** However, since this is an American slang phrase, it certainly could be applied to anyone who's lively, no matter where his or her ancestors were born.

The trouble with discussing this phrase is the "shedding light on it" part. *The Oxford English Dictionary*'s earliest citation for it is from its mention in *The American Thesaurus of Slang* (1942, by Lester V. Berrey & Melvin Van Den Bark), but we have a citation in our files from Steinbeck's 1938 *The Grapes of Wrath:* "'How ya keepin' yaself?' 'Full a piss an' vinegar.'" If Steinbeck had a character use a phrase in speech and didn't gloss it, then the phrase had to have already been familiar for some time before he recorded it. There are also plenty of citations going forward from that date, all the way up to Bart's declaration in a 1994 episode of *The Simpsons:* "I'm full of piss and vinegar."

However, we still haven't turned up anything earlier than the Steinbeck citation, which makes it hard to know where the phrase comes from. There is certainly a similar expression with the identical meaning, "full of beans," which goes back to 1854. There's "full of piss and wind" which means 'full of blustering talk; pretentious' that dates to 1922. And there's also Kyne's "He's full of pep and vinegar" (*They Also Serve,* 1927) that may indicate a euphemistic treatment of *piss;* certainly the sense of *vinegar* alone meaning 'vitality' was already part of campus slang in the 1920s.

It could just be that the common 1920s provenances of *vinegar* meaning 'vim', *piss and wind,* and *pep and vinegar* means that some slick-haired co-ed came up with the combination of pungent liquids in the expression **piss and vinegar.**

In fact, they've been combined before: there is an expression "to piss vinegar" that goes back to 1602, meaning 'to be miserly'. This gave rise to the 18th-century *vinegar-pisser,* a 'miser'. If there is any connection between these meanings and **piss-and-vinegar** vitality, it seems exactly the sort that a college student might make.

~*WRN*

plight

ARISTODEMOS WROTE: I have been wondering about the old wedding vow "thereto I plight thee my troth," in which **plight** means 'pledge'. The noun **plight** means 'peril' or 'predicament'. Any thoughts on why the word has such different meanings?

The verb **plight** in the sense of 'pledge' was well-established by the time Thomas Cranmer used it in the marriage service of the Anglican *Book of Common Prayer* in 1549.

If we look back at this word in Old English, however, we find a different meaning. *Pliht* (pronounced with a short *i*) meant 'danger' or 'risk' from its first appearance in the 9th century: *mid micclan plihte,* 'with great danger'. The Old English verb *plihtan* meant 'to bring danger upon an object'. It gradually came to mean 'to bring danger upon an object by risking its forfeiture'. If one made a pledge, one had a solemn responsibility to fulfill it; failure to do so could place life and property in peril, especially if the **plight** was a vow of allegiance to a ruler.

By the 14th century, the verb **plight** had come to mean 'to give in pledge' or 'to pledge (one's faithfulness or oath)'. It was used both in a general sense and with reference to betrothal or marriage. "I thee plight" meant 'I promise you'.

Now on to the other **plight,** meaning 'predicament'. The Middle English form of this word is *plit, plyt,* or *plyt.* It derives from the Old French *pleit* or *ploit* 'fold' and is related to English *plait.* In addition to 'fold', *ploit* meant 'an act or manner of folding' and—here's the important bit—'a manner of being' or 'condition'.

The sense 'manner of being' goes back to the 14th century in English. The 'condition' referred to was originally neutral or good. A "Treatise on the Passion of Christ" in 1534 says: "And [to] lyue here in suche pleasaunt plight as we shuld have lyued if Adam had not synned." When **plight** had a negative sense, that had to be specified. The author of the 14th-century *Sir Gawain and the Green Knight* wrote: "Thus in peryl, & payne, & plytes ful harde."

In some dialects, the *g,* the *h,* or the *gh* of the Germanic word **plight** meaning 'pledge' was already lost in the 14th century. This left a word that was identical in spelling with the word of French origin meaning 'condition', although the Germanic word was still pronounced with a short *i.* Through some mysterious process, both words came to be pronounced with the long *i* of the French word, but the spelling of both gradually shifted back to the Germanic **plight.** Something interesting happened to the meaning of the noun, too: originally a neutral word meaning simply 'condition', it acquired the sense of 'a harmful condition'—perhaps under the influence of the other **plight** with its sense of 'a risky pledge'.

~GSM

point man

I most often hear the term **point man** in a political context, as in "He's the point man for the new legislation." I have heard that the term has military or basketball origins.

Since the mid-1800s, the term *pointer* has referred to one of the cowboys riding at the front of a herd of cattle; **point man** in this sense is first recorded in 1903. The *point* is the position at the front of the herd, and these cowboys *ride, walk,* or *take (the) point,* making sure the cattle stay together and go in the right direction.

Point in the sense 'the leading party of a military advance guard' is first recorded at the beginning of the 20th century. The *point* is also the position at the head of a column or V-shaped wedge of troops. **Point man** meaning 'the lead soldier of a patrol' dates from the mid-1940s; like the cowboy, he is said to *ride, walk,* or *take (the) point.* (Actually he is sometimes at the back of the rear guard, also a dangerous position.)

The cowboy sense of *point* and **point man** is directly connected to the military meaning, both uses implying a person in a leading or dangerous position. The **point man** risks loss of life and limb by going out on a limb.

The Middle English phrase *in point* meant 'in immediate danger'. There are also slang uses: a **point man** is a lookout who is *on (the) point* or *stands point* while a crime is being committed. A hunting dog *makes* or *comes to a point* by standing rigid and facing the game. Even the sports senses imply danger or peril. In box lacrosse, the **point man** is the player in the middle of the attacking zone when the team is on the offense. In ice hockey, he is in the offensive position inside the attacking zone. The basketball *point guard* (not **point man**) is the guard in the front court who directs the team's offense.

Point man in the sense 'a person in the forefront' usually refers to someone who leads an attack on a proposal, or a movement in defense of a proposal. This person *takes the point* or is *on (the) point,* often receiving the criticism or blame. Most often, the context is a public (political) issue, because the **point man** (or *point person* or *point woman*) is usually in the public eye. This extended sense of **point man** is fairly recent, probably dating from the late 1960s. Here's a 1983 cite that alludes to the military meaning: "Just as John Glenn became the point man for the original seven astronauts, Ed Harris [playing Glenn in *The Right Stuff*] emerges as the squad leader of this talented troupe."

~*CGB*

preposition at end

DR. RICHARD A. SACHS WROTE: In a recent posting, you said ". . . so you'll know whom to quibble with." Am I being old-fashioned to prefer that we not end sentences with prepositions? Sometimes it does seem awkward to recast sentences otherwise, but certainly ". . . so you'll know with whom to quibble" flows quite well.

You're being as old-fashioned as the poet and dramatist John Dryden, who started the vogue for objecting to this usage in the 17th century, and as modern as Beverly Brooks and Sid Waxman, who also wrote to ask about this one.

Dryden, for no good reason I can ascertain, decided mid-career that English should follow Latin in its structure (this sentiment is also likely to be at the root of the objections to the split infinitive that arose in the 19th century). He went so far as to go back over his earlier writings and remove the offending sentence-final prepositions once he had decided they ought not to be there. Thus the shibboleth that one must eschew such constructions can be traced to the fancy of one individual—albeit a very influential individual—and has nothing to do with what is 'proper' in English.

Nor does this imposed Latin convention work well in practice with English verb structures. Latin uses inflected endings on verbs, nouns, and other parts of speech to denote cases such as the *nominative* (subject), *accusative* (object), and *genitive* (possessive). English retains little in the way of inflection outside of verb tenses; it survives in our possessive 's and in certain pronouns (*she/her, my/mine, who/whom*). In the majority of instances, English now uses prepositions to fill the role that inflections formerly held in indicating grammatical relationships. Phrasal verbs such as "quibble with" are prime examples of this.

The reality is that English phrasal verbs simply don't fit into Latin constructions. The most obvious examples of this are intransitive phrasal verbs: no one would ever say "Up speak!" instead of "Speak up!" Transitive phrasal verbs are a bit more complex: some have separable particles (the adverb or preposition that follows the base form of the verb) as in "look up a definition / look a definition up in your dictionary"; others are not separable, as in "See what I have to put up with?"

In natural, idiomatic English, the components of a phrasal verb should remain together if they are not separable by an object. In other words, if one were to recast the sentence "I'm talking about your manners" as a question, one would say, "What are you talking about?" not "About what are you talking?" Enter "quibble with": as a transitive phrasal verb, it is not separable, and therefore the preposition must remain with the base form of the verb. If "with whom to quibble" sounds natural to you, it is probably because there are three centuries of hypercorrection brainwashing you.

~WRN

private language and idioglossia

BRAM CARTMELL WROTE: I'm curious about **private languages.** I've heard of **idioglossia,** which I assume is related. Do these languages tend to derive from dialects and develop entire grammatical structures? What exactly makes a language private as opposed to a language spoken by a small group? How common are they?

A **private language** is an exclusive language intelligible only to a restricted group of people. The reasons for using such a language are to maintain secrecy, to distinguish group members from outsiders, or just to have fun. These secret languages are found in many cultures and subcultures. The "in-group" may be large or small. Some private languages are fairly intelligible, while others are completely opaque.

Private languages sometimes invent new vocabulary and grammar. More often, they use distorted spellings or pronunciations of commonly used words, or they give new meanings to everyday words. For example, pig Latin is derived from everyday English.

Sometimes the words of a private language seep into the standard language. *Moniker,* meaning 'a nickname or alias', and *bloke,* meaning 'a fellow', may have come from Shelta, a private language spoken by the tinkers (or Travelers) in Ireland.

You mention **idioglossia.** This is a form of private language invented by one child or by children in close contact. It's been said that 40 percent of twins develop some form of private speech. Also, families will sometimes make up words or use existing words in idiosyncratic ways.

Language codes are a form of private language. The Navajo "code talkers" baffled Japanese eavesdroppers in World War II, as by using Navajo bird names for warplanes. Another example is *cant,* the private language of the underworld. Even teenage slang and technical jargon can be considered private languages. And among some Australian Aborigines, it's taboo to converse freely with certain relatives; a private "mother-in-law language" is used whenever the taboo relative is nearby!

Boontling, a moribund private language of Boonville, California, probably originated in the hop fields and among sheep shearers. One elderly Boonter, Bobby Glover, gives this account: "Back in the 1880s, a girl from San Francisco got herself pregnant and was without benefit of clergy. Her family sent her to Boonville. . . . Well, the women who worked in the hop fields found out about this and wanted to talk about the girl. So they invented code words so the children wouldn't be able to understand. . . ."

Philosophers have argued about the concept of a private language. Ludwig Wittgenstein explained it this way: "The words of this language are to refer to what can be known only to the speaker; to his immediate, private sensations. So another cannot understand the language." But Wittgenstein concluded that such a private language is impossible because the originator would be unable to establish meanings for its signs; you can't name anything you aren't acquainted with. For example, even the sensation of itching derives its identity from a shared use of language.

~*CGB*

props

KATIE MCHUGH WROTE: Where does the slang phrase **mad props** come from, and what exactly does it mean?

This two-word slang expression has its origin in Black English, specifically, in the hip-hop culture of young African-Americans. In this particular phrase, **mad** is an adjective meaning 'many, much, plenty of', as in "mad publicity, mad dough, mad friends." But it can also be an adverb meaning 'very, extremely', as in "mad cool, mad funny, mad scared." This use of **mad** dates from the early 1990s, though the adverb *madly* (as in "madly talented") is much older.

Though **props** has several slang senses, here it means 'proper or due respect; compliments, credit, admiration, or praise'. Since the term implies public recognition, it's usually used of a performer or other person in the public eye. For example, if a musician "gets (his) props," he's gained public recognition for his accomplishments; to "give him his props" is to give him the respect he deserves. However, in my opinion, successful people who have gotten their **props** should then "give props to their peeps," that is, they should (at least partially) credit their parents and friends.

According to Clarence Major's *Juba to Jive: A Dictionary of Black American Slang*, the Black English term **props** also refers to any form of support or protection. So your **props** can include your friends, your family, and even your switchblade.

Though **props** in the sense of 'proper respect' is obviously derived from the adjective *proper*, the sense recorded in Clarence Major's dictionary overlaps with the standard English sense of *prop*, 'support; mainstay'.

Written evidence for **props** goes back at least ten years. And the synonymous slang term *propers*, as recorded in Geneva Smitherman's *Black Talk*, is much older. Both these terms are still current slang, especially in verbal use and in alternative (nonmainstream) publications. Searching the archives of Internet chat rooms, I found *propers* sometimes misspelled as "proppers."

$\sim$*CGB*

p's and q's

LINDA ARCHER WROTE: How many times did your Mother say, "**Mind your P's & Q's**"? Just what was she asking [you] to do? I always understood it to mean "Behave," but there are no *p*'s or *q*'s in that word. Maybe, just maybe, I'm still not "Minding my P's & Q's."

Various sources define **p's and q's** as 'manners; behavior; conduct'; and define minding them as watching your step, being careful or polite. The earliest citation for this use in *The Oxford English Dictionary* (1779), "You must mind your P's and Q's with him, I can tell you," expressed the need for careful behavior in the face of potential criticism . . . or worse.

Where the phrase comes from is another matter. Frankly, it would be difficult to find another English expression that has spawned more putative origins than this one. Here are some classified samples, each offered as if true:

Pronunciations and Puns: (1) The term, reduced to *peas and kyous,* comes from p(l)eas(es) and (than)k yous. (2) In the court of Louis XIV, dancing masters cautioned fledgling courtiers to *mind their pieds* (dancing feet) *and queues* (full wigs—*periwigs* or long *perruques* worn by fashionable men, sometimes including a longer braided strand hanging down the back). What with all that bobbing and curtsying, it would have been awkward if courtiers tripped on their hair. (3) In an earlier citation (1602), "Now thou art in thy pee and cue," the references are to a "pea coat" and probably again to a "queue."

Pubs: A cumulative tally of bills for befuddled customers, showing how many pints and quarts they had each imbibed, was kept on a board near the bar, using these letters as abbreviations. Barkeepers were warned not to confuse the expensive *Q* with the piddling *P*. A hastily scrawled circle with a tail pointing vaguely downward from its bottom could wind up looking ambiguous.

Printing: Early printers had to deal with text as a mirror image. Try it with lower-case *p*'s and *q*'s and you'll see why apprentices risked error. But why wasn't that risk attributed as easily to *b*'s and *d*'s?

Pedagogy: Children learning to read and write, having ascertained that objects stay constant whichever way they're turned, now find that *p*'s and *q*'s are not like cups with handles, which remain cups with handles. Instead these letters switch identities when the "handle" moves from left to right. Once more, why not *b*'s and *d*'s?

Each theory has its own appeal. Etymologists have been unwilling to commit to one, although there is some leaning toward the pedagogical explanation. I can only speculate about the drift from an admonition to distinguish letters to an admonition to behave. Perhaps when **mind your p's and q's** became a parent-to-child cliché, it—like other protective warnings—was interpreted simplistically by young children as the more general "Behave!" Ask any parent.

~EP

quark

JESSE GORDON WROTE: I'm trying to impress a young lady . . . [who] is a graphic artist who uses the **Quark** program and wonders about its origins. All of the dictionaries I can find talk about its scientific meaning, viz., a subatomic particle. But as I recall, James Joyce made up the word in *Finnegans Wake* and some scientists adopted it from there because of some common aspect of threeness . . . and what is the etymological connection, if any, to the popular graphic design program?

James Joyce did indeed make up the noun **quark.** He used it only once, in the second of the four books of *Finnegans Wake.*

James speaks of "the stout ship Nansy Hans" sailing away, then breaks into a song that begins:

Now follow we out by Starloe!
Three quarks for Muster Mark!
Sure he hasn't got much of a bark
And sure any he has it's all beside the mark.

There's no consensus on what Joyce meant by a **quark.** He may or may not have been aware of the rare verb *to quark,* which is used occasionally in 19th-century texts instead of 'croak' or 'caw'. If he did know of this verb, he might have written "three quarks for" on the analogy of "three cheers for," since cheering might sound like croaking or **quarking** if you'd been doing it loudly enough. This in turn conveniently rhymes with the other *-ark* words in the song. At the end of the song, Joyce also says:

Overhoved, shrillgleescreaming.
That song sang seaswans.

—which does seem to put the whole thing into the mouth of a bird.

Demystifying Joyce has been, and continues to be, the occupation of myriad academics' lifetimes. It was also an interest of Murray Gell-Mann, one of the two scientists to put forward the theory that subatomic particles, the building blocks of matter, could essentially be classified into three groups. Gell-Mann, in a 1978 letter to the editor of *The Oxford English Dictionary,* said "the allusion to three quarks seemed perfect." Gell-Mann favored the theory that "three quarks" was "three quarts"—of ale, in a pub.

As for the computer application: the company called *Quark* was founded in 1981 by Tim Gill, who indeed named his firm after the subatomic particle. He wrote the first word-processing program for the Apple III and appears to have liked the concept that his program was also a building block.

$\sim$*WRN*

ravel and unravel

RANDY LAUER WROTE: I recently discovered that the words **ravel** and **unravel** mean the same thing. How can this be?

It's worse than you think. Not only do both **ravel** and **unravel** mean 'to disentangle; come apart' (as the threads of a cloth), but **ravel** can mean its own opposite—'to tangle'! Threads that were neat (aligned, coiled, etc.) can become **raveled**—i.e., twisted and knotted. As fabric frays, loose threads become disentangled from the fabric but entangled with each other. Confusion existed from the beginning; the word comes from the Dutch *rafelen* or *ravelen* 'to unweave; fray' and 'to tangle' (from *rafel* or *ravel,* 'a thread').

To explain why we have both **ravel** and **unravel,** we have to examine the prefix *un-*. When affixed to verbs, it commonly reverses their meanings, a function it has had since Old English. Middle English saw such formations as *unbend, uncover,* and *unhasp,* still in use. Reversive *un-* is so productive that it attaches itself spontaneously to verbs representing any action that can be undone: "You hired that person? Well, go unhire him!"

More rarely, the prefix is not reversive but redundant. From Middle English we have *unloose,* and from Modern English *unthaw,* synonymous with *loose* and *thaw.* Redundant *un-* normally intensifies the verb. With **unravel,** however, it is difficult to determine whether *un-* reverses the 'tangle' sense of **ravel** or intensifies the 'untangle' sense.

Centuries of usage would seem to point to the latter. Almost without exception, a search for **ravel** through old and new writings yielded the 'untangle' sense. From an address to the alumni of Harvard in 1866, a literal use: "And before new armies in hostile encounter on American soil shall unfurl new banners to the breeze, may every thread and thrum of their texture ravel and rot . . ." From an 1875 issue of *Scribners Monthly,* the metaphorical sense: "Then the General retired, went to his house . . . and, in less than an hour, was absorbed in raveling the snarled affairs connected with his recent disastrous speculation" (J. G. Holland, "The Story of Sevenoaks"). I found only one citation, in a recent book review, that used **ravel** to mean 'tangle': "In 'Speak You Also', . . . Steinberg cryptically ravels and unravels his past" (Susan Shapiro, *New York Times*).

On the other hand, *un-* is so rarely redundant that we overwhelmingly perceive it as reversive. That is why you were perplexed enough to ask your question. And the earliest citations for **ravel** in *The Oxford English Dictionary* (1585–1600) are for the now rare sense of 'tangle'. **Unravel** appears shortly thereafter (1603), barely *before* the first known occurrence of **ravel**'s 'disentangle' sense (1606). Consequently, most major dictionaries have concluded that this *un-* reverses the *less* common 'tangle' sense. Unravel that if you can.

~*EP*

right and left

MARK GRANNIS WROTE: What connection is there among the disparate senses of the word **right?** How has it come to mean 'correct', 'the opposite of left', and (as a noun) 'an entitlement or claim'?

Arnie Kurczaba and R. Rodek both asked about the political senses of *left wing* and *right wing*.

The basic sense of **right** is 'straight' or 'stretched out'. It derives from the Indo-European root **reg-* and gives us hundreds of words through Greek *oregein* 'to stretch out' and *orektós* 'stretched out' and Latin *regere* 'to lead straight', therefore 'to guide or rule', and *rogāre* 'to stretch out one's hands for', therefore 'to ask', as well as *rectus* 'straight'. French *droit* 'right' or 'law' comes from Latin *dīrectum* 'legal right'. I could fill a page with cognates!

By the time the adjective appeared in English in the 9th century, the literal sense of 'straight' had already been extended to mean 'upright' or 'righteous'. It also had the sense of 'correct and proper' in Old English. The noun was used by the Venerable Bede to mean 'law', by King Alfred to mean 'one's duty', and by the *Beowulf* poet to mean 'that which is morally just'.

Right was also used to mean 'legal or moral title or claim' as early as 900. By the 13th century, people spoke of someone's "right to" something: "A fals king that nadde no right to the kindom" (Robert of Gloucester, 1297). The plural form meaning the permission to publish an author's work, as in *serial rights,* was first used in the 1890s.

The term *right hand,* meaning the hand that is for the majority of people the stronger one, was used as early as the 10th century. It came to be considered the "right" hand because the majority of people use that hand. The word was extended to refer to that side of the body and to corresponding parts of other objects.

As a verb, **right** meant 'to make staight' or 'to guide' in Old English. The sense of "righting a wrong" appeared in the 14th century. Shakespeare wrote in *Titus Andronicus:* "I am Revenge sent from below, to join with him and right his heinous wrongs."

Left comes from a Germanic root meaning 'weak or worthless'. It is found in the Old English word *lyftadl* 'paralysis' and was used to refer to the less-used hand by the early 13th century and then extended to that side of the body.

The political senses of **right** and **left** originated in the French National Assembly of 1789: the nobles, who were conservative, were seated on the presiding officer's **right** (the *côté droit*), and the members of the Third Estate, who favored sweeping reforms, were seated on his **left** (the *côté gauche*). In legislative assemblies in Continental Europe, the more conservative members are still usually seated to the president's **right.** The terms *right wing* and *left wing* come from military usage.

$\sim$*GSM*

'S (apostrophe-s)

MEL RUSSELL WROTE: Recently our corporate mavens came out with this decree: THE POSSESSIVE FORM IS NOW "XEROX'S." [. . .] The previous spelling— Xerox'—is no longer appropriate. As I recall from my grade school grammar—which was admittedly some time ago—the possessive form of words ending in *s* or an "ess" sound was formed by adding an apostrophe. Adding apostrophe-*s* makes the noun plural. What is the correct style? Am I a bizarre old fogie?

You're being hard on yourself. But let's clarify one thing: adding apostrophe-*s* doesn't make a noun plural except in certain cases; it makes the noun possessive: the boy*'s* side of the back seat. Or, it is a marker for the old genitive case: his sister*'s* incursion onto his side. You would write "we all had bloody marys" rather than *mary's.*

The "certain cases" are quite varied. For instance, if a word or compound that is not normally pluralized ends a quotation, it is allowable to use **'s:**

How many "no comment's" are we going to hear from the mayor?

I think this is bizarre—I would have written "no comments"—but there it is in my *Chicago Manual of Style.* More commonly, **'s** is used for the plural of lowercase letters, and is optional in the plural of uppercase letters:

There are three m's in mummify.
M&M's candies

With decades written as numbers, you can use an apostrophe or not:

the 1920s/1920's

Abbreviations with more than one period in them usually get an apostrophe:

She has two M.A.'s.

However, abbreviations with just one terminal period do not:

yrs./eds.

Now, as for the possessive forms, in general the preferred style is to use **'s.** There are, as ever, some exceptions; most have to do with euphony, and the others mainly come from familiar, fixed phrases:

for goodness' sake
Moses' staff
Hermes' speed

So in fact, the spelling *Xerox'* is an example of hypercorrection based on an old-fashioned notion that if a noun ends in an (s), (ks), or (z) sound, it cannot be pluralized with another *s.*

Originally, the apostrophe marked the omission of the letter *e* in the old genitive ending, and also in the transcription of some plurals. The standardization of the use of the apostrophe and its restriction to possessives (with the above exceptions) didn't happen until 1725. The fact that native speakers (native spellers?) and second-language learners alike have problems remembering the rules isn't too surprising. Many people add an apostrophe to plurals, even in cases where doing so results in the misspelling of the form, as in these recent examples from my local supermarket:

Tomatoe's $1.29 lb.
Free Delivery's

I'm pretty sure this is on the analogy of *ATM's,* and not at all helped by the fact that IT'S means "it is" and ITS, sans apostrophe, is the possessive form.

~*WRN*

Sam Hill

LYN WASSERMAN WROTE: I was dining with friends the other night, one of whom was named **Sam Hill**. A discussion ensued regarding the derivation of the phrase "What in the **Sam Hill**," and we set about to try and find out. No one has been successful up to this point.

What the **Sam Hill** are you asking this for? Who in **Sam Hill** are you, anyway? Why in the **Sam Hill** can't you just leave it alone? You're making me work like **Sam Hill**!

No, no—sorry, I wasn't yelling at you; I was just illustrating some typical **Sam Hill** syntax. As you can see, **Sam Hill** is a strangely satisfying euphemism for 'hell'. (Try saying it, and you'll see what I mean.) This kind of euphemism allows you to swear without swearing. The term has been around in print since the 1830s but isn't used much now—certainly not by those members of our culture who don't bother with euphemisms.

In *WH*-questions (questions beginning with *who, what, where, why,* or *how*), **Sam Hill** is usually preceded by *in* or *the* or *in the*. And **Sam Hill** isn't always the hellish euphemism of choice. If I presented you with blanks to fill in, like "By ____," or "To ____ with that," you might choose *heck,* for example. And in some phrases, like "Go to ____," no euphemism seems adequate to replace what you really want to say.

As for derivation, the most likely source is simply the similarity in sound between *hell* and *hill.* You can get away with *hill* in mixed company. Similar phonetic alterations have resulted in *goldarned, gosh darned,* or *dadblamed* for 'goddamned', the highly reduced and now archaic *zounds* for 'by God's wounds', and numerous others.

There is one theory floating around that purports to involve a real **Sam Hill.** The story goes that a Colonel Samuel Hill, in Guilford, Connecticut, at some unknown time in the early 1800s, perpetually but unsuccessfully ran for political office. Hence, "to run like Sam Hill." However, Guilford's historical records do not yield his name or any other corroborative evidence.

I hope your friend has learned to live with a name used as a "mild oath." It could be worse.

〜*EP*

same difference

I can't blame you. Most dictionaries are no help with this one. But I wish I'd been a fly on the wall, listening to your debates; I'd sure like to know what all the definitions were. I can think of only two uses, one very literal and the other an idiomatic response.

The literal meaning is easy. The meanings of *same,* 'identical to or agreeing with', and *difference,* 'unlikeness; dissimilarity', are just what you'd expect. But when you use **same difference** together, you're not comparing two things; you're comparing the *difference* between one pair of things with the *difference* between one or more other pairs. You're saying that those *differences* are analogous. Here is an example from an 1841 issue of the *United States Democratic Review:*

> There is a wide difference between the rational gratification of human desires, and the abusive indulgence of them. There is the same difference, as between eating and gluttony—between drinking and drunkenness—between mirthfulness and satire—between justice and vengeance (A Phrenologist, "On Rights and Government").

Here's a simpler one: "There appeared the same difference between the leaders as between the armies" (Gibbon, *The History of the Decline and Fall of the Roman Empire*, 1776–88).

But the idiomatic use of **same difference,** which materialized in English in the mid-1940s, is more interesting. It's an interjection. Syntactically, it can stand alone—a conventionalized, frozen response to a petty, irrelevant correction or some niggling distinction. It's a verbal shrug, a signal of indifference or mild annoyance. A recent citation from a British newspaper, the *Sun,* illustrates both the meaning and the mood:

"What the hell is that, Derek?"
"It's a gerbil, Rodney."
"It looks more like a hamster to me, Der."
"Hamster, gerbil, same difference."
"It's 6 ft tall, Derek."

Same difference means 'same thing; no difference'. No one can say for sure how the expression arose, but very likely it was through a blending of these two phrases. Formulaic expressions are often fads; they come and go. People today are more likely to say, "Whatever."

I hope that makes the waters less murky. Or should I say *muddy?* **Same difference.**

⁓*EP*

saturnine (SAT-ur-nine) **and**
saturnalian (sat-ur-NAY-lee-un)

JOHN MANDEVILLE WROTE: How did it happen that the adjectives **saturnine** 'gloomy' and **saturnalian** 'wildly merry' have opposite meanings?

Both **saturnine** and **saturnalian** derive ultimately from the name of the Roman god Saturn, who was an early Italic god associated with agriculture. In classical times, Saturn came to be identified with the Greek god Kronos, also a very ancient and somewhat obscure agricultural figure who is the subject of a number of myths. One story tells that under the rule of Kronos (or Saturn), humans enjoyed a Golden Age in which people lived long and virtuous lives, there was no war and no need for laws; everyone lived together in harmony, enjoying the abundance of produce which the earth brought forth without human labor.

The Romans held an annual harvest festival honoring Saturn, which was called the *Saturnalia* and occurred around the 17th of December, at the time of the winter solstice. It lasted about a week and was a time of general unrestrained merrymaking. Since it was regarded as a return to the Golden Age under Saturn's rule, all people were equal. Even the slaves were allowed to celebrate and were waited on by their masters. All trials, executions, and wars were suspended during the Saturnalia.

When the date for the celebration of the birth of Christ was fixed in 336, it was made to correspond to the festival of Saturnalia so that it would replace rather than compete with the pagan feast.

Saturnalia referring to the Roman festival appeared in English in the late 16th century. In the 18th century, the word began to be used with a lowercase *s* to mean 'a period of unrestrained license or revelry'. The adjective **saturnalian** is first attested in English early in the 18th century.

The five planets known to the ancient world were named by the Romans in honor of the gods: Mercury, Venus, Mars, Jupiter, and Saturn. Saturn was the farthest from the sun and, because of its remoteness and slowness in motion, was believed by astrologers to have an unhappy effect on human affairs and to cause a gloomy and sluggish temperament in those born under its sign. Such people were called **saturnine,** which first meant simply 'born under the influence of Saturn' but came to mean 'gloomy'.

During the 1996 presidential election, Senator Bob Dole was frequently referred to in the press as **saturnine.** Several years later, a writer for the *Washington Post* mentioned President Clinton's "**saturnalian** appetites."

One other meaning of **saturnine** should be mentioned: in alchemy, *Saturn* is the technical name for 'lead' because the planet was thought to have leadlike properties. So **saturnine** can also mean 'suffering from lead poisoning' or 'caused by absorption of lead'. *Saturnism* is lead poisoning.

And then there's *Saturday,* the only day of the week that retained its Roman name in English following the invasions of the Angles and the Saxons. Latin *Sāturnī diē* became *Sœternesdœg.*

~*GSM*

say/says

PATRICK MORIARTY WROTE: A friend of mine recently asked me about the proper usage (or whether there is one) of **said** versus **says** when describing a conversation in the past. For example, I might say, "So I'm standing there and this guy said to me . . .," or I might say, ". . . and this guy says to me . . ." [. . .] And this also brings to mind that I've heard elderly people, my own grandmother included, say things like, "And so I says . . ." Is it a matter of grammar, convention, or preference?

You've really got two phenomena here. One is a storytelling device, used to make the action more immediate, that doesn't normally violate the agreement of subject and verb. In other words, the story will go something like this: "So she says, I don't believe you, deep-fry a turkey? and I say, see for yourself, they're doing it on TV, so she finally comes and looks and she still doesn't believe it, she thinks it's a joke."

In much the same way that my punctuation of the quoted story "violated" rules to give a better sense of the rhythm and flow of the storytelling, a storyteller "violates" the time element to heighten the drama of the story. It's not a question of proper grammar, but of storytelling license. The other phenomenon, however, is definitely grammatical, a legacy of the Scots tongue.

Because of your surname, I'm guessing you may have heard some stories from your grandmother, if she's anything like the Scots-Irish settlers of Appalachia and the Ozarks, or their ancestors in the lowland Scottish border country. In the early 17th century, James VI confiscated the lands of the

Celtic chiefs in Ulster (the area now known as Northern Ireland) and granted territory to Scottish lowlanders, many of them Presbyterian, who came to farm the land and (ironically) to find religious freedom. A great majority of the Scots-Irish who migrated to America came from Scotland via Ulster in this way.

These "Irish" of Scottish origin maintained both their penchant for storytelling and certain peculiarities of the language called Scots. In the present tense in Scots, if a personal pronoun is right next to the verb, it agrees in the way we'd expect it to: "They say he's owre auld" ('They say he's too old'). But move the pronoun away from the verb, and the -s ending is uniformly applied: "Thir laddies says he's owre auld" (quoted from *The Oxford Companion to the English Language*).

Now, according to that grammar, "I says to him" is still ungrammatical, but it's an easy step to make over generations of separation and diversification from the ancient dialect. Whether your grandmother is using "I says" only in storytelling or as a preferred form, she's reflecting a dialectal variant. It's now more regional than specifically ethnic; many Scots-Irish blended both linguistically and physically with the Pennsylvania Dutch after they were made unwelcome further north and thus greatly influenced the speech of the Ohio Valley area and beyond.

~WRN

scalawag (SKAL-a-wag)

ARYEH COHEN WADE WROTE: We're studying Reconstruction in school and are using the term **scalawag** to refer to Southern whites who participated in the Southern radical governments. What's the origin of this word?

Scalawag actually came into existence before the Civil War. It's definitely of American origin and first appeared in print in 1848. In *The American Language,* H. L. Mencken writes that "scalawag originated in western New York and at first meant 'a mean fellow, a scapegrace'." (A *scapegrace* is a 'complete rogue or rascal'.) **Scalawag** also meant a 'poor or worthless animal', usually a horse or a steer. The latter was sometimes called a *scalawag steer.* Here's an example of that last meaning in use from *Social Relations in our Southern States,* a book published in 1860: "He will tell you he wants no scallywags about him—no horses of unrecognized or uncertain pedigree." In its history, the word has been rendered as *scallywag, scallawag, scalliwag,* and *scallowag.* After the Civil War it was applied to the white Southerners who collaborated with the occupation, and since then it has been used to designate any lowdown politician.

The eighth edition of *A Dictionary of Slang and Unconventional English* has three or four speculations about the origin of **scalawag.** (No one knows for sure.) One that appeals to me is that it's a cognate of the Scottish *scurryvaig,* 'a vagabond', which itself may be derived from the Latin *scurra vagas,* 'a wandering buffoon'. *A Dictionary of Americanisms* suggests that it may derive from the word *scallag* used in Scotland for 'a servant, rustic'. But the 'animal of little value' meaning has led some lexicographers on a journey to Scotland—specifically to Scalloway, one of the Shetland Islands. The speculation is that Scalloway's so-called undersized and ill-fed horses (i.e., Shetland ponies) became synonymous with the island's name and that Scalloway eventually was transformed into **scalawag,** hence signifying those 'animals of little value'.

Back to Reconstruction. The Civil War Society's *Encyclopedia of the Civil War* says that **scalawag** was a term used "to describe Southern whites who joined the Republican Party after the Civil War." In doing so, they were considered traitors to many who remained loyal to the Confederate cause. Over 20 million Southerners joined. "All scalawags had one thing in common," says the *Encyclopedia.* "They felt they stood a better chance of achieving their goals by cooperating with a Republican administration than by joining the anti-Reconstruction camp." In Thomas McCorvey's 1868 *Alabama Historical Sketches,* I found this: "The scallawag is the foul leper of the community. Unlike the carpet-bagger he is native, which is so much the worse."

Today, **scalawag** has much less of a sting to it. It means 'scamp' or 'rascal' and is often applied affectionately.

~*RG*

scat

SARAH WRIGHT WROTE: A friend of mine with a rodent problem was told by the exterminator that the beasts' **scat** led him to believe her problem was bats. I assume **scat** is the root of *scatological.* Is it also related to the way Ella Fitzgerald used to sing? Any chance my friend's bats will treat her to a cooler version of "Blue Moon" à la the mice in *Babe?* And what are people really telling you when they tell you to **scat?**

What a useful skill that exterminator had! You would think that **scat,** in the sense 'animal excrement', would be related to *scatological/scatology,* borrowed from a Greek word meaning 'dung'. But some etymologists see this Greek word as an unlikely source of English **scat,** given the popular character of the word, its late (1920s) appearance in English, and the unusual derivational pattern. As an alternative derivation, Random House Webster's dictionaries cite the dialectal British verb **scat,** meaning 'to scatter, fling down, bespatter'.

And it would seem reasonable that **scat,** meaning 'to go away hastily', would be a shortened form of *scatter,* but not all etymologists agree. Alternatively, *The Oxford English Dictionary* mentions the 1830s phrase *quicker than s'cat,* meaning 'very fast', giving a clue as to the real origin of **scat.** It may be derived from what we say when we want a cat to vamoose—we make a hissing sound (written as *'ss*) followed by the word *cat.* Personally I think **scat** may be an alteration of *scoot,* as in this quote from *Uncle Remus:* "W'en ole man Rabbit say 'scoot', dey scooted, en w'en ole Miss Rabbit say 'scat', dey scatted."

None of which has anything to do with Ella Fitzgerald's *scat singing,* a vocal style that uses onomatopoeic and nonsense syllables instead of words, sometimes using the voice to imitate a musical instrument or instrumental phrasing. The word **scat** itself is probably of onomatopoeic origin, being one of the common nonsense syllables used in this vocal style.

Supposedly, Louis Armstrong invented *scat singing.* In 1926 he accidentally knocked the lyrics sheet off the music stand during a live recording session, forcing him to improvise. Though Armstrong was the first to popularize *scat singing,* especially in his recordings "Heebie Jeebies" and "West End Blues," it was around well before Armstrong, according to Jelly Roll Morton: "People believe Louis Armstrong originated scat. I must take that credit away from him, because I know better. Tony Jackson and myself were using scat for novelty back in 1906 and 1907 when Louis Armstrong was still in the orphan's home."

Scat syllables are actually transcribed on sheet music, written under the notes as lyrics would be—here's part of Fitzgerald's rendition of "Flying Home": rri-ti-u t'li t'la d'li bah!

~*CGB*

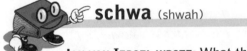

schwa (shwah)

JAN VAN IERSEL WROTE: What the heck is a **schwa??**

Ah, the **schwa**—the linguist's name for the most common sound in English and for its phonetic symbol ə. The sound is that slight "uh" that serves as the vowel in an unstressed syllable, like the *a* in "alone" and the *u* in "circus." It also occurs in other languages—as for the *e* in the second syllable of German *schlafen* 'to sleep'.

We make vowel sounds by using the lips and tongue to vary the shape of the mouth cavity as we speak. Although the role of the lips is easy to see [compare the rounded sound of (oh) with the unrounded (ee)], without training it's hard to perceive exactly what we're doing with our tongue. But if we say *yeah* and concentrate on what's happening, we can feel ourselves moving the tongue down as the word progresses, and with *you* we can feel ourselves pulling it back. This controlled movement of the tongue—higher, lower, frontwards, backwards in the mouth—allows us to make the variety of vowel sounds in human speech.

The **schwa** sound is more or less in the middle—the position to which the tongue tends to return in unstressed syllables, or when we're pausing to . . . uh . . . think of what to say next. The minimal activity required to produce it takes place in the *mid* portion of the vertical (high-low) axis of the mouth and in the *central* portion of the horizontal (front-back) axis, making it a "mid-central" vowel. The sound is *neutral* because the tongue is relaxed. So we can define the **schwa** technically as 'a mid-central, neutral vowel, typically occurring in unstressed syllables'.

The word **schwa** itself comes from the Hebrew *shewā*, the name for a diacritical mark representing either the absence of a vowel or a neutral, unstressed vowel in that language. (In English, too, unstressed vowels sometimes disappear entirely; see SYNCOPE AND ASSIMILATION.) In the International Phonetic Alphabet (IPA) and in modern dictionaries, however, the **schwa** is symbolized by ə, informally called an "upside-down *e*." It is better to think of it as a "turned *e*," however—rotated 180 degrees. I remember teaching students that it was neither a *6* nor a *9*.

When *The American College Dictionary* (forerunner of today's *Random House Webster's College Dictionary*) came out in 1947, it adopted the **schwa** from IPA, introducing it to the pronunciation systems of American lexicography. This was a daring innovation. I'm told that hundreds of letters came into Random House from upset dictionary buyers, threatening to return the dictionary because our *e*'s were upside-down! I guess it took a while for people to get used to the symbol, but it is now found in virtually all dictionaries that show pronunciations.

~EP

secesh (si-SESH)

ELAINE BECKER WROTE: I have come across the word **secesh** in literature on the Civil War in Kentucky. I gather that it is a term for *secessionist,* but I would like to know if it was used outside of Kentucky, or even outside of the Bluegrass region of Kentucky, and if it was just a derogatory term used by Union supporters.

Secesh is indeed a short form of *secessionist,* but it was actually used in a wider range of meanings, and across a range of regions—from states that eventually did secede, such as Arkansas and Virginia, to states that ultimately did not, such as Illinois and Ohio. It's hard to pinpoint the earliest use of the term; our first citations are from 1861, the same year in which the final states that seceded did so.

These earliest citations are for the adjective meaning of *secessionist* rather than the noun: "Miss Cuttle is . . . strongly 'Secesh.' " "All the 'secesh' women in the south." The fact that the term **secesh** is appearing in quotation marks shows that it was quite new. It does seem to be used almost exclusively by people who were pro-Union, but we do get "I was one of the original 'Secesh' " in *A Fool's Errand* (1879, by Albion Winegar Tourgée).

Interestingly, we have no citations for **secesh** being used in the singular to refer to one secessionist. Instead, we get the mouthful *secesher* (as if "secessionist" weren't hard enough to say three times fast): "The front yard of some secesher's deserted house" (1861); "Thick . . . as Seceshers down to Memphis" (1862). **Sesesh** is used as a plural noun: "Presently my dragoon cocked his carbine and exclaimed, 'There's Secesh in the woods' " (1863); "You are the boys who can whip all the G-d d-md Secesh in Arkansas" (1862; author's censorship, not mine).

We're not done with the parts of speech on this one. **Secesh** was also used as a verb: "Under no circumstances whatsomever will I secesh" (1862); "I woodent hev secesht" (1866). Its other noun role was as a short form of *secession:* "Secesh doesn't prevail . . . in this village" (1863); "Secesh is played out" (1892).

That last citation is the latest one we have, and nearly all of our citations cluster around the years 1861–63. This would indicate that **secesh** was obsolescent as a slang term not very long after the end of the Civil War, and obsolete by the turn of the 20th century. It's now regarded as historical slang, used only by history teachers, historical novel writers, and perhaps the odd elderly Yankee with a long memory.

~*WRN*

shebang

BOB BEATTIE WROTE: I've used **shebang** as in "that's the whole shebang" for years. What does it mean?

Shebang has only been around for a hundred and fifty years or so, but it has been through three huge changes in meaning that leave us wondering whether the various **shebangs** are related at all.

The **shebang** that you are asking about, the one that means 'everything', is probably most closely related to the old **shebang,** which referred to some kind of dwelling. Walt Whitman wrote about Civil War soldiers' bush **shebangs** in 1862. In the years following the Civil War, **shebang** went with the flow of post-war semantic drift, describing fewer barracks and more civilian structures.

How is this **shebang** related to the one that means 'everything'? Well, in many early citations, military officers are left "running the shebang," as in S. C. Wilson's *Column South* (1864). It isn't clear whether this **shebang** is a military camp or just means 'the whole thing', so the derivation of 'everything' **shebang** from 'dwelling' **shebang** is possible.

The spoiler for this line of reasoning is Mark Twain's 1869 letter to his publishers in which he says that he believes "the chebang will be a success." Spelling differences aside, this citation date is very close to the date of the first written citation (1862) for **shebang** meaning 'dwelling'. The dates are close enough to raise a doubt, but this connection is not nearly as shaky as some others in **shebang**'s history, so I'll let it slide for now and pursue **shebang** one generation further to the question that has etymologists scratching their heads: What is the origin of the 'dwelling' **shebang?**

One guess is that it comes from French *char-à-banc,* a word that referred to horse-drawn carriages with bench seats. This etymology is logical for another meaning of **shebang,** 'a vehicle', as in Mark Twain's *Roughing It:* "This shebang's chartered, and we can't let you pay a cent" (1871). The connection between a horse-drawn carriage and a shelter is either the whitewater-rapids version of semantic drift, or just plain wrong.

The alternative brings us to another **shebang,** the one that refers to a saloon or tavern, as in W. Wright's *Big Bonanza* (1876): "I was told down the street . . . that there was a . . . row in one of the shebangs up this way." This **shebang** appears to be a variant of the Anglo-Irish *shebeen,* referring to a place where liquor is sold illegally. It probably comes from the Irish *séibín* meaning 'small mug' or 'bad ale'.

We could hook up the 'shack or shelter' **shebang** with the 'illegal bar' **shebang** and they would make a perfect couple if only the date of the 'shanty-shelter' **shebang** didn't precede the date of the 'liquor-house' **shebang.**

So, **shebang** 'the whole' has three possible sources: **shebang** 'the tavern', **shebang** 'the shack', and **shebang** 'the carriage'. With reasons to doubt all three of these etymologies, and suspicious gulfs of time and meaning to cross, *the whole shebang* falls short of telling the whole story.

⁓HGB

showstopper

F. Dodge wrote: In engineering use, a **showstopper** is an aspect of a project that is so bad it threatens to cancel the project unless it is corrected. However, isn't **showstopper** also a term used to indicate that part of a show is so good that the audience literally stops the show by clapping? If so, how did this phrase come to mean the opposite in engineering?

The reason for this divergence of meaning is that there are two logical ways of interpreting the word **showstopper.** A person or thing can literally or figuratively "stop the show" in a negative or positive way.

Showstopper is first recorded in the context of a vaudeville show: "The first half [of the program] held two show stoppers in the Dixie Four . . . who stops the show . . . with their 'itch' dance finish" (*Variety,* 1926). So the earliest meaning was 'a performer or performance that wins enthusiastic applause'. A closely related meaning is 'a spectacularly arresting or appealing person or thing'. For example, the term **showstopper** was used to refer to an actress at the Academy Awards—evidently, she "stopped the show" even though she wasn't performing: "[Annette Bening] was nine months pregnant, and her radiant face and cap of curly hair were showstoppers above a soft and feminine black gown" (*Houston Chronicle,* 2001). Other examples of **showstoppers** capable of attracting lots of attention: a flashy new sports car or a chef's pièce de résistance.

About 25 years ago, the term **showstopper** was co-opted by engineers to refer to 'something about a product or project that presents an insurmountable obstacle'. The problem is usually a serious engineering defect but could also be a restrictive government regulation or high development costs.

As a recent development from this negative use in engineering, the term **showstopper** is often used in computer contexts. It refers to 'a serious hardware or software bug that must be fixed'. In his book, *Showstopper! The Breakneck Race to Create Windows NT and the Next Generation at Microsoft,* G. Pascal Zachary tells of a software bug that plagued the Windows NT operating system up until a week before its scheduled release. Microsoft programmers rewrote the offending lines of code at the last minute, and the project became a huge success.

The technical (negative) sense of **showstopper** has led to its use in any context that presents an insurmountable obstacle: "'We can't seem to get that accomplished with existing staff', she said. That has been the real showstopper'" (*Dallas Morning News*, 2001).

~*CGB*

sixes and sevens

MARK ROBBINS WROTE: I would very much like to find out the origin and meanings of the British expression **at sixes and sevens,** as in "His unexpected message left her feeling all at sixes and sevens." Its contextual meaning . . . implies a feeling of confusion and uncertainty, discomfiture, perplexity, being disconcerted. . . . But what in the world do the *sixes* and *sevens* refer to? And how and when did this phrase enter into currency?

You've got the meaning right, though I'd like to add one: if two people or groups are **at sixes and sevens,** they are 'in disagreement or dispute'. The expression is more common in Britain than it is in the United States. Although it goes back to Chaucer, it is still very much alive in the United Kingdom, as evidenced by the following headlines: "Phone Codes at Sixes and Sevens"; "Church of England at Sixes and Sevens over Child Communion"; and from Hong Kong in 1997: "Our Future Will Still Be at Sixes and Sevens."

There are two proposed origins for the phrase for which no evidence exists. One has to do with the position of the medieval guilds in the Lord Mayor's parade. The other finds a derivation in Job 5:19, "He shall deliver thee in six troubles; yea, in seven shall no evil touch thee."

The clearest evidence points to the origin of **sixes and sevens** in a complicated medieval dice game called "hazard." The two highest numbers on a die are five and six, and the original expression was probably "to set on cinque and sice" (from the French numerals). Anyone who tried for these numbers was regarded as taking a tremendous risk (with the possibility of "hazarding" his whole fortune). By Chaucer's time there was a play on these words, and "five and six" became "six and seven," an impossible throw of the dice. To *set all at six and seven* or to *set the world on six and seven* meant 'to risk everything': "Lat nat this wrecched wo thyn herte gnaw, But manly sette the world on six and sevene" (Don't let this wretched woe gnaw at your heart, but be a man and risk it all) (Chaucer, *Troilus and Criseyde,* c1425).

Risking one's whole fortune on a throw of the dice involves an element of carelessness about the consequences of one's actions, and by the 16th century, **six and seven** began to take on the sense of disorder or confusion. By the 18th century, the plural forms had become standard, and Grose's *Dictionary of the Vulgar Tongue* gives the following definition for *left at sixes and sevens:* 'in confusion, commonly said of a room where the furniture, etc. is scattered about, or of a business left unsettled'.

As evidence that the phrase is alive and well, see the following lines from "Don't Cry for Me, Argentina":

You won't believe me
All you will see is a girl you once knew
Although she's dressed up to the nines
At sixes and sevens with you.

~GSM

skank and skanky

ROB RICHARDSON WROTE: I've come across **skanky** several times recently, usually in jokes told by or about rednecks. I checked your unabridged dictionary on CD-ROM (I don't have the dead-tree version), and all it lists is **skank,** referring to a way of dancing. What does the adjectival form mean? I infer it is somewhat the opposite of *swanky*.

Yes, come to think of it, **skanky** is somewhat the opposite of *swanky*, though its origin is not in any way connected with that word. The adjective **skanky** probably originated in Black English in the senses 'nasty, repellent, ugly, malodorous', and it also meant 'sluttish, disreputable, immoral', almost always referring to a woman. The corresponding noun **skank** referred to 'a female prostitute or low-life'. Those senses of the adjective and noun have been in use since the early 1970s. One source derives **skank** from the words *skunk* or *stank,* but other sources say it is of unknown derivation.

In the 1980s, **skanky** was associated with Valley Girl slang, especially in the sense 'dirty, repulsive, disgusting', and it is still used in this way. There are many equivalent terms—*gross, scuzzy, groady* come to mind. **Skanky** can describe stringy hair, sleazy clothing, or even immoral acts: ". . . saying yes to [Bill] Clinton also appears to be their way of just saying no to Monicagate, meaning no to the very idea of making intimate personal behavior, even skanky behavior, the subject of a criminal inquiry" (*Time,* 1998).

The noun **skank,** originally referring to a female prostitute, now refers to a male prostitute or pimp, or anyone connected with that industry. By extension, it refers to any immoral or sleazy person.

It seems that both **skank** and **skanky** have evolved from a specific reference to an ugly or malodorous woman, especially a female prostitute, to their current use as general-purpose insults to males as well as females. I have seen references to "skanky Calvin Klein models" and "skanky lawyers."

The related verb **skank** has been used since the 1970s in the sense 'to dance with violent, jerky movements, usually to reggae music'. *The Oxford English Dictionary* describes the movements in more detail: rhythmically bending forward, raising the knees, and clawing the air with the hands in time to the music. The verbal noun *skanking* refers to this style of dancing, which probably originated in Jamaica.

$\sim$*CGB*

skedaddle

BOB BEATTIE WROTE: I've used **skidaddle** to mean 'to hurry along' as in "I've got to skidaddle" for years. Can you tell me about it?

As you might imagine, **skedaddle** has an elusive origin. Some people think it is of Swedish or Danish origin and may have been introduced into English by immigrant populations in England, but there don't seem to be any cognate forms in these languages. I'm more convinced by arguments that **skedaddle** comes from the Irish word *sgedadol*, meaning 'scattered'. It is also possible that the word entered English through a Scottish dialectal variant.

From around the time of the American Civil War, there are some citations that can finally be pinned down. **Skedaddle** seems to have been U.S. military slang for a hasty flight from battle. The term gained currency during the war years: "No sooner did the traitors discover their approach than they 'skiddaddled' (a phrase the Union boys up here apply to the good use the seceshers make of their legs in time of danger)."

In fact, the Canadian term **skedaddler** referred to 'an American that fled to Canada rather than fight in the Civil War'.

Today, as you mentioned, a **skedaddler** is anyone who hurries anywhere. There is no shadow of cowardice hanging over the modern word, so feel free to **skedaddle** away.

$\sim$*HGB*

skinny

MIKE JAMES WROTE: I was telling a coworker something lately, and when he was called away, he said he'd **get the skinny** from me later. I've heard this expression before but not very often. Where does it come from?

You're not the only one who's asked us to *get the skinny* on **skinny,** in the slang sense 'accurate information; confidential news or gossip'. But the evidence as to where this sense comes from is very thin. Some sources suggest it's from the notion of getting down to the bare skin, the bare and undisguised facts, or, as we say, the "naked truth." But the noun may be completely unrelated to the adjective in the meanings 'of or like skin' (16th century) and 'very lean, thin' (17th century). Other slang uses of the noun are definitely unrelated: for example, a late 1800s sense 'physics and chemistry'; an early-20th-century sense '10-cent piece'; and a current Australian sense 'a girl or young woman'.

The slang sense you ask about is first recorded in 1938: "... the straight skinny on what's going on ..." (John Geary). After that early quote, the written evidence is spotty until the 1950s. An article appearing in 1980 in the journal *American Speech* gives this cite from 1956: "The skinny was always: You married specifically against death" (R.V. Cassill). Cassill goes on to say: "I first heard [skinny] persistently and widely used by nearly everyone in the Army and Navy in World War II." The earliest cite in *The Oxford English Dictionary* is from a 1959 article in the same journal: " 'What's the skinny?' means 'What's up?' "

So the evidence shows that this particular slang meaning probably originated in the military, as a large percentage of slang does, but it was not widely known and used until the 1960s and 1970s. However, it's a slang term with proven staying power and currency: "He killed two people there while they slept—that was the skinny of it" (*New York Magazine,* 1994).

$\sim$*CGB*

slang

C. C. Goodman wrote: What is the origin of the word **slang?** When I look in the dictionary to find out, I come to a dead end.

The term **slang** is like old money. If you go back far enough, you'll uncover its disreputable past. When the word first appeared in print over 250 years ago in England, it was associated with bad company indeed. **Slang** was applied to the special vocabulary of "low, illiterate, or disreputable persons," as *A Dictionary of Slang and Unconventional English* puts it. It was the cant of the underworld. That's clear in this quote from Henry Fielding's 1743 novel, *The Life of Mr. Jonathan Wild the Great:* "The master who teaches them [young thieves] should be a man well versed in the cant language, commonly called the slang patter." Think of *The Beggar's Opera* (1728) or William Hogarth's *A Rake's Progress* (1735). It was the age of gin alley, and the word **slang** was ready to burst into print.

The first substantial effort at recording English slang was Francis Grose's *A Classical Dictionary of the Vulgar Tongue* published in 1785. It's a delightful book, and though it's out of print, it was reissued as recently as 1963, so you can look for it in the library. In it, you'll find *corporation* meaning 'a large belly', *nutmegs* meaning 'testicles', and words like *pig-headed* and *pimp* whose meanings haven't changed to this day. The term **slang** was still being used to denote underworld speech eighty years later, as attested in this passage from Sir Walter Scott's novel *Redgauntlet:* "What did actually reach his ears was disguised . . . completely by the use of cant words, and the thieves-Latin called slang."

By 1800, however, **slang** was already beginning to move in better circles. The word was being used to refer to the specialized language of legitimate professions. Today, most of us are familiar with at least a few **slang** words or expressions used by people in various professions. We've learned that *whiskey* means 'rye bread' in the local diner. Or that a *gob* is a 'sailor'. And so on.

You'd hope that someone somewhere would have an idea where the word **slang** came from. No. **Slang** has that infamous label "orig. uncert." affixed to it, which, in layman's terms, means, "You tell me." But, as is always the case in these situations, there is no lack of speculation. **Slang,** some experts say, might have come from the Norwegian word *sleng* 'fling, toss' (as in insult?). A closely related Norwegian word, *slengenavn,* means 'nickname', which seems to fit nicely. But it appears the dates for this particular etymological conga line are wrong for that theory. So, it's probably going to stay "orig. uncert."

~*RG*

sleep tight

MELANIE CHALMERS WROTE: I put my sweet three-year-old daughter to bed tonight and told her to **sleep tight.** She said, "What does that mean? Are my covers supposed to be tight?" I told her that I don't know! Can you help me?

Some years ago, a guide at one of the historic houses in Westchester County told us that **sleep tight** referred to the ropes that were laced across the frames of early beds to serve as springs under the straw mattresses: the ropes had to be tightened periodically because the beds were more comfortable when the ropes were tight than when they were sagging.

This is the explanation that I've found at a number of sites on the Internet. One site says this explanation is "common knowledge among historians." Someone suggested that the phrase might have originated in the Navy because hammocks are also more comfortable if the ropes are pulled tight to reduce the amount of sag. I don't doubt that the ropes under the straw mattresses needed to be kept tight, but I haven't found any absolutely firm evidence for that origin of the expression **sleep tight,** which isn't attested until the 19th century.

There is one other possibility. *The Oxford English Dictionary* gives 'soundly, roundly' as a meaning for *tight* in the late 1700s. The adverb *tightly* was used in the late 16th century to mean 'soundly, properly' or 'well': "Hold Sirha, beare you these letters tightly" (Shakespeare, *The Merry Wives of Windsor,* 1598). Here's a quotation from 1898: "She had been so tight asleep" (Mary Annette von Arnim, *Elizabeth and Her German Garden*).

And then there's the unnamed nursery rhyme, which seems to support the 'soundly' meaning of *tight.* I haven't been able to find a date for it, but the final two lines have a distinctly Victorian flavor:

Good night, sleep tight,
Wake up bright
In the morning light

To do what's right
With all your might.

Most people are probably more familiar with the other version, which apparently originated in the United States in the 19th century: "Good night, sleep tight. Don't let the bed bugs bite."

~*GSM*

snarky

BECKY BALDWIN WROTE: I have recently seen the word **snarky** in the *New York Times* and in a cartoon in the *New Yorker*. What does it mean? Does it come from Lewis Carroll's "The Hunting of the Snark"?

"The Hunting of the Snark" (1876) is a nonsense poem about the quest to find an imaginary creature called a *snark*. The creature's name was coined by Lewis Carroll. Since they go on a sea voyage, Carroll may have intended a blend of *snake* and *shark,* though the poem gives no description of how the creature looks. The *snark* proves elusive, but the Baker does find a nasty *boojum,* a variety of the snark.

The poem has nothing to do with the word **snarky,** which means 'sharply critical'. More precisely, **snarky** means critical in an annoying, sarcastic, grumpy, wisecracking, or cynical sort of way. Maybe you're referring to the recent headline in the *New York Times:* "The Stars of Reality TV Are Snarky, Whiny, and Loud. But They Look Fabulous." The comedian David Spade has been called **snarky,** and so has talk-show host David Letterman. The young star of the TV show *Mal-*

colm in the Middle is very **snarky.** And a cantankerous CUR-MUDGEON is **snarky** by definition.

The following analysis of words beginning with *sn-* is from the *Guardian* (London): "And few groups of words are as useful for verbal snipers, those who sneer, snap, and snarl, who resort to the snide, sniffy, snarky, snooty, and snotty, as those which begin with an *s* and an *n.* That is not to say that all belong exclusively to the world of vituperation. Snug and snuggle are cosy agreeable concepts."

The adjective **snarky** is first recorded in 1906. It's from dialectal British *snark,* meaning 'to nag, find fault with', which is probably the same word as *snark/snork,* meaning 'to snort, snore'. (The likely connection is the derisive snorting sound of someone who is always finding fault.) Most dictionaries label **snarky** as "Chiefly British Slang." But for the last five or more years, it has become increasingly common in American publications, maybe ones infiltrated by British or Canadian writers and journalists.

$\sim$*CGB*

spam

ED WALCH JR. WROTE: How did junk e-mail or unwanted e-mail get to be called **spam** or spamming?

Spam—the electronic plague of the Internet Generation! No wonder so many of you have written to ask this question.

The term in this sense goes back, of course, to the canned meat product (itself probably a blend of "s[houlder of] p[ork and h]am" or of "sp[iced h]am"), but there is fairly general consensus that it was derived more directly from a classic, wonderfully absurd Monty Python sketch in which canned Spam was, to put it mildly, ubiquitous.

The sketch takes place in a cafe, where all the customers are dressed as Vikings. A waitress, when asked by two Viking customers, a Mr. and Mrs. Bun, what food is available, announces a long list of items that includes "SPAM, egg, SPAM, SPAM, bacon, and SPAM"; other absolutely endless Spam combinations; and—eventually—"lobster thermidor aux crevettes, with a mornay sauce, garnished with truffle paté, brandy, and a fried egg on top and SPAM." Nothing on the menu is Spam-free.

After protestations from the wife, the other Vikings start to sing "SPAM, SPAM, SPAM, SPAM, SPAM, wonderful SPAM, lovely SPAM," etc. They are screamed at and told to "shut up," but continue singing, with only brief interruptions—apparently unstoppable. No one can order food or have even a banal conversation.

The New Hacker's Dictionary (1991) defines **spam** as a verb, meaning 'to crash a program by overrunning a fixed-size buffer with excessively large input data'. Definitions for **spam** have expanded; as a noun, it means 'any unsolicited, widely distributed e-mail or newsgroup posting'. Typically, **spam** contains an advertising pitch, a get-rich-quick scheme, or an invitation to a porn site. Its verb senses now include 'to send such material', whether or not it crashes hardware or software.

The computer pioneers (*hackers* in the good sense) who borrowed the term for these meanings were inordinately fond of Monty Python and apparently sensed humorous analogies between the scene in the cafe (annoying, persistent singing, interruptions to any meaningful conversation, the sense of being overwhelmed by Spam) and the scene at one's computer (annoying, persistent influx of junk, interruptions to any meaningful work, the sense of being overwhelmed by **spam**).

A competing theory, outlined in *Random House Webster's Computer & Internet Dictionary,* proposes that **spam** may have come directly from Spam, so called by the computer group lab at the University of Southern California because it shares certain characteristics with the lunchmeat: Nobody wants it or ever asks for it; it is the first item to be pushed to the side; sometimes it is actually tasty or useful.

Both of these theories are amusing, but for the most part, **spam** itself is no laughing matter. There are high costs to all of us—in money, time, and aggravation.

$\sim$*EP*

spitting image

CHERYL SHARP WROTE: I have always heard this term used in reference to someone who bears a close resemblance to someone else. What is the derivation? And is it **spitting image** or **spit and image?**

Spitting image, meaning 'exact likeness; counterpart', has been around in one form or another for about a century. It first appeared as *spit and image,* but other early spellings include *spitten image, spit 'n' image,* and *spittin' image.* These are now rarely seen.

The shift to **spitting image** is the result of phonetic reconstruction (early dictionaries called it "corruption"). *Spit and,* said in rapid continuous speech, is pronounced (SPIT-n), to rhyme with *kitten. Spitting,* informally *spittin',* is often said in exactly that way. Interpreting (SPIT-n) as *spitting* instead of *spit and* was an understandable development. **Spitting image,** once considered a mistake, is increasingly the term of choice, although *spit and image* is still in use.

The *spit* in this term is the one that means 'saliva', not the one that holds your suckling pig over the fire. It derives from the Old English verb *spittan* through Middle English *spitten.* But how did "spit" come to be associated with the idea of 'likeness'? DNA tests were far in the future.

The verb *spit* has been attested in statements about familial similarity since the 17th century. C. Nesse, in 1690, wrote, "We are of our father . . . as like him as if spit out of his mouth." From this verb a noun sense emerged, and *spit* came to mean 'exact image'. We find examples from the 1820s like: "She's the very spit of her," or "He's the dead spit of the old man."

"But," you ask, "doesn't that make *spit and image* redundant? Who would want to say 'he's the image and image of his father'?" Bergen and Cornelia Evans, in their 1957 *A Dictionary of Contemporary American Usage,* mention an alternative theory that posits a slurred pronunciation of *spirit and image* as a source of the term. This not only avoids semantic repetition but suggests a resemblance in both inner selves and outer appearance. Pretty as that theory is, the Evanses and most other historians of the language reject it.

Besides, redundancy has long been a feature of English. James E. Clapp, in his *Random House Webster's Dictionary of the Law,* says at the entry for *to have and to hold:*

The English language often places a higher value on rhythm, rhyme, and alliteration than on concision ... redundant expressions, like *nooks and crannies, each and every, hale and hearty, part and parcel, safe and sound,* are part of everyday speech, and the language would be poorer without the music they provide.

I couldn't have said it better.

~*EP*

squash

LAYJER WROTE: I was cooking a stuffed acorn **squash** for my wife for dinner when we got into a discussion about the origin of the word **squash.** It started out with me asking her whether the vegetable was named after the verb, or vice-versa. So, was it: "The inside of that vegetable is all squashed?" Or: "That thing you stepped on looks like the inside of a squash? He, he, you SQUASHED it!"

This is one of those cases in which two words, though they sound exactly the same and are spelled exactly the same, have totally different origins. (These are called *homonyms*.) The verb **squash** is completely European in origin, whereas the **squash** that you were so kindly preparing for your wife is distinctly American—Native American, in fact. (Hold on, though. There is a bit of a curiosity here. I'll get to that later.) The verb, as we all know, means 'to crush or beat into a pulp'. It first appeared in print in England in 1565 in Thomas Staple-ton's translation of Bede's *History of the Church in England:*

"Yea must, I saye, teare them, rent them, and squashe them to peeces."

Squash comes from the Middle French word *esquasser,* which in turn is from a likely form **exquassāre* in Vulgar Latin. It's probably onomatopoeic in origin. The **squash** that we eat, on the other hand, is a Native American word, like *succotash.* Both words are from the Narragansett language, which is part of the Algonquian group. (Notice the *-ash* suffix they share.) **Squash** is from *askūtasquash,* which literally means 'the green things that may be eaten raw'. Its first appearance in print in America was in Roger Williams's *A Key into the Language of America,* printed in 1643: "Askutasquash, their Vine apples, which the English from them call Squashes, about the bignesse of Apples, of several colours, sweet, light, wholesome, refreshing."

Here's the curiosity: the **squash** meaning 'to crush' had a noun form once that is now obsolete. It meant 'the unripe pod of a pea'. *The Oxford English Dictionary* says it "was also applied contemptuously to persons." Shakespeare uses the noun **squash** three times. (He does not use the verb.) In *Twelfth Night,* Malvolio says, "Not yet old enough for a man, nor young enough for / A boy; as a squash is before 'tis a peascod." Leontes, in *A Winter's Tale,* says, of his son, "How like, methought, I was then to this kernel, / This squash, this gentlemen."

So, do we have a connection, even a tenuous one, between the American gourd and the English vegetable? Most likely, says Dr. Ives Goddard, curator and head of the Division of Ethnology, Department of Anthropology, Smithsonian Institution. Dr. Goddard is one the leading authorities on Native American Languages. "I think there was convergence," Dr.

Goddard said, "in that the Southern New England word [*askūtasquash*] was not shortened randomly but ended up homophonous with an existing word."

Something like this just makes my day.

~RG

squaw

KENNETH J. DORAN WROTE: This one has a particularly strong political edge, but lexicographical duty calls: **squaw.** Many Native Americans consider it so pejorative that they have campaigned, sometimes successfully, to have it classified on a par with the legendary *N*-word and prohibited in place names. Others, including some other Native Americans, contend it is an entirely benign Algonquian/Narragansett word for 'woman', documented in translation since 1643 and still in use. Your verdict please, with public policy recommendations.

To answer what has indeed become a politically charged question, I laid **squaw** on the doorstep of Dr. Ives Goddard, curator and head of the Division of Ethnology, Department of Anthropology, Smithsonian Institution. He is also linguistic editor of the *Handbook of North American Indians.* Dr. Goddard is rightly considered the leading expert in this area. His response is worth quoting in full:

"Squaw was borrowed into English in the Plymouth and Massachusetts Bay colonies in the 1620s and 1630s from the local Indian language, called Massachusett (no -s), where it meant 'younger woman'. It came through the local pidgin, in which it was the general word for 'woman, female'; it is first attested in the pidgin expression 'Squa Sachim', glossed 'Massachusetts Queene', i.e., Indian queen Mourt's *Relation*, 1622; from Plymouth."

Dr. Goddard goes on to speak of the contention by some Native Americans—and by others as well—that **squaw** means 'vagina'. This, of course, would be considered highly insulting. But is it true?

"The false claim that squaw means 'vagina' has been repeated endlessly, even after the facts became easily known, most recently in connection with the decision by the State of Maine to follow other states to expunge squaw from place names. I have no doubt that some speakers of Mohawk sincerely believe that it is from their word *ojískwa* 'vagina' (though I know that other Mohawks laugh at the whole idea), but the resemblance (if there is one) is entirely accidental. 'Vagina' was not a meaning that was ever known to the original users of the word, and although it appears in a college anthology published in 1973, it was not widely known before Suzan Harjo's appearance on the Oprah Winfrey show in 1992.

"I have always been careful to point out that the word is generally considered disparaging (as dictionaries rightly say), though it is still widely used in compounds like *squawbread*."

Indeed, *Random House Webster's College Dictionary* corroborates this in its usage note for **squaw,** saying the word is "insulting to Native Americans." Further, *The Thesaurus of Slang* (Lewin, 1997) has **squaw** as one of the synonyms for 'prostitute'.

Dr. Goddard's reference to Maine's action to expunge **squaw** from place names is correct. Any river, lake, mountain, etc., in Maine with the word **squaw** in it will now have to be replaced with a name without it. It would appear clear that **squaw** may be historically innocent, as Dr. Goddard puts it, but it's politically incorrect—if not worse.

~RG

star

ROBERT PATRICK WROTE: When and where was the word **star** first used for a charismatic performer?

Today we are familiar with the use of **star** to refer to celebrities because of the legacy of the Hollywood *star system.* However, the metaphorical use of **star** to refer to a performer who shines more brightly than the rest dates from the 18th century: "The little stars, who hid their diminished rays in his [Garrick's] presence, begin to abuse him" (Warner, *Selwyn & Contemporaries*, 1779). By the middle of the 19th century, theater owners had something in common with modern studio executives: "Our theater was . . . commodious; but the manager could not draw audiences without stars" (Knight, *Passages of a Working Life during Half a Century*, 1864).

Early in cinema history, there were no **stars;** the actors were not even credited by name. All of that changed in 1910 when Vitagraph Company introduced and promoted the Vitagraph Girl, Florence Lawrence. By 1920, Hollywood was dominated by the *star system.* Studios would discover young **stars** and *starlets,* sign them, and cultivate an image through heavy publicity and script development. Most film historians name Charlie Chaplin (and his "Little Tramp" persona) as Hollywood's first **star.** Throughout the Golden Era (1930–50), the *star system* dominated the silver screen. But in the 1950s, a series of antitrust suits broke the power of the large studios, freed actors from restrictive contracts, and ended the Hollywood *star system.*

Of course, that was not the end of the Hollywood **star.** Actors, agents, and screenwriters still understood the appeal of *stardust.* So even today, personas are guarded, formulas are adhered to, and **stars** are born.

~HGB

story

DAVID MAXWELL WROTE: I was thinking about tall buildings the other night and came to wonder how the word **stories** came to denote 'floors of a building'. Can you shed any light on this?

I always had assumed that the two distinct meanings of **story** (or *storey* as the British spell the word meaning 'floor of a building') must have derived from separate roots. Not so.

The view that the architectural sense of **story** comes from Old French *estorer* 'to build, furnish' is generally discounted because the evidence points in a different direction.

Story in the sense of 'a narrative' appeared around 1200. It came into English through Old French from Latin *historia* 'account, tale, story'. The ultimate origin is Greek *historía* 'learning or knowing by inquiry' from the verb *historein* 'to inquire' and the noun *histor* 'a wise man or judge'. English **story**

originally meant 'a historical narrative', but by the 16th century, *history* came to be used for a factual narrative of past events, and **story** meant 'a fictitious tale': "Sum singis, sum dancis, sum tellis storeis"—Some sing, some dance, some tell stories (Dunbar, *Poems,* 1500–20).

So that's all very straightforward, etymologically speaking. But take a look at this quotation from Robert of Gloucester's *Chronicle* in 1400: "Hii begonne her heye tounes strengthy vaste aboute, Her castles & storys. . . ." The reference is to fortifying towns and adding **stories,** or upper levels to castle towers.

Records from the 13th and 14th centuries indicate that the Anglo-Latin word *historia* had the meaning of 'a picture' or 'a tier of painted windows or of sculptures'. A 12th-century abbot completed "unam istoriam" in the main tower on the abbey's west side. In a 1398 history there is mention of "una historia octo fenestrarum" (one historia of eight windows). Think of a medieval cathedral with rows of stained glass windows all telling **stories** from the Bible.

By the 15th century, the English word **story** had acquired from the Anglo-Latin *historia* the sense of 'each of a number of tiers or rows of columns, windows, etc., placed horizontally above each other'. Various parish records from the 16th century tell of payments made to workmen for jobs like "making a foot of glass in the upper story of the middle aisle" or "trimming four stories of old iron."

Although the Romance languages use derivatives of Latin *historia* to mean 'history' or 'story', the development of the sense to 'something that tells a story' and then to 'the location of something that tells a story' is peculiar to Anglo-Latin and therefore to English. Why? Who? Another fascinating little etymological mystery.

~GSM

syncope and assimilation

TIMOTHY Q. NOHE WROTE: *Federal, general, veteran* — these . . . are like fingernails on a chalk board when I hear them pronounced as two-syllable words. Isn't it obvious that they are three syllables each? And while we're at it, how about *vegetable* (four syllables and no "ch" in sight)? Why do so many people who speak so well otherwise seem to get so lazy when they say these words?

Let's start with the mysterious (ch) that crops up in *vegetable*. It results from **assimilation**—the tendency of a sound to become more like a neighboring sound. For those who say (VEJ-tuh-bul), the sound of (j) is likely to be influenced by the immediately following (t). Whereas (j) is normally "voiced" (pronounced with vibration of the vocal cords), (t) is a "voiceless" sound. In this case, the (j) loses its voice, so to speak, becoming the devoiced (ch). The same kind of anticipatory **assimilation** is often heard in *congratulate,* resulting in an opposite effect this time; the standard (ch) becomes voiced to conform to the following *u,* and we get (kun-GRAJ-uh-late).

As for that reduction in number of syllables, there are people out there who agree with you, and some of them wield a certain authority. Charles Harrington Elster, in his *The Big Book of Beastly Mispronunciations* (aptly subtitled "The Complete Opinionated Guide for the Careful Speaker"), says about *temperature,* another word for which the number of syllables varies, that it is "Properly, TEM-pur-uh-chur. Now often TEM-pruh-chur (acceptable) or TEM-pur-chur (beastly) or TEM-puh-chur (very beastly)." You can practically see him shudder at the final two, but the first of the three-syllable pronunciations is one that he finds good enough.

On the other hand, where pronunciation is concerned, one person's "lazy" is another person's "normal and relaxed," and one person's "careful" is another person's "stuffy." Even Elster acknowledges that what we have here exemplifies a very common phenomenon in the continuing evolution of spoken English. He explains that

> *Temperature* has become a victim of *syncope* . . . , the loss or omission of sounds or letters from the middle of a word. This natural and often ineluctable process affects numerous English words. For example, long before any of us were born syncope had . . . pruned *interesting, vegetable, several, diaper,* and *vacuum* to IN-tris-ting, VEJ-tuh-bul, SEV-rul, DY-pur, and VAK-yoom; and mostly since the mid-20th century it has been hewing the middle vowel sounds from *family, grocery, chocolate,* and *conference,* leaving FAM-lee, GROHS-ree, CHAWK-lit (or CHAHK-lit), and KAHN-frints.

The major dictionaries are all over the place, showing the full number of syllables only; showing it first or second; giving the reduced number first; or . . . you get the idea. Those who pay attention to such matters tend to think that their own choices are correct and all other speakers are either sloppy or old-fashioned. As for me, I still order a three-syllable *omelet* in coffee shops, although I know in my heart that (AHM-lit) is what most people say.

~*EP*

synesthesia (sinn-us-THEE-zhuh)

AIMEE HAIRE WROTE: There is a word for the confusion of your senses that occurs when you take a drink of what you believe to be iced tea and it is actually cola. I know this word, but I have forgotten it.

I'm not sure there's a word for the kind of disjunction you describe between an expected taste sensation and the one you actually experience, but could the word hovering at the edge of your brain be **synesthesia?** It certainly fits "confusion of your senses." *Syn-* comes from the Greek for 'with; together'. *Esthesia* or *esthesis,* also from Greek, is 'perception; sensation; feeling'. So **synesthesia** involves commingling our five senses. The term has drifted from psychology into other contexts ranging from linguistics to art, but its primary meaning is the psychological one, regarding confused perceptions. According to Dr. Richard E. Cytowic, a neurologist, psychologist, and the guru of **synesthesia,** the word "denotes the rare capacity to hear colors, taste shapes, or experience other equally startling sensory blendings whose quality seems difficult for most of us to imagine."

Unlike the incident you described with tea and cola, which seemed to be a momentary confusion, the true synesthete's propensity for "seeing" a sound as a particular color or "feeling" a color as a particular texture is stable over the person's lifetime; the same perceptual associations remain from childhood through adulthood. In addition, this rare kind of perception runs in families, the most well-known of which is the Nabokovs. The Russian novelist, Vladimir Nabokov, described in his memoir *Speak, Memory* how he perceived the sounds of language as distinct colors. The long *a* in English had the tint of weathered wood; while a French *a* was the color of polished ebony. The sounds of *x* were steel blue, and *s* was "a curious mixture of azure and mother-of-pearl" (1966).

This phenomenon is not considered pathological in the world of psychology. There are, however, certain characteristics common to synesthetes. One is "non-right-handedness" (meant to include ambidexterity as well as left-handedness). Other traits are intelligence, creativity, mental balance, and excellent memory. Less helpful ones include difficulty with math, right-left confusion, and a poor sense of direction.

The concept lends itself to metaphor. In fact, it virtually embodies metaphor. In linguistics, **synesthesia** describes a putative association between sound and meaning, exemplified by the (fl) sounds in *fly, flit, flame, flicker,* and *flutter.* A recent music critique in the *Boston Globe* speaks of a cornetist and percussionist who "create intimate, attractive textures spiced with electronics on the new 'Synesthesia'." And to return to taste, a September 2000 article from the *Tulsa World* states vividly that food "engenders a crossing of senses, a synesthesia, where taste produces color, where a smell zings the pelvis—we are enlivened. . . . When Shakespeare speaks of Cassius' 'lean and hungry look' or of Cleopatra in her 'salad days', we immediately know one for being a green thing and the other . . . a predator."

~*EP*

🖥️👉 take a gander at

> **ZOE GREENBERG WROTE:** I'm wondering where the phrase **to take a gander at** came from, as in, "Take a gander at some of those rhinoplasty samples, and when I come back in a few minutes, you can tell me which you've chosen." Is it somehow related to geese?

Gander meaning 'the male of the goose' goes back to Old English, but several other meanings developed over the centuries. Since your question involves a modern usage, we'll **take a gander at** the earlier senses first.

From the 16th through the 19th centuries, a *gander* was 'a stupid person' or 'a fool' (perhaps because geese are generally regarded as rather stupid birds).

A *gander* is also slang for 'a married man, especially one not living with his wife', and a "gander party" is a party for men only (as opposed to a "hen party" for women only). The citations for that meaning are from the 19th century, but the expression *gander month* or *gander moon* goes back to the 17th century. Grose's *Dictionary of the Vulgar Tongue* (1796) defines *gander month* as 'that month in which a man's wife lies in: wherefore, during that time, husbands plead a sort of indulgence in matters of gallantry'. *The Oxford English Dictionary* speculates that the term might be an allusion to "the gander's aimless wandering while the goose is sitting."

In *Sexual Slang* Alan Richter says that a *gander* is 'an active homosexual'. An Internet search yielded the information that *gander* is the name for 'the active partner in gay sex'. Another slang glossary says that *gander* is 'street slang for a pimp' (and that *goose* is 'street slang for a prostitute').

Gander was first used as a verb in the 17th century. One meaning was 'to wander aimlessly or with a foolish look' (like that of a *gander*). The other meaning, related to *gander moon*, may be illustrated by a 1687 quotation: "To go a gandering, whilst his wife lies in, chercher à se diverter ailleurs. . . ."

In the 19th century, the verb acquired another meaning: "Gonder, to stretch the neck like a gander, to stand at gaze. 'What a't gonderin' theer fur?'" (T. Darlington, *Folk-Speech of South Cheshire*, 1887). The *Cincinnati Enquirer* wrote in 1903 that to *gander* means 'to stretch or rubber your neck'. So there's the connection with geese: if you stretch your neck to look at something, you're "gandering."

The verb first appeared in Britain, but the noun *gander* meaning 'a look' is first attested in the United States in Jackson & Hellyer's 1914 *Vocabulary of Criminal Slang*. The earliest instance of the phrase **take a gander** that I've found is in Raymond Chandler's *The Big Sleep* (1939): "I go over and take a gander into it." You can also "get a gander" at something. And in Britain, you can say "give us a gander."

~*GSM*

tattoo

BILL KEELER WROTE: You mentioned that the only words you know of from the Tongan language are *taboo* *(tabu)* and *kava*. I was under the impression that **tattoo** was also Tongan. Could you tell me the origin and history of the word **tattoo?**

Actually, it's Tahitian. So says *Random House Webster's Unabridged Dictionary. The Oxford English Dictionary* more broadly claims the derivation of **tattoo** as Polynesian. Tongan is part of this language group that includes Tahitian, Somoan, and Marquesan.

In Tahitian and Tongan, the original word for **tattoo** is *tatau*. In Marquesan, it's *tatu*. Broadly speaking, it means to mark the skin with indelible patterns by making punctures and inserting pigments. In that sense, it can be anything from the traditional sailor's *Mother* to ritual designs having deep cultural significance. Not to mention the butterfly on your daughter's ankle.

The first citation for **tattoo** in the *OED* comes from a famous man—Captain James Cook—in 1769. Cook (1728–79) was on what was to become a famous and historical three-year voyage (1768–71) aboard the ship *Endeavour*. The purpose of the voyage was to observe Venus transiting the sun, a rare event. Cook reached Tahiti in April 1769. It was in July that he recorded this entry in his journal: "Both sexes paint their Bodys, Tattow, as it is called in their Language. This is done by inlaying the Colour of Black under their skins, in such a manner as to be indelible." Cook continues, demonstrating that getting **tattooed** was never a breeze: "This method of Tattowing I shall now describe . . . As this is a painful operation, especially the Tattowing of their Buttocks, it is performed but once in their Lifetimes."

Probably the most famous **tattoos** in history are entirely fictional—those of Qeequeg, the Polynesian harpooner in *Moby Dick*. Herman Melville had been to Tahiti (landing in jail there for joining a mutiny), so he must have seen his share of **tattoos.** In fact, in *Moby Dick,* Melville describes a particularly fearsome—not Moby Dick—whale: "thou terror of all cruisers that crossed their wakes in the vicinity of the Tattoo Land."

Actually, there is a second **tattoo.** It has an entirely different meaning and derives from entirely different roots. It's a signal to soldiers—on a drum or trumpet—to let them know it's time to return to quarters. It came into use around 1580 from the Dutch word *taptoe,* which means, essentially, that the tap room is about to shut.

All this talk about **tattoo** made me recall the classic television series *Fantasy Island*. In it, the late, lamented Hervé Villechaize played a character named Tattoo. I wondered how Tattoo came to be named Tattoo. Alas, after many phone calls to Los Angeles—not recommended on a daily basis—going from former distributor to former distributor, I reached a dead end.

Anybody know?

$\sim$*RG*

termagant (TER-me-gent)

KAIRIN WHITESIDE WROTE: Someone called me a **ter-magant,** and I was wondering about the origin and usage of the word.

It sounds as if someone thought you were being an uppity woman.

Termagant (with a capital T) was the name given by medieval Christians to an idol or deity supposedly worshiped by the Muslims. The name appeared in Early Middle English as *Tervagant,* in Old French as *Tervagan,* and in Italian as *Trivigante.* Skeat's *Etymological Dictionary,* published in the 19th century, speculates that the name was originally *Trivagante* 'thrice wandering' and referred to the moon, who wandered under three names: Selene (or Luna) in heaven, Artemis (or Diana) on earth, and Persephone (or Proserpina) in the lower world. Others have suggested a Saxon origin, *tyr magan* 'very mighty', or a Persian one, *tir-magian* 'Magian lord or deity'.

The Crusaders tended to lump all non-Christians together under the name "Saracens," and Termagant was called "the god of the Saracens" or "the co-partner of Mahoud" (Mohammed). In the legend of *Syr Guy,* the Sultan says, "So helpe me, Mahoune, of might, / And Termagaunt, my God so bright." In the *Chanson de Roland* (c1100), the pagans, having lost the battle at Roncevaux, become angry and overthrow the idols of their gods because they failed to protect them: "Apollyon's grotto they make for in a rout, / With ugly insults they threaten him and shout . . . / Termagant gets his carbuncle torn out; / Into a ditch they boot away Mahound / For pigs and dogs to mangle and befoul" (translation by Dorothy L. Sayers).

Termagant was introduced into the medieval morality plays as a violent, turbulent, overbearing person in long, flowing Eastern robes. In Hamlet's speech at the beginning of Act III, Scene 2 (which is Shakespeare's commentary on the actor's art), he tells the players not to rant and rave: "I could have such a Fellow whipt for o'erdoing Termagant: it out-

Herod's Herod." Termagant and Herod were both portrayed as raging tyrants in early plays, and **termagant** came to mean a 'a savage, violent person' or 'a bully'. Because the Termagant character wore long gowns like those worn in Europe by females, the name came to be applied to women rather than to men.

The usual meaning of **termagant** now is 'a violent, turbulent, or quarrelsome woman'. A columnist for an Australian newspaper, writing about a female politician who had been heavily criticized, asked sarcastically, "How much more can we take from this whingeing termagant?" A soprano was praised for her portrayal of "a beautiful, termagant Queen of the Night" in *The Magic Flute.*

Like *virago,* **termagant** has been adopted by some feminists as a term for a strong, assertive woman. You might want to assume that the person who called you one had that meaning in mind.

~*GSM*

testify and testicle

BYRON ANNIS WROTE: A couple of years ago, I read in a novel that the word **testify** is derived from the same Greek root as **testicle.** It was explained that in ancient Greece, men giving testimony were required to cover their genitals with their hand. . . . I looked up the word . . . and found only one citation which indicated that it was derived from Latin and was related to Roman custom, but there was no mention of the aforementioned male appendages. Can you elucidate?

This etymology has appeared in a number of places, in print and on the Internet, but it isn't true. There is no evidence anywhere that a Roman or a Greek had to put his hand on his **testicles** in order to validate his testimony when swearing in court.

The words are interesting, and the relationship between them isn't completely clear. The Latin word *testis* originally meant 'witness'. It comes from the Indo-European roots **tre-* meaning 'three' and **sta-* meaning 'stand'. A witness was 'a third person standing by'. From the noun came the verb *testificari,* which evolved into Middle English **testify** in the 14th century.

Where it gets confusing is that *testis* also—although not originally—meant 'testicle' in Latin. If *testis* meaning 'witness' and *testis* meaning 'testicle' are indeed the same word, then the etymology could be that the **testicles** are 'witnesses' or evidence of virility.

There is also a theory that *testis/testicle* comes from Latin *testa,* 'pot'.

The *Oxford Latin Dictionary* says that *testis* meaning 'testicle' is probably "a special application" of *testis* meaning 'witness' and refers the reader to the Greek word *parastátēs,* which means 'one who stands alongside another'. In addition to singular and plural, Greek has what is called a "dual" that denotes two of whatever is being talked about; it is used for things that come in pairs, like hands and feet. The dual form of *parastátēs* means 'testicles', which are 'two glands standing alongside each other'. It is conceivable that Latin simply took these two senses of the Greek word and translated them with *testis.* That seems to me to be the theory that makes the most sense.

In the book of Genesis there are several passages in which a man who is taking an oath puts his hand "under the thigh" of the man to whom he is swearing: "And Abraham said unto his eldest servant of his house . . . Put, I pray thee, thy hand under my thigh: And I will make thee swear by the Lord. . . ." The Hebrew word in this passage is *yarek,* which means 'thigh' throughout the Old Testament. My biblical expert says that this ritual seems to come from the idea that the thigh is the locus of power, probably because it's near the genitals. He also notes that some modern interpreters of the Bible envision it as a swearing *on* the genitals, with "under the thigh" being a euphemism that goes all the way back to the Hebrew.

I think it is very likely that these biblical passages are the source of the popular notion that **testify** derived from **testicle.**

$\sim$*GSM*

than (usage)

PETER CHANG WROTE: In the following sentence, "I enjoyed that talk more **than** (her, she)," please indicate which word fits in the parentheses: "her" or "she."

Well, that depends on what you mean by that sentence. If it's "I enjoyed that talk more than she enjoyed it," use *she.* If it's "I enjoyed that talk more than I enjoyed listening to it with her," use *her*—or better still, amend your sentence and say what I just said to avoid confusion.

Your question points to the real usage issue, which is

whether **than** is a conjunction or a preposition. If it's a conjunction, then the subjective case (I, she, he, etc.) is appropriate; if it's a preposition, then you need the objective case (me, her, him, etc.). And your example sentence neatly shows that **than** can in fact function as either a conjunction or a preposition, and that if you aren't careful about the difference, you could end up saying something you didn't mean.

The use of **than** as a conjunction is far older than its use as a preposition—Old English versus sometime in the 16th century. There's a classic example from Milton of the prepositional use that every usage book seems to cite, in which he uses the construction "than whom" in a line about Beelzebub. When Robert Lowth wrote his *A Short Introduction to English Grammar* in 1762, he couldn't get around the fact that Milton had inconveniently and famously messed up his perfect theory that **than** could be used only as a conjunction, so he had to make up a convoluted explanation as to why "who" wouldn't work in that sole construction. Lowth was a classic example of the type of sergeant who made the English language do Latin exercises in the 18th-century Enlightenment boot camp.

Some will tell you that in careful formal writing, you should still take pains to use the subjective case if the implied clause would have been in that case—so you should say "I work harder than she" because "she does" is implied. I would say that if you know that your audience might contain a Lowth fan, use the subjective case when you write, but for Pete's sake don't do it when you speak, because it sounds painfully forced.

~*WRN*

thinking outside the box

DAVID ISAACSON WROTE: I know that this phrase means unconventional or creative thinking. But what is meant by the reference to a box here? Is it a specific kind of box or just any old box that's "square" and therefore ordinary?

You're right; "any old box" would support the metaphor. If you want to think creatively—even within the limits of reality—you don't want your thoughts confined by rigid barriers or solid walls or anything else that limits the scope of your imagination and intelligence. And the opposition between the ordinary "square" box and free, unconventional thinking works too.

But a more likely source for **thinking outside the box** is a well-known mathematical puzzle called the *nine dots puzzle*. In it, you're asked to put nine dots on a piece of paper so that the first row has three dots, the middle row three dots directly under those, and the bottom row three dots lined up with the others. You've now formed a pattern like this:

```
•   •   •


•   •   •


•   •   •
```

Aha! The nine dots form a two-dimensional box! The fiendish puzzle makers want you to connect all nine dots, using only four straight lines, without lifting your pencil from the surface of the paper and without drawing over any of the lines you already have. Lines may cross, however.

You've probably guessed by now that you simply can't solve this puzzle unless you **think outside the box.** As Professor Daniel Kies of the College of DuPage points out on his Web site (oddly enough, a site dedicated to English, not math), "When most of us look at the field of nine dots, we imagine a boundary around the edge of the dot array. In doing so, we limit ourselves to trying solutions to the puzzle that only link the dots *inside* the imaginary border. The result is futility. We can only solve the puzzle if we realize that there is no border."

There are several sites on the Web that offer solutions, most of which are identical except for the direction in which the resulting design points. You can find the sites by searching for *nine dots puzzle* or *join the dots puzzle.* But why don't you try to solve it for yourself before peeking at one of them or looking below? After all, it's a children's puzzle.

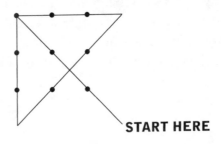

START HERE

$\sim$*EP*

thou / thee / ye / you

S. AND L. MEIN WROTE: When and how did **you** take the place of **thou?**

Ye have posed a most interesting question. I hasten to answer you.

From the beginning of Middle English, **thou** was the second-person pronoun used to address another person, and **ye** was used to address more than one person. The objective singular was **thee,** and the objective plural was **you.**

In the 13th century a distinction developed between the use of **thou/thee** and **ye/you,** depending on the social situation. **Thou/thee** was used familiarly, when speaking to children and other family members, lovers, or social inferiors. Since the occasional misuse of **thou** in more formal situations was interpreted as patronizing, it developed a contemptuous or scornful connotation. In Shakespeare's *Twelfth Night,* Sir Toby Belch urges a letter to be written to Viola: ". . . taunt him with the license of Inke: if thou thou'st him some thrice, it shall not be amisse." (Meaning: If you speak familiarly and insultingly to him, . . .) Sometimes it looks as though Shakespeare made mistakes in using these pronouns. In fact, Shakespeare and other writers were not consistent, or at least, modern readers can't always figure out why one or the other pronoun was used.

In formal social situations, the historically plural **ye/you** began to be used in the singular, as a sign of respect when speaking to a person of higher rank. This distinction spread to England and throughout Europe because of the similar use of *tu/vous* in French (and in many modern languages).

By the 16th century **ye/you** was beginning to be used in all social situations. Originally **ye** was in subject position and **you** was in object position. But because they were pronounced alike, **ye** and **you** eventually became interchangeable. By about 1600 **you** had replaced **ye,** except in liturgical and other elevated language.

Thou/thee had disappeared from standard English by the 18th century but survives in certain British dialects, and in poetry and liturgy. Quakers still use these pronouns, considering all human beings equal before God, though they often use **thee** in subject position. **Ye** also survives in dialectal use and in liturgy.

The distinctions were so confusing, no wonder **you** is now used in the singular and plural! To avoid confusion *youse* can always say *you-all* or *you guys.*

~CGB

to wit

CHRIS NELSON WROTE: I've heard **to wit** in a context that suggests it's synonymous with "for example" but haven't been able to find the phrase in any dictionary.

If you're *at your wit's end,* Chris, then may I recommend the *wit and wisdom* of *Random House Webster's Unabridged Dictionary,* which you must have *unwittingly* missed in your search, but which I'm sure you would have checked had you not apparently *lost your wits.* Yes, the preceding are all slightly different senses of *wit,* but only one of them is close to the one you want. *Keep your wits about you* now, and I'll try to sort them out.

The noun form of *wit* is the one we are most familiar with, with several senses relating to the mental faculties, in particular, nimbleness of mind, intelligence, and sense. This *wit* predates the 10th century, coming from an Old English word of the same spelling meaning 'mind or thought'. It is related to the German *Witz,* meaning 'joke'. The *wit* in the phrase *wit and wisdom* is wisdom's clever counterpart, in that it denotes 'quickness of mind and humorous verbal play' as opposed to wisdom's 'sagacity'. This meaning of *wit* is our modern sense of the word, first attested in the mid to late 1500s, and exemplified by this quote from William Hazlitt's 1819 *Lectures on the English Comic Writers:* "Wit is the salt of conversation, not the food."

Earlier, humorless senses of *wit* have left their traces in fixed phrases we call "fossilized forms," so named because they allow us to examine otherwise extinct species of words. *Wits* as 'mental faculties; senses' can be seen in the phrase *to lose one's wits.* To be *at one's wit's end* means to be 'at the end of one's ideas or mental resources.' To *live by one's wits* is 'to provide for oneself by employing ingenuity or cunning.'

But it is the adverb *unwittingly* that holds the real clue to the meaning of **to wit.** To do something *unwittingly* is to do it unknowingly, the adverb having been formed from the (now archaic) English verb *wit,* meaning 'to know'. This verb descends from the Old English verb *witan,* which binds an Indo-European root meaning 'to see' to a sense of pastness, giving 'to have seen', and hence, 'to know' (an obvious leap, providing one can trust one's senses). Relatives of this *wit* are German's *wissen* 'to know' and Latin's *vidēre* 'to see, to perceive (with the eyes)'. The phrase **to wit,** then, literally means 'to know'. It is a shortened form of the now obsolete phrase *that is to wit* and is used to mean 'that is to say' or 'namely', as in this 1711 quote from Sir Richard Steele: "Accounting for what we frequently see, to wit, that dull Fellows prove very good Men of Business." And this brings me, yes, to *wit's end.*

~HL

FOLLOW-UP QUESTION FROM DAVID RUBIN: Isn't **to wit** also equivalent to the less commonly used *viz.,* meaning 'namely'? And *viz.* is an abbreviation for *videlicet,* which comes from *vidēre licet,* meaning literally 'it is permitted to see'.

Yes, it is indeed equivalent to *viz.;* **to wit,** you are correct. Also, *i.e.* (Latin *id est* 'that is'). And, if you happen to be writing in Anglo-French, *cestasavoir.* The connection between "seeing" and "knowing" is obviously one that doesn't exist only in the Germanic languages.

~HL

transparent

LARRY ZAR WROTE: I have trouble with the word **transparent** as used by computer types. In the sentence, "The change was transparent to the users," the intended meaning is that the users will not notice anything different. If the change is not obvious or is hidden from the user, wouldn't calling it an "opaque change" be more appropriate? Where does this use of **transparent** come from?

Just recently, a Random House newsletter informed us about some changes to our phone system: "Don't worry! The switchover to the new system will be transparent to outside callers, and your old voicemail will be operative until the new phones are active." I naturally interpreted this to mean that outside callers won't notice any change—the switchover will not be obvious to them.

This meaning of **transparent** is indeed the opposite of the usual meaning, 'easily recognized or detected; obvious'. It seems that you have uncovered a good example of a *Janus word,* one that has two opposite meanings.

Transparent, in the sense of 'not obvious; not noticeable', is used by techies or "computer types," and has been part of their vocabulary for at least 15 years. In this particular use, the term **transparent** refers to a computer device, system, or software function that operates in such a way as to have no visible effect. To say it another way, it is invisible to the user. For example, if you can't see the formatting codes inserted in your document by your word-processing program, the codes are said to be **transparent.** According to *Random House Webster's Computer & Internet Dictionary,* "Transparency is usually considered to be a good characteristic of a system because it shields the user from the system's complexity." Another example: A computer graphic is **transparent** if the color in part of the image disappears into or blends with the background color of the Web page or other display.

In your example, "The change was transparent to the users," I wouldn't substitute the word *opaque,* since it means 'hard to understand or explain'. However, in its basic sense, 'impenetrable to light', *opaque* is the usual antonym of **transparent** and is distinguished in meaning from *translucent.*

Why the two opposite meanings of **transparent?** Here's the basic meaning: 'transmitting light through its substance so that objects on the other side can be distinctly seen'. **Transparent** windowpanes are visible barriers, but light can pass through them. **Transparent** lies or excuses are also visible, but you "see through" them and penetrate to the truth on the other side. Similarly, you "see through" **transparent** software functions and processes, but you don't notice them because they are invisible.

$\sim$ *CGB*

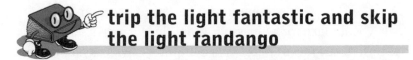

trip the light fantastic and skip the light fandango

JIM LASSETER WROTE: Trip the light fantastic or **skip the light fandango**—what on earth is the origin of these colorful but mysterious figures of speech?

Trip the light fantastic means 'to dance', the verb *trip* meaning 'to step lightly and nimbly'. Probably the best-known use of this fixed expression is in the 1894 song "Sidewalks of New York." Here's part of the chorus:

Boys and girls together,
Me and Mamie O'Rourke
Tripped the light fantastic
On the sidewalks of New York.

Trip the light fantastic is a strange alteration of lines from Milton's "L'Allegro," written in 1632:

Haste thee, Nymph, and bring with thee
Jest, and youthful Jollity, . . .

Sport that wrinkled Care derides,
And Laughter holding both his sides.
Come, and trip it as you go,
On the light fantastick toe.

Here, Milton seems to be describing the *light* (nimble) and
fantastick (fanciful or fancy) footwork that is characteristic of
dancing. Milton's lines were occasionally echoed by later writers: "Mr. St. Ledger . . . prided himself . . . on his light fantastic
toe" (Disraeli, *Vivian Grey,* 1826). Other authors have used the
term *fantastic-footed* to refer to fancy footwork—reference to
feet rather than toes does seem to make more sense.

Though **trip the light fantastic** goes back to Milton's
poem, reference to *tripping (it) on one's toe* is found in Shakespeare's *The Tempest,* written in 1611:

Before you can say come, and goe,
And breathe twice; and cry, so, so:
Each one tripping on his Toe,
Will be here with mop, and mowe.

(Here, *mop, and mowe* means 'a grimace'.)

Now, strange as it may seem, the lines from Milton are recalled several centuries later in "A Whiter Shade of Pale," a
1960s ballad sung by the rock group Procol Harum. This time
Milton's lines take on new life in the expression **skip the light
fandango,** also meaning 'to dance'. (The *fandango* is a lively
Spanish dance accompanied by castanets.) This rock ballad
is about a man who has had too much to drink and dances
with a woman, maybe in a barroom or dance hall:

We skipped the light fandango,
Turned cartwheels 'cross the floor

I was feeling kinda seasick
But the crowd called out for more.

Incidentally, the story told in "A Whiter Shade of Pale" is said to parallel the plot of "Tam O'Shanter," a poem written in 1791 by the Scots poet Robert Burns. Tam is a drunken man who passes by an old church late at night and sees a group of witches dancing to bagpipe music:

Warlocks and witches in a dance;
Nae cotillion brent-new frae France
But hornpipes, jigs, strathspeys, and reels,
Put life and mettle in their heels.

So **trip the light fantastic** and **skip the light fandango** are expressions that describe dancing, maybe drunken and wild dancing, and both have their roots in poetry and songs about nymphs, witches, and wild women.

~CGB

unaware and unawares

STEVE LUNT WROTE: In a recent story on CNN I heard the correspondent report that an individual was **unawares.** It caught me as strange, and since then I have heard other people use **unawares** instead of "unaware." Am I just "unawares" of this usage?

If the CNN reporter was using the adverb **unawares** as an adjective—an **unawares** person, a person who was **unawares**—then it's the reverse of the usual mistake of not bothering to use an adverb when an adjective will do. ("How are you doing?" "Real good.") I'd be interested in more detailed citations of this usage. One would think that the mistake would have been to use **unaware** in an adverb position rather than the other way round.

If, however, the reporter used **unawares** in an expression such as "So-and-so was caught unawares," the usage is correct, because *caught* calls for an adverb complement, not an adjective. The verb *caught* is used with many such complements: participles (caught napping), adverbial prepositional phrases (caught with his hand in the cookie jar), or a word that is usually an adjective taking the role of an adverb (caught red-handed). Another example of a word with a dual role as adjective and adverb is *blind*: one would hope there are no blind drivers on the road, but if you're driving blind, you may be able to see but you have no idea of where you're going.

Still, in the case of **unaware** and **unawares,** you don't have dual-role forms that are spelled the same: the adjective and the adverb have different forms. The *-s* suffix goes back to an Old English genitive ending and was used to form adverbs from other parts of speech, especially adjectives and prepositions. This is where *always* comes from, as well as such creaky terms as *betimes* and *needs* (as in the expression "if needs must"). We see it more commonly in prepositions that become adverbs: "a backward glance" but "he glanced backwards."

Unawares has been in use since the early 16th century, both in the meaning 'without being aware of something' and in the meaning 'without being noticed'. So you could in theory say "She trashed his hard drive unawares" as well as "After that, she had to be careful in dark alleys, lest he come upon her unawares." Well, you probably wouldn't, but you could.

Any confusion in usage likely comes from the first meaning, because the difference between 'not aware of something' (**unaware**) and 'without being aware of something' (**unawares**) is so subtle.

~*WRN*

vaudeville

NAN FRASER WROTE: The dictionary definition of **vaudeville** doesn't make much sense to me. Is there more to it than that? A recent Public TV show got us all thinking about this word.

There are actually three meanings of **vaudeville** that trace the way the word has evolved: a satirical cabaret song; a light theatrical piece with songs and dances; and a theatrical entertainment with a number of acts involving comedians, singers, dancers, acrobats, etc.

The town of Vire, capital of Calvados in Normandy, was an important settlement in the Middle Ages, and the composing and singing of songs that satirized the events and personalities of the region was a popular entertainment. These songs were known as *chansons du Vau de Vire,* 'songs of the valley of Vire'. This was eventually shortened to *vau de vire.* The name was first given to songs composed by Oliver Basselin, a poet and fuller of Vire in the 15th century. By 1500 *vaux de vire* was applied to popular, satirical songs composed anywhere in France.

While the *vaux de vire* were folk-based, there was another type of song in 16th-century France called *voix de ville,* or 'voices of the city', which were songs of courtly love. A collection of the *voix de ville* was published in 1555. Eventually, the two names were confused, and *vaux de ville* was the result. In 1573 there was a collection of courtly songs called *Premier livre de chansons en forme de vau de ville.* By the end of the 16th century, **vaudeville** was in common use in France.

The term first appeared in English in 1611 in Cotgrave's *Dictionarie of the French and English Tongues,* which defined it as 'a country ballade, or song'. In 1739 Horace Walpole wrote in a letter, "I will send you one of the vaudevilles or ballads which they sing at the comedy after their 'petites pièces'."

During the late 17th and early 18th centuries, comedies that incorporated the old **vaudeville** tunes with new lyrics— *comédies-vaudeville*—became popular in France. The Théâtre de Vaudeville opened in Paris in 1792, and the word **vaudeville** gradually came to refer to the shows themselves rather than to the songs in the shows.

By the 19th century, the English music halls had taken over this form of entertainment: "I also had the honor . . . of being selected by her Royal Highness the Princess Elizabeth to write a sort of vaudeville farce," wrote a gentleman named Dibden in 1827.

When **vaudeville** reached the American stage, it became a variety show with the addition of other elements. **Vaudeville** thrived in the United States until the 1930s, but it was eventually displaced by the movies and disappeared completely by the end of World War II.

～*GSM*

vegetarian

JENNIFER COMEAU WROTE: Is the meaning of the word **vegetarian** undergoing a shift? Lately I've heard more than one person say, "I'm a vegetarian—I only eat fish and chicken."

A lot of people have shared your experience. So, what's the deal with *vegetarianism,* and what are we supposed to call people who do or don't eat one animal or another?

Vegetarianism itself is very old. Anthropologists have found evidence in Great Britain of a **vegetarian** diet in the Mesolithic period (8,000 years ago!). The first advocate of *vegetarianism* in the recorded history of the Western world is Pythagorus: "As long as man continues to be the ruthless destroyer of lower living beings he will never know health or peace. For as long as men massacre animals, they will kill each other. Indeed, he who sows the seed of murder and pain cannot reap joy and love" (quote attributed by Ovid, excerpt from the book *The Extended Circle* by Jon Wynne-Tyson). **Vegetarians** from the Renaissance to the 19th century were often called "Pythagoreans."

The term **vegetarian** is attributed to Joseph Brotherton, a member of the Vegetarian Society of the United Kingdom at Ramsgate in the mid-19th century.

Most anthropologists will agree that *vegetarianism* is a choice that people within a culture make for any number of reasons (health, environment, animal rights, etc.). This choice is not to be confused with a lack of resources (another historical reason Homo sapiens have eaten a meat-free diet).

But of course, *vegetarianism* is not a black-or-white

choice. A person who follows the strictest path of *vegetarianism* is a *fruitarian*. *Fruitarians* do not eat any food if their doing so will hurt another living thing. So, a *fruitarian* will eat oranges, but not carrots. (The orange tree survives, the carrot does not.) *Vegans* exclude all animals and animal products from their diet. This includes meat, eggs, dairy, honey, and sometimes yeast. (The term *vegan* was coined by Donald Watson in the 1940s.) *Lacto-vegetarians* are like *vegans,* but they include dairy products in their diet. *Ovo-vegetarians* are like *vegans* who eat eggs. *Lacto-ovo-vegetarians* are the largest group of **vegetarians.** They eat eggs and dairy, but no meat of any kind. A *pescatarian* eats everything a **vegetarian** eats and adds fish. The person you describe in your question sounds like a *semi-vegetarian* or a *pseudo-vegetarian*. They usually eat everything except beef and pork. That's about as high on the food chain as you can climb and still call yourself a **vegetarian.**

But why the explosion of terms? The earliest of the classifications dates from the 1860s (*ovo-lacto vegetarian*). The latest term is from the 1940s (*vegan*). It seems that as *vegetarianism* develops, and people make **vegetarian** choices for different reasons, they choose different paths of *vegetarianism*. Then these people have to decide what they will call themselves. And so the word **vegetarian** covers a lot of ground.

⁓*HGB*

vis-à-vis (vee-zuh-VEE)

Don Lewis wrote: I hear **vis-à-vis** used by many in the media to mean 'as to' or 'concerning'. I was under the impression, since its literal meaning is 'face to face', that it means 'as opposed to', as in "The pro-lifers' stance vis-à-vis the stance of the pro-choicers is. . . ." Your comments, please.

You're right. The French term **vis-à-vis** literally means 'face to face; facing another person or each other'. The English adverb is sometimes used in this sense: "After two months of e-mailing each other, we found ourselves vis-à-vis for the first time." (Translation: They decided they needed some face time.) The English preposition is used in the corresponding literal sense 'facing; opposite': "I found myself vis-à-vis the most handsome man in New York." (Now, there's a happy ending.)

Some older usage guides caution about the perils of using a foreign term and giving it far-fetched Anglicized definitions. But *The Oxford English Dictionary* shows that the preposition **vis-à-vis** has been used since the 18th century in the sense 'in relation to; compared with, as opposed to'. (In fact, it's also used this way in French.) Here are some examples: "They had a major advantage vis-à-vis their competitors"; "The [Czech] crown weakened vis-à-vis the euro." These are just figurative extensions of the literal meaning 'face to face; facing', and therefore most modern usage guides don't object.

However, you are right to question the use of **vis-à-vis** to mean 'concerning, regarding'. Although this sense is increasingly common, the consensus is to avoid it as an error. A recent newspaper article discussed Syria's policy **vis-à-vis** Israel and Israel's strategic goals **vis-à-vis** Syria. Despite objections, this use of **vis-à-vis** is actually similar to the literal meaning 'facing; opposite' and the figurative meaning 'in relation to; compared with, as opposed to', because the context often implies a confrontation, opposition, or comparison.

~CGB

Wassup?

RON JOURARD WROTE: Wassup? Is this now a word? If so, is there a term for a word formed from two others (what's up), without an apostrophe, which would be a contraction?

Is it a word? I guess that depends on what you mean by *word*. If you limit your sense of *word* to the discrete bits of vocabulary we ordinarily think of as words, you may hesitate to include a term like **Wassup?** But dictionaries commonly define *word* more loosely than you might expect—as a unit of language smaller than a sentence, which contains one or more morphemes, consists of one or more spoken sounds or their written representation, and communicates a finite meaning. We recognize **Wassup?** in appropriate contexts; it conveys a particular message, and it's a single unit in writing. Moreover, it can be thought of as a compound—formed by putting two or more words together, like *bluebird* or *nevertheless*. At the same time, we can't easily give it a part-of-speech label. Also, it functions as a question—a full sentence. It's rather like *fuhgeddaboudit;* I'd be reluctant to classify either one of them as a word.

Is it a contraction? Contractions are formed by omitting parts, yielding *e'en* from *even* or *he'll* from *he will.* You're right to recognize the apostrophe as a typical signal, especially in English, that points out where one or more sounds or letters are missing. But the apostrophe isn't always necessary. Older dictionaries included abbreviations like *Dr.* or *oz.* (for ounce/ounces) as contracted forms. Perhaps **Wassup?** can loosely qualify as a contraction.

But there's a better label: *pronunciation spelling.* Expressing continuous, rapid speech, words like *gonna, gotta,* and *lemme,* for *going to, got to,* and *let me,* are frequent and conventionalized enough to have found a place in dictionaries. These spellings abound in fiction and nonfiction, where they convey a tone of informality: ". . . star Keanu Reeves, currently making back-to-back sequels to *The Matrix,* proclaims, 'It's gonna be very cool'. *Matrix 2* is due Dec. 25, 2002" (*Toronto Star*). **Wassup?** is still transitional—a *wannabe,* seeking enough acceptance to be added to dictionaries.

Wassup? is also *phatic.* A phatic term, such as a greeting, creates an atmosphere of shared feelings and goodwill. It doesn't impart or ask for real information. No one expects an actual answer to "What's up?" or "How are you?" A common feature of such forms is that they can quickly disappear. So at the moment, we're on hold—waiting to see what's up with **Wassup?**

~*EP*

wax (e.g., poetic)

HOLGER MAERTENS WROTE: Just today, I once again heard someone **wax poetic.** Apart from not knowing the etymology of the term, I realized I was also unsure how to handle it grammatically.

For instance, how can I qualify the phrase? Does a person "wax nicely poetic"? Does he "wax poetic nicely"? Or does she "wax nice poetic"? . . . And what else can I **wax** without making a fool of myself (apart from floors and skis, that is)? Or should I say, HOW else can I **wax?**

In the Marx Brothers' movie *Horse Feathers,* Groucho Marx, playing waggish university president and professor Quincy Adams Wagstaff, is informed by his secretary: "The Dean is furious. He's waxing wroth." To which Groucho ripostes: "Is Roth out there too? Tell Roth to wax the Dean for a while." Aside from the very funny image of two distinguished professor types buffing each other to a nice shine, the question this raises is: What's *waxing?* And, for that matter, what's *wroth?* (Bonus word of the day within word of the day: *wroth* means 'angry'. Think 'wrath', and also 'writhe'.) *Wroth* is an adjective, as is *poetic,* and this is your clue, Holger, that nowadays one typically neither *waxes* a thing, nor *waxes* "how." Now, excuse me while I *wax pedantic.*

Wax the verb (when not referring to actions involving the use of real or metaphorical beeswax-like substances) derives from an Old English word *weaxan* meaning 'to become'. The earliest sense of the verb **wax,** first attested in the 8th century, was 'to grow; to increase in extent, quantity, intensity, power, etc.'. It was used intransitively with subjects both animate and inanimate, so that one might say of oneself "Ich am wel waxen" (c1300), and of things less tangible, "His Art, still wexing, sweetly marrieth / His quavering fingers to his warbling breath" (1598). This usage of **wax** has waned in modern times, except in reference to the moon, and in opposition to its more popular sibling, *wane.*

From the 13th century on, we find constructions of the **wax poetic** sort, where **wax** is followed by an obligatory subject complement, here a predicate adjective. The verb **wax** in this context had further developed the nonconclusive durative sense of 'to grow' into the conclusive 'to become', in the process taking on a copular (or linking) function, much like the verb 'to be' in English. How do you know when you have a linking verb on your hands, you ask? Try dropping the complement, and see if the meaning of the verb changes. You're becoming smart. You're becoming. Holger *waxes enthusiastic.* Holger *waxes.* Totally different meanings, right? Any old adjective won't do, however—people can't *wax quadratic,* for instance, and plants don't *wax bombastic,* though some people you know might. As for how to modify this type of phrase adverbially, it depends on whether you are modifying the verb and complement together, so that "He waxes poetic nicely," or the adjective only: "As uncharacteristically poetic as he waxes, I find myself falling for him anyway."

~HL

wh-

DAVE MAXWELL WROTE: I was taken aback to learn from a competitor's "Word of the Day" that the first word in **White Elephant** was pronounced (wite). . . . It had always been (hwite) to me. I checked my *Random House Unabridged* and read that the first pronunciation was (hwite) and the second (wite). I then polled the household: the two children (14 and 18) said (wite), my wife (hwite). (The dog didn't have an opinion.) "Hwot" was the original pronunciation and when/where did it change? Is there a regional preference? . . . And why is *who* only (hoo) and not also (woo)?

Your family (including the dog) reflects the real English-speaking world. And thanks to you, we have the *sound* of the day—representing yet another case of a pronunciation slipping into oblivion.

The use of (hw) is a relic of Old English forms spelled with *hw*. Sometime during the Middle English period (c1150–c1475), *h* and *w* switched positions, but the pronunciation did not. Long considered the norm, (hw) was, until the mid-20th century, the only pronunciation in both American and British dictionaries. In one of the first such works to show pronunciations at all, John Walker's *A Critical Pronouncing Dictionary, and Expositor of the English Language,* Walker stated unequivocally that "*w* before *h* is pronounced as if it were after the *h*, as *hoo-y, why, hoo-en, when,* &c."

Other major dictionaries followed suit, showing only (hw). Not until the 1960s did virtually every major U.S. dictionary acknowledge the increasing use of (w) by giving both pronunciations. Many British dictionaries, including the *New Shorter Oxford English Dictionary* (1993) now show only (w). They have gone directly from (hw) to (w), eliminating the interim phase.

The traditional (hw) pronunciation can no longer be described, as it was by Arthur J. Bronstein in his 1960 text *Pronunciation of American English,* as "the normal American pronunciation of all **wh** words, except *who, whom, whose, whole, whore, whoop,* and their derivatives." These are patterned differently, perhaps because (hw) plus (oo) or (oh) is just too difficult to say.

Dialects—regional *and* generational—that include (hw) distinguish between *where* and *wear, when* and *wen,* and *which* and *witch.* Those who say only (w) depend on context to differentiate meanings. I grew up using (hw) and still do in words like *overwhelm* or *wherewithall.* It has virtually vanished in my casual speech, though, particularly in common words like *what, where,* and *when.* And here's a generational bellwether; I have never heard a teenager utter *Whatever!* with an initial (hw). The (w)-users are oblivious to (hw) and perfectly happy.

~EP

whammy

BORIS WROTE: "KaZING! KaZING! KaZING! You've got the whammy!" Such were the words of some big kids around me as a child many years ago, spoken along with a double-handed gesture as if flinging the thing with all fingers so it sticks. Aside from the strange nature of this mock curse, I must ask what a **whammy** might be. My childhood imagination still envisions something akin to Dr. Seuss's green eggs and ham. Am I even close? Even worse, do I still have it?

That's funny, because when I picture the **whammy,** I think of the cartoon character designed for the *Press Your Luck* show.

Well, any way you picture it, the **whammy** is bad news. No, it is not contagious, but it tends to be pretty serious. The **whammy** is, in fact, 'the evil eye'. The wicked force it represents is old and cross-cultural. The ancient Egyptians were said to have worn eye and lip makeup to prevent this spirit from entering their bodies through their eyes and mouths. The Greeks and Romans would spit to protect themselves from it. Shamrocks, garlic, and bells may also protect you. If you feel you may still have the **whammy,** I would try these and then consult an older woman from your village. (Traditionally they are the ones who can help.)

The name for this evil force tends to follow from the method in which people give it to you. The *evil eye* can be cast with a look. In Italian (*far le corna a*) and French (*faire les cores à*) you give it by holding your middle two fingers and extending your index finger and pinkie in the shape of horns (an image that may be related to HORNS and marital misfortune).

In English, the name **whammy** seems to have originated as a diminutive of the sound of **wham.** This name may represent the figurative noise of impact ("Goody Smith just looked at my cattle and wham! they dropped dead"), or from the sound produced with your hands when you give the **whammy** to someone. The gesture in the United States is either a forward moving fist strike into your palm or the move you described (double handed with extended fingers). The **whammy** was first recorded as a name for the evil eye in the 1940s. "Interest round the field now centered in the Kid's chances for a no-hit game . . . On the bench everyone realized it too, but kept discreetly quiet on account of the Whammy. Mustn't put the Whammy on him!" (Tunis, *Kid from Tomkinsville,* 1940).

The **whammy** tends not to be the threat it once was. (It's been years since it wiped out the neighbor's cattle.) Now the **whammy** tends to frequent playgrounds and game shows.

You can still hear about misfortune and the **whammy** in the common expression *double whammy*.

~HGB

which vs. that

JOYCE MOORE WROTE: What is the rule regarding the use of **which** and **that?**

The short answer is that you use **that** for restrictive clauses, and **which** for nonrestrictive ones. In other words, if a sentence cannot be understood without a given clause, use **that,** and if it can be understood just fine without the clause, use **which:**

> Sarah broke the necklace that I just gave her. (You don't know which necklace without the **that-**clause.)
> Sarah broke her necklace, which I just gave her. (The first part of the sentence could stand alone, but you add the second part because you're mad about it.)

However (and there's always a "however"), the rule about nonrestrictive clauses isn't really that fixed.

The confusion comes because **which** and **that** are both relative pronouns—words that stand for a noun and relate information in a clause back to the subject of a sentence. Of these pronouns (*that, which, what, who, whom,* and *whose*), **that** is the oldest (Early Middle English), and it used to be used in any context, restrictive or nonrestrictive. After **which** entered the language (14th century), it was used almost interchangeably with **that,** and both were used instead of **who** as well—think of all the "He that's" and the "Our father, which art in heaven" of the King James version of the Bible (1611).

By the 20th century, the restrictive-only use of **that** was fixed. **Which,** however, does get used for restrictive clauses as well, more often in Britain than in the United States. For instance, the British lexicographers I worked with in England would define a *leaflet* as 'a piece of paper which gives information about something', rather than using '. . . that gives information.'

The choice of **which** or **that** in restrictive clauses is more of a stylistic one—what you think is clearer, what sounds more mellifluous. Sometimes, however, the choice is pretty darned obvious: Nietzsche's "That which does not kill me makes me stronger" would be ludicrous as "That that."

$\sim$*WRN*

whole cloth

BOB BAGG WROTE: Why does the metaphor **to be cut from whole cloth** mean 'to be a complete and total lie or fabrication'?

(I could make this up out of **whole cloth,** but I'll resist.) As you can see, the current metaphor has some minor variations. You can **cut** or **make up** something **out of** or **from (the) whole cloth.** The usual figurative sense 'without foundation in fact; fictitious', has completely obscured the earlier literal meaning. There is at least one other common, closely related, figurative meaning. But first, some history:

In the 15th century, **whole** (or **broad**) **cloth** referred to any full-size piece of cloth that had not yet been cut up, especially to make clothing. It was intact, as when manufactured. Often, **whole cloth** meant cloth woven on a wide loom. To have a garment **cut out of whole cloth,** not fabricated from leftover material, was highly desirable. A quote from 1525 in *The Oxford English Dictionary* illustrates a request for "your hole cloth . . . to make a large Gowne and a Kyrtell."

Authorities disagree about how the meaning of the idiom got so completely turned around. Some sources derive this switch from 'great' to 'contemptible' from the fact that something made from **whole cloth** is created fresh, with no history, and is therefore a lie. But that's something of a stretch; a fresh creation is not necessarily fictitious. Note the intent in this quote from Mark Twain's *Life on the Mississippi:* "And, mind you, emotions are among the toughest things in the world to manufacture out of whole cloth; it is easier to manufacture seven facts than one emotion." This is the other sense I mentioned. There is no lie referred to here—just 'something made without the materials you usually need for making it'. If you *could* manufacture an actual emotion, it would be genuine by definition.

True, something created with no foundation can turn out to be a lie. But various sources postulate a more direct connection between **whole cloth** and 'prevarication'. It is said that by the 18th century, custom tailors were not above trying to deceive their customers by advertising that they made clothing out of **whole cloth** when they actually used leftover pieces. The 'lie' metaphor, then, emerged from a public reaction to these claims that was resoundingly cynical. While I could find no clear evidence to confirm this origin, it is mentioned in more than one source and seems reasonable.

The idea that a *fabrication* is made out of **whole cloth** made me look for a pun. But wait! Recent ads from today's fashion industry describe, say, "a long skirt made out of wool fabrication." We're moving from the lie back to the cloth! What can we expect? These are the people who keep trying to sell us a *pant.*

~*EP*

wicked

PETER MICHAUD WROTE: The word **wicked,** meaning 'very', seems to be gaining widespread acceptance. It has been in use in Maine for several years, and there is even a musical group called the "Wicked Good Band." Any idea where this usage originated?

The word **wicked** stretches back to the Old English *wicca* meaning 'wizard'. For eight hundred years it was a word that lived on the dark side. Gluttony, sloth, lust, jealousy, impure thoughts—there were lots of **wicked** things.

Then, in the 1960s, **wicked** went the way of *bad*. Things got so **wicked** that they were good. People disagree about who turned **wicked** around. It might have been the hippies, or it might have been the street gangs. It really caught on once it hit the playgrounds.

Wicked, also spelled *wikkid,* became a popular synonym for 'cool', especially in the Northeast: "That concert was wicked!" (V. Chen of Massachusetts, 1997).

In the 1980s, **wicked** morphed from adjective to adverb (what I like to call the "super" transformation). So, just like *super cool, wicked cool* means 'very cool'. The adverb use was confined to the Northeast for almost a decade, but it is on the move today, spreading down the eastern seaboard. As it begins to creep westward, **wicked** will face some competition from *hella,* a western synonym that is spreading eastward.

What will happen when **wicked** and *hella* square off against each other somewhere in Kansas? I don't know, but the showdown promises to be hella-wicked pissah cool.

~HGB

widdershins (WID-er-shinz)

JEFFREY COUNTS WROTE: I know that the word **widdershins** means 'anti-clockwise', and I've usually seen it associated with the practice of witchcraft or the occult. Where did we come up with such an unusual word to mean 'anti-clockwise', and is there a corresponding word for *clockwise* itself?

I've always thought **widdershins** is a much more interesting word than "anti-clockwise"—or, the more usual term in the United States, "counterclockwise."

The other form of **widdershins** is **withershins,** which is the preferred spelling in some dictionaries. The word came into English in the early 16th century. It originated in Middle High German *widersinnen,* meaning 'to go against'. The German prefix *wider-* means 'against or in opposition to'. This prefix became *wither-* in Old English, which is probably why two forms developed. The German verb *sinnen* meant 'to travel or go'. The *s* on the end of **widdershins/withershins** is a suffix used to form an adverb.

The earliest meaning of **widdershins** was simply 'the wrong way'. This quickly came to mean 'in a direction contrary to the apparent course of the sun' when one is facing south, and that's how the word is used today (by those who use it, mostly people in Scotland).

Widdershins has unlucky associations, probably because the direction goes against the natural path of the sun, which has got to be bad. In Dorothy L. Sayers's *The Nine Tailors* (1934), Lord Peter Wimsey "turned to his right, knowing that it is unlucky to walk about a church widdershins." *Going widdershins* figures in several superstitions, which might be why you associate it with witchcraft. It was said that if you *walked widdershins* around the church three times at night, you would see the devil looking out at you from the church porch.

The Oxford English Dictionary also has an entry for **withershin(s)/widdershin(s)** as an adjective meaning 'moving anti-clockwise' or 'unlucky, ill-fated'. D. H. Lawrence used it this way in *The Plumed Serpent* (1926): "She made up her mind, to be alone, and to cut herself off from all the mechanical widdershin contacts."

If you don't want to say *clockwise,* you can say *deasil* (pronounced DEE-sil) instead. Cognate with the Latin *dexter,* meaning 'right', this is a Scottish Gaelic and Irish word meaning 'turning right'—or 'in a direction following the apparent path of the sun'. Since the ancient Celts found it auspicious to follow the path of the sun, *deasil* has lucky connotations. A traveler in Scotland reported in the 18th century that, following a marriage or baptism, a procession was made round the church "deasoil, i.e., sunways."

Watch those left turns, especially if you're going round a church.

~GSM

window

CIA MARIA RISING WROTE: I love the words *fenestration, defenestrate, fenestra,* etc. Where and how does the word **window** come to us? Obviously, *fenêtre*, the French word for 'window', comes from the same place as my favorite words. Please discuss the word **window**.

Window provides an excellent example of foreign influences at work in the development of English.

A bit of background first: Both the Celtic inhabitants and the Roman occupiers of early Britain left their mark on English chiefly in place names, so the history of the English language really begins with the Angles, Jutes, and Saxons who invaded Britain in the 5th century. The various dialects of their West Germanic language became what we call Old English. Beginning in the 8th century, the Vikings invaded and then settled throughout Britain, adding their own North Germanic words to English. In 1066 the Normans arrived, French became the language of the court in England, and English was revolutionized. Although English is part of the West Germanic branch of INDO-EUROPEAN, it was influenced in the early stages by the North Germanic Scandinavian languages and later, and more significantly, by French.

During the Old English period, the word for 'window' was *eagthyrel,* a compound of *eage* 'eye', and *thyrel* 'hole'. (*Thyrel* survives in Modern English in *nostril* 'nose hole'.) *Eagthyrel* appeared in King Alfred's translation of the Venerable Bede's *Ecclesiastical History of the English People* in the 9th century and in the *Lambeth Homilies* in 1175: "the sunne scineth thurh the glesne ehthurl" (The sun shines through the glass eye-hole). The latest example of a form of *eagthyrel* appeared in 1225 in a guide for anchoresses called the *Ancrene Riwle:* "thurh eie thurles death haueth hire ingong into the soule" (Through eye-holes death has its entrance into the soul).

Another manuscript of the *Ancrene Riwle* contains the earliest evidence of the word **window,** a product of Scandinavian influence, borrowed from the Old Norse *vindauga,* a compound of *vindr* 'wind' or 'air' and *auga* 'eye', thus 'the wind's eye'. (Note that Old Norse *auga* is cognate with Old English *eage.*)

So the Scandinavian word replaced the Old English word. But that's not the end of the story. Around 1300 we find the following in a poem called *The Land of Cockaygne:* "All the fenestres that beth of glasse . . ." (all the windows that are of glass). The Old French word *fenestre,* derived from the Latin *fenestra,* has replaced the Scandinavian **window.** For about 250 years, both **window** and *fenester* (or *fenestre*) were standard. In Edward Hall's *Chronicle* in 1548, the two words appeared side by side: "In the Fenestres and wyndowes were images resemblynge men of war." Shortly after that, **window** won, and *fenester* disappeared, leaving *fenestra, fenestrated, fenestration,* and *defenestration.*

Why the Old Norse word, rather than the Old English or the French, became standard in Modern English is one of those mysteries that makes language study so fascinating.

~*GSM*

wreaked (reekt) and wrought (rawt)

BRIAN TUNG WROTE: Wreak, it seems, is only used with a couple of things you wreak, like *havoc* or *vengeance.* What else can you **wreak,** and have people previously **wreaked** other things that they no longer do? Along the same lines, what is the past participle of **wreak?**

Wreak means 'to inflict or cause'. The most common thing one can **wreak** is havoc, though one can also **wreak** most of havoc's dire synonyms: great destruction, devastation, harm, ruin, evil, damage, disorder, or confusion. (The word *havoc,* from Old French *havot,* was originally a command for invading soldiers to start pillaging. Shakespeare used it in *Julius Caesar:* "Cry 'Havoc!' and let slip the dogs of war.") Though havoc is usually dire, it is not always so, as shown by a recent headline in the *New York Times:* "High Gas Prices Wreak Havoc in the Land of the Car." Less commonly, one can **wreak** vengeance, justice, or punishment, as colorfully put by the 19th-century writer George Meredith: "The woeful retribution Nature wreaked upon a life of indulgence."

Wreak also means 'to give vent or expression to'. One can **wreak** rage, hatred, malice, or most any strong emotion. With less serious effect, ill-humor can be **wreaked** on one's family after a hard day at work.

The past tense and past participle of **wreak** is always **wreaked:** "The eruption of Mount Usu has wreaked havoc in Japan." However, **wreak/wreaked** is sometimes replaced by another verb, *work/worked:* "The volcanic eruption has worked havoc." Occasionally, the archaic past tense of **work** is used: "The volcanic eruption has wrought havoc." So

wrought is not an incorrect substitute for **wreaked,** but rather an archaic variant of *worked.* In this particular use, the verb *work* means 'to bring about or cause'. This meaning is similar to that of **wreak,** and like **wreak,** the reference often concerns damage or destruction. Or just as often, a good night's sleep can *work* miracles, or change can be **wrought** by computer technology.

$\sim$*CGB*

Yankee

SHANNON WROTE: I have heard a variety of stories about the origins of the word **Yankee** but none I find convincing (my husband tells me it's related to the Yangtze River in China, for example). None of my dictionaries even attempt to explain it. I'm guessing it has some American Indian origin. Any ideas?

There are indeed a variety of stories about **Yankee,** but the Yangtze River connection is a new one.

Among the myriad theories are several involving Native American origins. It has been suggested that **Yankee** came from the Cherokee word *eankke,* 'slave, coward', or from the name of a Native American tribe, the *Yankoos,* 'invincible ones'.

The most persistent theory in the 19th century originated with the Rev. John Heckewelder in 1819. He wrote that **Yankee** resulted from the Native Americans' attempts to pronounce the word *English.* James Fenimore Cooper was a proponent of this theory and referred to it in *The Deerslayer* in 1841.

In *Knickerbocker's History of New York* (1809), Washington Irving wrote that **Yankee** came from a Mais-Tschusaeg (Massachusetts) word *yanokies,* 'silent men'. Irving was joking, but some people took him seriously.

Another hoax appeared in the *Monthly Review and Boston Anthology* in 1810 in a letter that was supposedly written by Noah Webster. It claimed that **Yankee** came from a Persian word *jang-ju* 'warlike man or swift horse' and that Genghis Khan meant 'Yankee King'. The piece was actually making fun of Webster's writings on etymology, but not everyone got the joke.

The word **Yankee** first appeared in the 17th century when it was used as a nickname in connection with Dutch pirates in the West Indies: "Yankee Duch," "Captain Yankey," and "the pirates Yanky and Jacob." Most scholars now believe that **Yankee** comes from Dutch, although there is disagreement about which Dutch word is the source.

Random House Webster's College Dictionary suggests that **Yankee** comes from *Jan Kees* (or *Jan Kaas*), 'John Cheese', a nickname for the Dutch. The *-s* at the end sounded like a plural to English speakers and was dropped. Proponents of this theory believe that the name was first applied to Dutch pirates by the English and later used by the New York Dutch for their Connecticut neighbors. The other popular theory, favored by *The Oxford English Dictionary*, is that **Yankee** comes from Dutch *Janke* (or possibly *Jantje*), 'Little John', the diminutive of *Jan,* which was used as a derisive nickname by either the English or the Dutch in the New England states.

The earliest recorded use of **Yankee** as a term for Americans is in a 1758 letter by General James Wolfe (of Battle of Quebec fame) in which he used the word pejoratively of the

American troops assigned to him. In 1775 the British troops used **Yankee** as a derogatory term for the citizens of Boston. The song "Yankee Doodle Dandy" was played by the British on their 1775 march to Concord as an insult to the Americans (the original lyrics were bawdy—"doodle" was a slang word for 'dolt' or 'penis'). After the battles at Lexington and Concord, the Americans adopted the song as their own and taunted the retreating British with it. **Yankee** thus began to acquire a complimentary sense. The version of the song that we know dates from 1776.

~*GSM*

zed or zee

DAVE SCHREIBER WROTE: The recent *Canadian Joe* .commercial for Molson beer shows Joe proclaiming, among other things, that it's pronounced (zed), not (zee)! Why do the Canadians pronounce **Z** as (zed), while Americans pronounce it (zee)?

The real question is, "Why do Americans say (zee)?" We're just about alone out here. **Zed** is the name in the rest of the (former) British Empire and in French. Canadians, hearing it from all sides, are largely in the (zed) camp. But like their spelling practices, their pronunciation exhibits connections to both Britain and the United States, and (zee) is not unknown there.

Actually, **zee** and **zed** are only half the story. There are older names. From Johnson's 1755 dictionary, for example, we have: "Z . . . [Name] **zed,** more commonly *izzard* or *uzzard,* that is, *shard*." These names, so bizarre to our modern ears, had not entirely vanished by the mid- to late-20th century. A 1947 opinion from the Court of Appeals of Kentucky included the following: "If this contract is valid, its provisions are all binding and effective from A to Izzard." A more recent "On Language" column by William Safire read, ". . . inventive native speakers also express their disdain for the dopes for not knowing the time of day, night from day, A from izzard, enough to come in out of the rain . . . " (1983). But these terms are now rare or dialectal.

Not only does **Z** have a plethora of names, it has a checkered past. When the Romans borrowed 21 of the 26 letters of the Etruscan alphabet, they included *zēta.* However, some time after 250 B.C., the Greek *zēta* was dropped. Latin words did not require it. Later, when Rome conquered Greece in the first century B.C., **Z** was taken back into Latin to enable the Romans to transliterate Greek borrowings.

Zed came into late Middle English from Middle French *zède,* derived from Latin *zēta,* in turn from Greek *zēta.* American **zee** has more mysterious origins. Etymologists, if they speculate at all, point to the analogy with our pronunciation of *B, C, D,* etc. But Noah Webster, advocate for a distinctive American English, must have exerted considerable influence. The statement in his *American Dictionary of the English Language* (1828) was unequivocal: "Z . . . It is pronounced zee."

Not that (zee) triumphed immediately; here is an 1882 quote from *The Oxford English Dictionary:* "The name . . . given to the last letter of the alphabet . . . in New England is always zee; in the South it is zed." That has changed. The standard U.S. pronunciation is now (zee). Canadian dictionaries, however, show either (zed) alone or both (zed) and (zee). I guess if (zee) were not a real possibility, Canadian Joe might not be as fervidly insistent upon (zed).

~EP

zydeco (ZY-di-koe)

JOSEPH MILLER WROTE: You folks at Random House are quite good at finding word origins, so here is a test: Where do we get the term for **zydeco** music?

Zydeco music, for those of you who are not familiar with it, is a blues-influenced kind of Cajun dance music. Like a lot of fun and delicious things in Louisiana, **zydeco** music is the product of the multicultural tossed salad that has characterized that state's history.

Zydeco is pretty young as a music genre, first appearing in the 1940s, but its roots reach back into the rich history of the Cajun people. The Cajuns were really Acadians, French immigrants to Acadia (present-day Nova Scotia and New Brunswick) in the 1600s. They had a nice community there for about 200 years; however, during this time, the French claim to the territory was disputed by the English. In 1713, the French government gave Acadia to the English. A variety of political and religious conflicts between the Acadians and the English ensued, and in 1755 all of these Acadian folks were expelled from the British territory. Many of them found their way to Louisiana, which was governed by the Spanish at the time. These Acadians settled in the southwest of Louisiana and became Cajuns. (Elide the *a*, palatalize the glide, and denasalize the vowel. Acadien = Cajun, see?)

The Cajuns had their own music, and they shared it with their neighbors in rural Louisiana. The Cajun music was reshaped by the vocal calls of the Native Americans, the accordion (introduced by German immigrants in the 19th century), and the syncopated hand clapping and stomping (called *juré*) of the African-Americans (who also contributed the early *frottoir*, the washboard instrument in Cajun music).

In the late 1940s, Cajun music was strongly influenced by blues and jazz, and a new style—**zydeco**—was born. In the mid 1950s, "the king of zydeco," Clifton Chenier, recorded the song "Les haricots sont pas salés" (The green beans ain't salty). The title was a comment on hard economic times when there was no salted meat to add to the beans. It is also the origin of the word **zydeco.** Don't believe me? Check it out: "les haricots" is really *lay za ree ko*. Now, drop the "lay" because that is just the article (the) and not really part of the word. Now we've got *ZA ree ko*. Change the *r* to a *d* (a normal change for an intervocalic *r*), dipthongize the stressed vowel, and reduce the others (because that's what English likes to do), and—voilà: **zydeco.**

Zydeco music underwent a huge revival in the 1980s and is enjoyed by people all over the world today. As the New Orleanians say, "Laissez les bons temps rouler!" (Let the good times roll).

~*HGB*

Bibliography

This is a list of the sources the experts consult most often. If you'd like to try your hand at word sleuthing, these books will give you a good start toward rooting out interesting facts, and uncovering surprising secrets, about whatever words you want to pursue. The books offer a range of approaches. Within a specific category—slang, for example—there are several choices and subcategories. Many of these books are expensive, and some you just won't find in your local bookstore, so you will want to consult them at your library. Good hunting!

American Heritage Dictionary of Indo-European Roots. Edited by Calvert Watkins. Boston: Houghton Mifflin, 2000.

You can look up a modern English word in the index and be referred to the IE root from which it comes; you'll also find other English words derived from this root. A fascinating and useful book.

American Speech. Journal of the American Dialect Society. Durham: Duke University Press. Published quarterly.

Published continually since 1925, this journal has articles on various linguistic trends and issues concerning English in North America. It is often cited in specialized dictionaries, such as the *Random House Historical Dictionary of American Slang,* so you can find out much more about a citation here. Index online.

An Anglo-Saxon Dictionary. Edited by T. Northcote Toller. Oxford: Oxford University Press, 1973.

If your word's etymology leads you to an Anglo-Saxon word, and you want to keep digging, this is the place to go. Includes citations from Old English literature.

The Century Dictionary: An Encyclopedic Lexicon of the English Language. 12 vols. Edited by William Dwight Whitney. New York: The Century Co., 1889–1911.

One of the greatest achievements of American lexicography. It gives a good historical perspective on how words were defined—and how their etymologies were traced—over 100 years ago. Like the *OED*, it has quotations, which makes it both interesting and practical.

The Chambers Dictionary of Etymology. Edited by Robert Barnhart and Sol Steinmetz. Edinburgh: Chambers, 1999.

(Previously known as *The Barnhart Dictionary of Etymology*.) Probably the single most interesting volume on etymology. It presents the first recorded dates of words, discusses their derivations, and traces their semantic development. This volume has many contributors who are experts in various fields; it has the singular virtue of appealing to the layperson, student, and linguist.

A Dictionary of Americanisms. 2 vols. Edited by Mitford Mathews. Chicago: University of Chicago Press, 1951.

For those trying to root out the meaning and origin of American words, this is well worth consulting. Its most appealing features: the quotations, and the first recorded dates of words.

Dictionary of American Regional English. 3 vols. Edited by Frederic Cassidy and Joan Hall. Cambridge, MA: Belknap Press, 1985-96.

Often referred to by the acronym *DARE*. It demonstrates how words are used in different parts of the country. With lots of citations, many delightfully nonliterary. The three published volumes contain entries for the letters *A* to *O*. Volumes Four and Five are not expected to be published in the near future.

Dictionary of American Slang. 3rd ed. Edited by Robert L. Chapman. New York: HarperCollins, 1995.

Based on a classic study of the same name by Harold Wentworth and Stuart Flexner. It contains both words and phrases. Accessible and easy to use, although its etymologies should not be taken as definitive without corroboration.

Farmer, J. S., and W. E. Henley. *Slang and its Analogues*. 2 vols. Millwood, NY: Kraus Reprint, 1986.

Originally published in 1890, this British work—it contains American slang, too—even today contains citations and leads you won't find anywhere else.

Hendrickson, Robert. *The Facts on File Encyclopedia of Word and Phrase Origins*. Rev. ed. New York: Checkmark Books, 2000.

With emphasis on *encyclopedia*. That is, it's discursive in nature. A good book for younger Mavens who might be turned off by the fastidious *OED*. Note: this should not be the sole book you consult; it is not nearly as scholarly as many of the other books listed.

Juba to Jive: A Dictionary of African-American Slang. Edited by Clarence Major. New York: Penguin Books, 1994.

Contains over 500 pages of African-American slang. Mostly from the 20th century, but some entries go back to the 1700s. Most important, each word or phrase is given at least one source, often two or three. Extensive bibliography.

Liddell & Scott Greek-English Lexicon. 9th ed. Revised by Henry Stuart. Oxford: Oxford University Press, 1996.

First published in the 19th century, revised several times since then. *The* source for anything to do with Classical Greek.

Middle English Dictionary. Edited by Hans Kurath, Sherman Kuhn, and Robert Lewis. Ann Arbor: University of Michigan Press, 2001.

Completed in 2001 after 71 years of work. Covers English vocabulary between 1100 and 1500 A.D., with numerous citations illustrating changing meanings. It was published in 115 fascicles, with the last one just published. There is also a Middle English Compendium of scans of original sources that can only be accessed online by means of a site license.

The Oxford Dictionary of English Etymology. Edited by C. T. Onions. Oxford: Oxford University Press, 1966.

This is a more accessible route to much of the *OED*'s etymology and, in some cases, it's more up-to-date.

The Oxford English Dictionary. 20 vols. 2nd ed. Prepared by J. A. Simpson and E. S. C. Weiner. Oxford: Oxford University Press, 1989.

The unrivaled *OED* gives each word's first known appearance in print, its earliest forms, and its derivation—which can take you back hundreds, even thousands, of years to ancient Greek, Sanskrit, Icelandic, or Hebrew, as the case may be. (Note: At least part of the scholarship—which, in some cases, was done in the 19th century—is out-of-date. It's best to consult other works as well.) Contains citations that are often wonderfully arcane.

Oxford Latin Dictionary. Edited by P. G. W. Glare. Oxford: Oxford University Press, 1982.

There are lots of smaller Latin-English dictionaries, which are fine for getting a quick sense of a word's meaning, but Oxford gives extensive definitions with citations, which help in tracing a word's development.

Partridge, Eric. *A Dictionary of Slang and Unconventional English.* 8th ed. New York: Macmillan, 1984.

The late Eric Partridge was the author or editor of scores of books on words and slang. He is always worth consulting and is conversant with both British and American slang. This book, however, has its detractors in scholarly circles.

Quirk, Randolph, et al. *A Comprehensive Grammar of the English Language.* London: Longman, 1985.

A massive book—1,700 pages—for which the word *comprehensive* is completely apt. With numerous example sentences and a slavish attention to detail.

Random House Historical Dictionary of American Slang. 2 vols. Edited by J. E. Lighter. New York: Random House, 1994, 1997.

A landmark work of scholarship. It covers an enormously wide range of American slang, from every level of society, and from numerous professions and pastimes. Its most distinctive feature is its citations, which are rich, varied, and exhaustive. Two volumes so far: *A–G* and *H–O.*

Random House Webster's Unabridged Dictionary. 2nd ed. New York: Random House, 2001.

Excellent for getting a basic feel for a word. It gives the researcher succinct, salient information on many aspects of a word, including meaning, usage, and etymology.

Smitherman, Geneva. *Black Talk: Words and Phrases from the Hood to the Amen Corner.* Boston: Houghton Mifflin, 1994.

Mostly modern slang, with no citations.

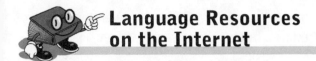

Language Resources on the Internet

http://www.americandialect.org
The American Dialect Society is a scholarly association dedicated to the study of the English language in North America—and not only dialects. Its Web site includes an index to its journal, *American Speech,* and also the archives of ADS-L, the association's electronic mailing list.

http://www.alt-usage-english.org
Mark Israel's original FAQ (frequently asked questions) document and its later supplements deal with a wide range of language topics, such as word origins, grammar, and usage. The newsgroup *alt.usage.english* is for everyone interested in language, not just linguists.

http://listserv.linguistlist.org/archives/linguist.html
The postings on this discussion list are of primary interest to linguists, though there is useful and interesting information for all readers.

http://www.wordorigins.org/home.htm
David Wilton's Web site discusses word and phrase origins and gives an overview of the history of the English language. There is also a discussion forum.

http://www.word-detective.com
The Word Detective is an online version of an entertaining

newspaper column written by Evan Morris. Selections were recently published as a book.

http://www.wordspy.com

The Word Spy, written by Paul McFedries, deals with new words, or existing words being used in a new way. Each article gives a definition and citations, and usually includes background information about the word.

http://www.worldwidewords.org

Michael Quinion's Web site investigates international English from a British viewpoint. His articles are divided into categories such as topical words, turns of phrase, and weird words.

http://wordsmith.org/awad

This is Anu Garg's Web site for the mailing list A.Word.A.Day, which sends a vocabulary word to subscribers every day, along with a definition, citations, and commentary. Words are usually selected around a weekly theme.

Index